SOUL
GRAFFITI

SOUL
GRAFFITI

MAKING A LIFE IN
THE WAY OF JESUS

MARK SCANDRETTE
FOREWORD BY SHANE CLAIBORNE

JOSSEY-BASS
A Wiley Imprint
www.josseybass.com

Published by Jossey-Bass
A Wiley Imprint
989 Market Street, San Francisco, CA 94103-1741   www.josseybass.com

Jossey-Bass books and products are available through most bookstores. To contact Jossey-Bass directly
call our Customer Care Department within the U.S. at 800-956-7739, outside the U.S. at 317-572-3986,
or fax 317-572-4002.

Jossey-Bass also publishes its books in a variety of electronic formats. Some content that appears in
print may not be available in electronic books.

Credits appear on p. 250.

Library of Congress Cataloging-in-Publication Data
Scandrette, Mark.
  Soul graffiti : making a life in the way of Jesus/Mark Scandrette;
foreword by Shane Claiborne.
      p. cm.— (Emergent)
Includes bibliographical references.
ISBN 978-0-4702-7662-4 (paperback)
1.   Conversion–Christianity. 2.   Christian life. I. Title.
BV4921.3.S33 2007
248.4–dc22
                                        2006101793

Printed in the United States of America

FIRST EDITION
PB Printing 10 9 8 7 6 5 4 3 2 1

A Living Way: Emergent Visions

Contents

To my wife Lisa Beth, who with quiet confidence, lives in the epic story of greater wholeness better than I could ever tell it

—M.S.

A Living Way: Emergent Visions Series Foreword

I'm dubious of grand, historic-sounding proclamations, but when enough people say that we're in the midst of a spiritual reformation-even an old fashioned revival-it might be time to pay heed. Americans, and people around the world, are not becoming less religious; headlines make that clear. But we are becoming *differently* religious. We're thinking about God in new ways, and we're pioneering new ways to seek after God.

Of course, not all innovations in spirituality are salutary. Some strain the very fabric of the human community. Some tear it.

But others are beautiful and helpful and salubrious. It's these that we desire to publish.

For a decade now, a group of friends has been gathering under the banner, "Emergent Village." Officially, we describe ourselves as "a growing, generative friendship of missional Christian leaders." But amongst ourselves, we know that we're a band of spiritual renegades who have committed to live into the future *together*. We share life in profound ways, we care for one another, and we laugh a lot. I can't imagine a better group of friends.

And out of this cauldron of friendship and disillusion with religion-as-usual have come some ideas and some practices that have marked me indelibly. New ways of being Christian, of being spiritual, of following God have bubbled up in this group. We've tried, on occasion, to capture the magic before, like vapor, it slips away. That's not always easy, but sometimes it happens.

When our friends at Jossey-Bass approached us about capturing some of this magic in the pages of some books, it seemed like a great idea. It also seemed daunting. *Who are we to tell others how to live?*, we wondered, *We're just figuring it all out ourselves.*

But it's become clear that it's the conversation that matters, not the conclusion; the journey, not the destination. Of course, this isn't a new thought in the history of spirituality-it's probably the oldest thought.

So, slowly and carefully, we enter into this realm, and we offer to you, dear reader, our humble attempts at what it means to follow God in this beautiful, worrisome age. We offer "A Living Way," for we firmly hold that God is alive and active in the world today; our job is to cooperate with what God is already doing. And we offer "Emergent Visions," because, even as we embrace them as our own in the here-and-now, we lean into the future, toward which God is beckoning us.

We welcome the conversation that we hope these books will provoke. And we look forward to meeting you down the road so that we can have this conversation together.

Grace and peace to you.

Tony Jones
A Living Way: Emergent Visions
Series Editor

Foreword

There's a story in the Scripture where folks are about to kill an adulteress. Jesus interrupts the scene by coming into the middle of the circle of violent men. He draws in the dirt with his finger. Maybe he was just buying some time to figure out what to do next, but I think he was playing in the dirt to disarm those dudes who had forgotten how to be like a child, and were about to kill another one of God's kids who had already experienced enough pain in her life.

Whenever he finds himself in a bit of a pinch, Jesus always seems to do something bizarre-like pull money out of a fish's mouth, walk on water, or play in the dirt. On one occasion he uses two of the most unlikely substances-spit and mud-to restore a blind man's site. . . a little scandalous in a society with a strict purity code and a keen eye for cleanliness. It is peculiar to have a God that uses the most unlikely, dirty things to bring about restoration. This book is about a God who makes ugly things beautiful.

In neighborhoods like Mark's (and ours in Philly), where graffiti tags are strewn about like billboards, beauty sometimes gets suffocated. And it takes eyes like those of Mark to remind us all that behind every sinner there is a potential saint, and behind every graffiti vandal there is a creator of beauty. This book is the quest to find God's holy ''tag'' branded on every human heart.

Mark Scandrette sees the promise of beauty in the ugly and forsaken. Soul Graffiti is that search for beauty, for God's image in people who are made from dirt, brought to life with the breath of God. So this book is Mark's little project of playing in the dirt.

One of the most profound images in scripture happens as Jesus is dying on the cross—the veil of the temple is ripped open. This veil was a curtain that took dozens of people to move, a curtain that historians say was as thick as your hand and almost as big as a football field. Ripped open! God is busting out of the holy of holies and setting free all that is sacred into the world. The temple no longer has a monopoly on the things of God. After all, that is exactly what got Jesus in so much trouble—he offered forgiveness, healing, and all the things folks thought you had to buy or beg for at the temple. Not only did Jesus redeem the broken but he set free the sacred. And *Soul Graffiti* is a book about finding the sacred and mystical in the ordinary and hidden. In this book Mark rips open the curtain to set truth free.

The mysteries of God are best told in stories like those that fill the pages of this book, stories that reveal the secret truths of the Spirit. And it is only when we live and create stories that our theology, ecclesiology, Christology, and any other -ology come to life. Mark, Lisa and their kids have their feet on the ground. Whether it's introducing their kids to homeless friends or making artistic messes with urban youth, they are creating stories with their lives. With people all around him talking theology and eschatology and epistemology, Mark is fleshing out his theology on the broken streets of San Francisco. In this book you can see what he believes by how he lives, as he brings the important but lofty ideas of academia down to earth, and puts them into a language Jesus loved... stories.

Like Mark, I get to hang out with Catholics a fair amount. They teach me about the Sacraments (sacrament means "mystery"), one of which is the Eucharist or the Lord's Supper. And in the sharing of this meal, God's Spirit is mystically present in the elements of wine and bread, the ordinary stuff of life. Bread is a simple stable food of the poor, which we are taught to pray for each day as "our daily bread". And yet, the other ingredient of the divine Meal is not water, but wine. Wine, as they know well out there in Napa Valley, is a fine, elegant luxury often enjoyed only by the rich. But at the feast of God the two elements come together, a symbol of the Divine Banquet where rich and poor come to the same table with the One who transcended all our categories of rich and poor, Jew and Gentile, slave and free, male and female.

Mark Scandrette is one who can appreciate wine and bread. He's one of those rare souls who can embrace both ascetic simplicity and elegant beauty... and find in each of them the heart of God. Amid the world of noisy consumerism, cluttered Christianity, and pop-counterculture, Mark has created a book of stories that nourish and refresh the imagination. He is hungry for the dreams of God, but stubborn enough not to allow those dreams to be boxed up in theological think-tanks or concrete buildings. His God lives on the streets, in the margins of empires and markets, busting out of the ghettos of poverty and wealth.

I remember hanging out with Mark and Lisa years ago down in the Bahama Islands (suffering for the Lord), dreaming together about what it means to be the Church, just as our communities were being born on opposite coasts. And we had fire in our eyes. Now a decade later (and after plenty of mistakes!), those dreams are still alive. This book is one more sign of a healthier Church, a Church that is closer to the poor and further from the drums of war. Mark is familiar with the embarrassing things that have been done in the name of God, and yet invites us to dig deep into Church history to find the treasures of our faith—the Celts, monastics, mystics. This is a book that reminds us of God's dreams for the Church, and beckons us to settle for nothing less.

Late Catholic activist Dorothy Day once said, "As I look at the world and read the scripture, I cannot help but ask—Have we even begun to be Christian?" This book is a gift to all of us who are trying to re-imagine what it means to be Christian today.

Shane Claiborne
December, 2006
Philadelphia, PA

Acknowledgments

I am deeply grateful for the support of my family during this book project: my wife Lisa, my daughter Hailey, and my sons Noah and Isaiah. Thanks for your patience and understanding when I had to close the bedroom door to keep writing when you really wanted to tell me a story or go for a walk. I promise that we will go camping soon and that I will finally finish remodeling the bathroom.

Many of the concepts included in this book were shaped or inspired by conversations and common experiences I had with the other founders of ReIMAGINE: Dr. Linda and Eric Bergquist, Rod Washington, Dieter and Val Zander, Ken and Kellie McCord, and Dave and Marcia Lantow. Many thanks to the countless people who endured our earliest experiments.

Thanks also to ReIMAGINE's current board of directors: Darren Prince, Steven Starfas, Keoke King, and Tim Locke. Your friendship and guidance have helped turn visions and dreams into reality.

I'm grateful for friends and traveling companions across the globe who have inspired me, provided solidarity and rich conversations: Doug and Shelley Pagitt, Andrew and Debbie Jones, Darin and Meeghan Petersen, Tony Jones, Michael Toy, Sean Blomquist, Ryan and Holly Sharp, Damien and Jen O'Farrell, Nate and Denise Eide, and Tom and Julie Larson.

My partners and colleagues in the work of ReIMAGINE have lived the vision of this book: Nate Millheim, Adam Klein, Amy Ross and Damon Snyder. Thanks to everyone who has participated in the Jesus dojo or contributed to the development of SEVEN. I hesitate to acknowledge all of you by name for fear that I will forget someone.

Three elders have guided and encouraged me during the past ten years: Rob Boyd, Dr. Red Ensley, and Dr. Floyd Roseberry.

I am also grateful for the many individuals and communities of faith who have supported our work over the years.

The example and guidance of my parents, Rich and Barb Scandrette, sowed the seeds for what I am still becoming. Dad, thanks for teaching me to consider new possibilities. Mom, I hope I have inherited a measure of your love for people and their stories. My editor, Sheryl Fullerton, has been a kind teacher and friend who patiently nurtured this project to completion. The team at Jossey-Bass has been great to work with. And thanks to Delia Ward and Charley Scandlyn, who read the manuscript and provided valuable feedback.

Mark A. Scandrette
October 25, 2006
San Francisco

Preface to the paperback edition

Why a book called soul graffiti?

What would you write on walls or sidewalks about your spiritual questions and longings if you could do so anonymously? In every literate society since ancient times people have acted on the impulse to scratch their names, their questions, their wisdom, or their subversive messages upon walls and other public spaces. Graffiti, as a medium of deconstruction, reveals a primitive hunger for renewal that makes space for what is emerging. *This book is for people with honest discontent and heartfelt questions about what it means to be truly spiritual in the times and places where we live.*

You and I are alive during a time that many believe to be one of the great turning points in history—a time when previous constructions are breaking down and we are searching together for solutions in an increasingly complex, mobile, interconnected, and fragmented world. This is a time of great possibility—for healing, reconciliation, and greater awareness about how we can live together in harmony with our Maker on the planet we call home. Yet these changing times have created fault lines, particularly within religious communities. As I write there is widespread intrigue and controversy about what some describe as "the emerging church." I suggest that this phenomenon, rather than representing a particular group or movement, is the historic and pervasive process of our response to an ever evolving and emerging flow of human consciousness. In this sense, the church of Jesus has *always* been emerging—wrestling with what it means to follow his message and teachings in particular times and places. I believe we are invited to add to the many scribbles of *soul graffiti on the walls of our religious landscape* as an integral part of the messy process of becoming.

Graffiti, in its most provocative form, is a tool for revolution that sounds the alarm and calls us to action. Among forward thinking people and younger generations there is tremendous dissatisfaction with religion as usual—a quest for perspectives and practices that integrate body, mind and spirit with moral, social and political consciousness to address tangible needs and opportunities in our world. *This book is for people searching for an integrative spiritual path that is not merely a way to believe, but a way of life.* I like to think of this book as a tool for the revolution—a collection of ideas, stories, and experiments that can awaken you to take new action to bring greater wholeness to our world.

We can't forget that most often graffiti is a form of vandalism. There is perhaps nothing more disruptive, scandalous, or criminal than the possibility that God might actually be speaking into our history and humanity, spraying a message of subversion onto the hard brick walls of our souls, disrupting our assumptions, guiding us toward a new way of being human and inviting us into the freedom we fear through the frailty of a messiah/prophet. *This book is for people who recognized the enduring scandal of the life, message and sufferings of a 1ˢᵗ century rabbi called Yeshua.*

Experts debate at what point graffiti crosses the line from art-crime to art work. Gradually the voice of dissent can become the voice of hope, generosity and beauty. It is my hope that we can move from being "haters" to creators—imagining and working towards a different and better future together. If we don't like the way things are, we can collaborate with our Maker to seek the kingdom "on earth as it is in heaven." *This book is for people who want to make beauty with their lives—expanding the boundaries of love in forgotten and unlikely places.*

The struggle for meaning among people of faith, at its root, has to do with our collective understanding of what "good news" is and how we live into that "good news." Over the past decade there has been increasing public interest in a more holistic and integrative understanding of the message of Jesus, often referred to as "the gospel of the kingdom of God." "Kingdom" language has now entered the popular vernacular of church leaders and earnest Christians from many traditions.

Pressing questions for many are, "How do we live into this reality?" or, "How do we recover from our reductionistic understandings and dualistic practices?" and, "How can we be about actually making a life in the way of Jesus?"

With this book I hope to address these questions from an applied perspective. The work is designed to provide a simple and lyrical exploration of the essential message of Jesus (as described in Mark 1:15) and relate that message to the experiences of contemporary spiritual seekers. I have sought to integrate theological insight with awareness of human psychology, culture, and life practice. I have attempted to speak of Jesus in a way that may appeal to the sensibilities of those who inhabit a post-Christendom milieu.

I have tried to approach questions of theology with realism and imagination, but understand that this style of investigation may be somewhat unfamiliar. Some readers may find the grittiness of certain stories or my inventive and poetic use of language unsettling.

My hope is that after having read the text, the reader will have greater motivation and guidance for taking action toward making a life in the way of Jesus.

GRAFFITI PUNCTUATING THE SILENCE

A few years ago I was invited to participate in a market research focus group. When I arrived at the sleek office suite I was greeted by an attractive receptionist who offered beverages and snacks and encouraged me to relax. The facilitator invited eight of us into a conference room, where we sat in comfortable chairs opposite a wall of mirrors. Behind those mirrors a team of analysts was observing our movements and responses. Our task was to give feedback on a proposed marketing campaign for a large health insurance company. The facilitator had us watch several pilot commercials highlighting the company's current marketing campaign, which emphasized preventative care through a healthy, active, organic lifestyle.

"How do the words make you feel?" the facilitator asked. "Do these images suggest health and wellness? Is this a company you could have confidence in?" In general, we all really liked the advertisements, which featured vibrant smiling people, young and old, doing fitness activities in slow motion, combined with images of falling water and green vegetables.

1

Finally one of the participants said, "It's a good concept, but how do we know it isn't just advertising spin?"

"Is the company changing its policies or doing anything practical to encourage and reward people who take better care of themselves?" I asked.

"Well, not exactly," responded the facilitator.

Another participant chimed in, "This is why people are so skeptical about advertising. It sounds like you have a great marketing campaign for a product that doesn't exist."

If you are like me, you are skeptical of offers that sound too easy or too good to be true. Today there is tremendous pressure on spiritual leaders to be spectacular and to "market" faith in ways that are simple, easy, and easily consumable. Too often the promise of "the life you've always wanted" is actually the life no one is living. Many of us wonder, Is there reality beyond all the words and hype? I even hear ministers and leaders lamenting, "I don't know if I can be the kind of pastor or priest I am expected to be and an authentic follower of Jesus at the same time."

My hope with this book is to have a conversation about what it might mean to follow the way of Jesus—not as an advertisement for an unattainable ideal, but as a messy, fertile experiment we can live into, that acknowledges the depths of our varied experiences and the complexities of contemporary society. I would like to explore how the generative life of the Creator can take root in the soil of our humanity.

MURMURS FROM THE UNDERGROUND

Every day we are bombarded with corporate advertisements trying to get us to buy things. This one-way communication is often slick and salacious. In urban areas, such as where I live, people have tangibly resisted the messages on billboards and bus shelters. With spray paint they scrawl their own names or tags across the advertisements or leave comments that question assumptions, turning one-way communication into public discourse. With wheat paste they hang homemade posters or artwork over corporate advertisements to subvert the dominance of the mass market, in an attempt to restore the voice of local people.

Tagging, the most primitive form of graffiti, is often seen as a way of marking territory or an attempt to claim personal space in the crowded metropolis. Writing tags on buses, trucks, or trains is like sending a message in a bottle, a cry to be known that will travel through the neighborhood and out into the wider world. Many underground artists tag or poster obsessively, addicted to expanding their names or causes at the risk of prosecution. Graffiti artists often leave messages for one another in their work, signatures that serve as a sign of respect or connection.

No matter our aesthetics, there is something in the motivation of the graffiti artist that we can identify with, a guttural yelp to be heard and understood, to talk back to the universe or to God when we feel helpless, abandoned, or overwhelmed. It may be that impulse we feel to find our place of significance in the wider world, or to initiate conversation with our Maker.

Not all graffiti is illegal or self-aggrandizing. Muralists and other underground artists eschew the pretentious nature of the gallery scene in order to bring beauty to the streets, where people live and work and die and love. Most people will never see the artwork that hangs on gallery walls unless the galleries are sidewalks, fences, and telephone poles. An artist I met named Dave hangs hundreds of simple, brightly colored paintings throughout the city, bringing smiles to the faces of people as they walk to the store or subway. Stenciled on the sidewalk at my feet I see proclamations left by neighbors: "Your existence gives me hope"; "Sluts against rape"; "Stop oil wars!" or, from a now deceased friend, simply the word "Grace" written with flowing cursive letters. One artist even fills the gaps in the concrete with rows of glass jewels. In our heavily pedestrian neighborhood, we have learned to look for the messages scrawled in chalk or stuck in the cracks of the sidewalk and to find beauty in small and hidden places. I am drawn to this kind of communication, because it speaks words of hope and life at the level where people actually live. And there the words don't sound like spin.

"Jesus went into Galilee proclaiming the good news of God" (Mark 1:14). I like to think that the message and method of Jesus was a lot like graffiti—immediate, street level, and personal. Jesus spoke as one who knew the struggles and joys of the people in his region. He spoke in words that connected with their longings.

And he spoke as one who also suffered. I'm convinced that the good news Jesus proclaimed is relevant for our day if the real issues of our lives, the places where we feel pain, loneliness, failure, and abandon, are acknowledged as part of the story. The "good news of God" must speak to the whole person: our bodies, our minds, our emotions, and our relationships with people and the planet we call home. And like graffiti at its best, the message becomes a two-way conversation of intimacy and respect.

SEARCHING FOR A WAY OF LIFE THAT WORKS

I purposely glanced away from the man I saw begging for change under the glow of the streetlight. In my solitary evening walk I didn't want to be disturbed. From behind I heard him call out to me, "Hey, aren't you that guy with three children who lives on 25th Street?" I turned around to see who was speaking and blurted out the first thing that came to my mind: "Jack, I'm glad to see you—I thought you were dead."

Jack, who used to live in an apartment down the street from our house, worked as a professional carpenter on high-end coastal homes. A friendly middle-aged man, Jack spoke with a distinct New England accent and showed his concern about safety in our neighborhood. Until a few months before, my kids and I would chat with Jack in the park where he walked his beloved dog. Once he told me how he had been robbed and assaulted late one night by three young men and was left with chronic pain. Over the next few months, Jack turned to heroin for relief. As we talked, I remembered how I had noticed that he had begun to exhibit tell-tale signs of heroin use: muscular degeneration, extreme weight loss, and open sores on his arms and face. He was also hanging out a lot in the park with the junkies he used to complain about. He began acting strange and tried to sell me things out of the back of his truck. Eventually we didn't see him anymore, and I felt bad that I hadn't been a better neighbor by naming the obvious and asking if he needed help.

Under the streetlight, Jack told me, "I took it just once, hoping that it would help with the pain—and I got hooked. I lost my job, my truck, my apartment, and even my dog because of the junk. Right now I'm trying to get myself together so I can see my kids again. I know what I have to do. I've been here before. I was an addict fifteen years ago and got myself cleaned up." Jack told me he was now on his way to rebuilding a life—attending daily meetings, occupying his time constructively, and finding new ways to deal with affliction and disappointment. "The challenge for me is to make good moment-by-moment choices. I am searching for a way of life that works."

Jack isn't alone. We have all found ways to misuse the good gifts of creation to cope with anxiety and stress: anger, working, drinking, consuming, eating, indulging in illicit escapes, and perhaps as many other things as there are people. Sometimes what promised relief become the habits that form us in ways that hurt our bodies, our souls, our relationships, and the Earth itself. In one way or another we are all reaching out to find a new rhythm of life that is healthy, generative, and sustaining. Discovering that transforming rhythm is the essence of good news.

A YEARNING TO BELONG

A man stood up at the funeral. He seemed not quite sure what to say. "My name is Richard. I am here representing Mrs. Banks, who due to illness wasn't able to attend today. I never actually met the deceased, but I'm certain she was a very nice person—from what others have said. . . ." For fifteen minutes he continued speaking about the woman he did not know. People quietly cringed and politely smiled, enduring his eulogizing.

A few days later I received a phone call from Richard. "You don't know me, but I was at the funeral last week. I'm a bit embarrassed by what happened." I assumed he was referring to his awkward tribute.

"I am not a religious person, but at that funeral I had a spiritual experience." I asked him to tell me more. "Well, I was sitting there thinking about myself and my group of friends back in the 1960s. We sincerely believed that we were a more sensitive and enlightened generation—and I imagined that in twenty-five years the world would be a better place because of us. It is now twenty-five years later and the world is not necessarily a better place, and I know that I'm not a better person. I somehow lost my way. Sitting there at that funeral, hearing a community of people talk about a person they knew and loved, I thought, 'If I died right now there wouldn't be a community to tell stories about me.' I am really alone. I realize I have lost my center and need to find it again, and I need a community where I can belong.''

Like Richard, you may know what it is like to look back with regret, having lost direction, vision, or hope and yearning for a place to belong. Though painful, the clarity to admit that we are lost or alone is a gift. And it is the place from which a new script for life can be written.

THE QUEST FOR PEACE AND A STORY THAT HELPS MAKES SENSE OF THINGS

It was almost 4 a.m. Michele, an Ivy League graduate from the upper east side of Manhattan, sat on our couch dabbing the bleeding mascara from her eyes. During late night coffee and dessert we discussed whether or not there is a God. I attempted to explain why I choose to acknowledge the presence of a Creator. Michele, whose Hungarian Jewish grandparents had been executed in the Nazi concentration camps, gave her reasons for not believing. I stammered momentarily, not knowing exactly what to say, and then ventured, "The Hebrew scriptures suggest that everything made somehow reveals the glory of God. The Earth, in a sense, is the voice of God romancing us. Michele, I think that if you went alone to a park, out into the woods, or on a walk along the beach and became very quiet—you would hear the voice of God speaking to you.''

Tears began streaming down Michele's face. "You don't understand how impossible that would be for me. I cannot be alone or still. I am constantly listening to music or talking on the phone. I rarely go to bed before 3 a.m. and usually not without more than a few drinks. I even sleep with the stereo turned up and the lights on. If I were alone I would have to face myself. And I am afraid of what I would find.''

I heard, in Michele's voice, a hunger for peace and longing for a story that makes sense of all that she has seen. We can become so entrapped in our chaotic patterns of distraction that, even if God is speaking, we cannot listen. We can be like children, asking question after question but not really listening for the answers.

Perhaps the first step toward discovering good news is learning to embrace stillness and quiet.

THE QUEST FOR HOLISTIC INTEGRATION

In a world that seems fragmented, we need a place to belong, a source of peace and rest, a way of life that works and a story that helps makes sense of all we see. These longings, I believe, reflect a quest for holistic integration. This is the primitive graffiti that we write with our lives. We have an intuitive desire for health, vitality, and wholeness in our bodies, minds, and relationships. And we search for connections, trying to understand how the parts relate to the whole, and how the demands of our daily lives reflect the destiny of what we were made to become. Where does our food come from? Where does our garbage go? Who makes the things we buy and under what conditions? Do these headaches have anything thing to do with what I eat? How is the time I spend at work affecting my family? A growing awareness of the ecological nature of our existence fuels our search for integration. We want to find a meaningful connection among the Earth, ourselves, and eternity.

One of my favorite graffiti artists weaves designs into wire fences using fallen leaves from neighboring trees. Often people who live in cities, perhaps due to limited open space, have an acute awareness of our responsibility to care for the natural world. My friend Andrew Jones, a Kiwi gypsy, speculates that current interest in organic produce and concern for the environment is related to our deeper quest for connection with the Creator. "I like to speak of spiritual realities in terms of organic symbols," he says, "beginning with the tree of life in the garden of Eden." Mountains and trees have often been places where humans waited to hear the voice of God. Ancient peoples wandered in the hills and wilderness seeking the will of the Creator. Prophets heard the voice of God in the silence of the desert. Devout Hebrews, such as Deborah the Judge, sat under trees to pray for wisdom, guidance, and just decisions. Trees symbolically represented the synchronicity between humans and the divine—a connection point stretching between Earth and eternity. After Jesus' death, Peter the disciple began speaking of Jesus being hung on *a tree* rather than a cross—alluding to the Nazarene as a bridge between Earth and eternity.

Today we are still being invited to wander in the wilderness, in mountains and among trees, and on the streets of cities to discover the connection between the eternal life of the Creator and the particulars of our lives in the here and now.

THE PROPAGANDA OF HOPE

I wonder, if Jesus were present in our time, what he might write on the sidewalks and walls. We know that he shouted along the Sea of Galilee, "Blessed are you who are poor, for yours is the kingdom of God. Blessed are you who hunger now, for you will be satisfied. Blessed are you who weep now, for you will laugh" (Luke 6:20–21). Jesus came offering the propaganda of hope. To people longing for purpose and wholeness he declared, "You are the salt of the earth! You are the light of the world!" (Matthew 5:13–14).

A COMPANION, ARTIST, HEALER, AND MYSTIC

Through what he taught and how he lived, Jesus addressed our hunger for a story, a way of life and a sense of peace and a place to belong. I've found it helpful to summarize the qualities of his example by suggesting that Jesus was (1) a companion, (2) an artist, (3) a healer, and (4) a mystic. As a *companion,* he lived with arms open wide to all people, making friends with the despised and forgotten, and sharing his journey with an expanding cast of characters. Jesus was an *artist* in the sense that he lived with an awakened imagination for the immediacy of God's kingdom, telling stories and taking prophetic actions to provoke and inspire. As a *healer,* he touched those who were hungry, thirsty, sick, lonely, or imprisoned, he advocated for the poor and the weak, and he identified with the sufferings and struggles common to humanity. Jesus was a *mystic* in the sense that he was conscious of the transcendent reality of God, accessing power to love through contemplative prayer, mindful surrender, and the practices of silence and solitude.

You begin "making a life in the Way of Jesus" by investigating the essence of his message and the example of his life—and by experimenting with following his path as a companion, artist, healer, and mystic. Each of the four parts of this book explores one aspect of his message and one of these four characteristics.

Neighbors call my friend Eric a Bodhisattva (the Buddhist term for an enlightened one who aspires to aid others), though Eric simply refers to himself as a follower of Jesus. Eric facilitates a community center in a neighborhood where many people are homeless or struggle with addiction, mental disorder, or generational poverty. I often hear Eric say, "I believe everyone has something valuable to offer to the community," and it shows in the way residents take ownership in caring for one another by preparing community meals and delivering groceries. For many neighbors the community center functions like a large extended family.

Christopher Robin is a twenty-five-year-old wandering poet who travels from city to city, often camping in parks and eating at local soup kitchens. One day he decided he was getting too settled, and in the spirit of Henry David Thoreau, he quit his job in New York, gave away all his possessions, and with $20 in his pocket hopped on a Greyhound bus headed to San Francisco. I met Christopher Robin at the community center the day after he arrived. We sat next to each other at breakfast, around a large table where a rainbow cast of characters assembled for a community workday. I had brought along six friends from a quiet farming town in the Central Valley of California. Together we repaired walls and electrical fixtures, installed block glass windows, and fixed a car. Christopher Robin and I drove around and bought hardware and supplies for these projects. It was inspiring to see homeless street kids working alongside older people and those who often feel useless having a sense of accomplishment and purpose. Lunch was prepared for all of us by a Tarot reader who lived in her car on the street nearby. The day was filled with lots of laughter and lively conversation. My friends from the farm town even went to hear an old rock musician we met play at a local dive bar that night.

On Monday, Christopher Robin went to Eric and told him that his experience with all of us on the workday gave him an epiphany: "I grew up in Catholic school, and then became an atheist. Through the kindness of new friends I see that love is real. I've started to believe in God again." Over the next week he had many conversations with Eric about Jesus and the ancient scriptures. In one conversation he asked, "How does God speak to us?" Before

Eric could answer, the Tarot-reading lady said, "I think God spoke through those men who were working here on Saturday."

In a world overwhelmed with words, sometimes the most powerful communication is action that is fueled and inspired by love. We are more likely to trust messages that are inhabited, like living, breathing three-dimensional graffiti.

Graffiti can be a plea for identity or a proclamation to puncture the darkness. It can also be prayer. One night I sat thinking about our collective longings for integration: a place to belong, a source of peace and rest, a way of life that works, and a story that makes sense of all we see. The fragmentation I recognize in the world and in myself weighed heavily upon me as I cut words into a waxed paper stencil. I prayed as I sprayed the paint through the stencil out onto the sidewalk:

CREATOR

RECREATE

HERE

NOW

INSTIGATE

A REVOLUTION

OF FAITH

HOPE &

LOVE
↓

CONVERSATION

Authentic messengers.   Who has been a presence in your life and has helped you believe that God is real? What about that person made them a good, trustworthy, or reliable messenger?

Hunger for greater wholeness.   As you think about your inter-actions with family, friends, neighbors, or coworkers, where do you sense the quest for greater wholeness? How do think spiritual longings are currently being expressed in our culture and society? Do you think this shows up in advertising?

EXPERIMENTS

Paint your own soul graffiti.   Where do you most long for greater wholeness or completion? What question or statement would you shout out to the universe or to God right now?

Go public with your yelping.   Write it with chalk on a sidewalk or post it on a Web site or message board and see what kind of response you get.

Identify your needs and desires.   *Good news* is only good if it connects to the real needs in our lives. In a journal or on a piece of paper write down 5–7 tangible needs that you desire to see fulfilled or resolved. If you have the courage, turn this list into a prayer.

PART ONE

HEARING THE MESSAGE OF JESUS IN THE HERE AND NOW

READING GANDHI
IN PALM SPRINGS

Commenting on his visit to the Gold Rush city, Mark Twain famously quipped, "The coldest winter I ever spent was a summer in San Francisco." People come to San Francisco from all over the world expecting beaches and balmy California sunshine—only to find themselves shivering and covered in goose pimples. The locals know who the visitors are because only the tourists wear shorts. The trinket vendors at Fisherman's Wharf make a brisk business of selling tourists fleece jackets and ponchos to face the chilling winds and fog that blanket the city in July and August.

Every August for the past five years our family has spent a week in Palm Springs, located in the desert east of Los Angeles. No one else goes to Palm Springs in August—the average temperature is 110 degrees every day—which is exactly what we want after wearing jackets and scarves all summer. We stay in a restored 1960s Tiki motel with a pool area surrounded by palm trees and decorated with Polynesian masks, grass cabanas, and Tiki torches. Elvis used to swim in the pool where our kids play all day while my wife and I sit and read, soaking up the sunshine and dry heat. I like to think of our week in Palm Springs as a nod to the contemplative desert fathers and mothers of the fourth century—only with a bit more luxury. (We do take some long meditative hikes in the arid wilderness of Joshua Tree.) This vacation gives us time to relax and do some soul searching as we reflect on our dreams and goals for the coming year.

My friend Adam recommended that I read the autobiography of Mahatma Gandhi, which I began while sitting by the pool. I called to mind the bronze statue of Gandhi I see by the bay in San Francisco, a sculpture of an older Gandhi wearing his iconic loincloth and striding with a walking stick in hand. He looks cold, and people often put a stocking cap on his head along with garlands of flowers around his neck. Gandhi is almost universally respected for his personal sacrifices and civil rights work in South Africa and India. Martin Luther King Jr. said that studying Gandhi's life inspired his own nonviolent civil disobedience. In the preface to his autobiography, Gandhi wrote that the goal of his life was to walk with God. He saw every act of his life as an "experiment in truth," a tool for learning how to love God and serve others. I was inspired by his dedication to play out this ambition in the details of his daily life, including his work, diet, exercise, financial affairs, and relationships.

Throughout the book Gandhi chronicled his spiritual development and particularly his contact with Christians and the "Christian" gospel. While studying law in London he read the Bible with a group of friends. During his early years in South Africa, he went regularly to a Christian church and ate Sunday dinners with a Dutch family. Many of the Christians he encountered were critical of his vegetarian diet and his deep sense of personal ethics. They suggested that through his lifestyle he was trying to earn his way to God; they were emphatic that the message of Jesus was exclusively about forgiveness of sins and eternal destiny but not about a new social ethic. This did not sound like good news to Gandhi, and with few notable exceptions, he didn't find much to admire in the daily lives of the Christians he knew. Gandhi couldn't see value in a message that had no hope or power for the here and now, and later stated, "I like your Christ, I do not like your Christians. Your Christians are so unlike your Christ."

Christ was born in poverty at the beginning of the first century AD. At the age of twelve he was found debating with prominent professors of religion, ethics, and philosophy. His early adulthood is veiled in mystery—though it is likely that he worked in the trades or wandered like a mad prophet in the wilderness. At age thirty he emerged from obscurity with a message *and* power that attracted the desperate masses. And at thirty-three he was executed as an insurgent. News that he was raised from the dead inspired his followers to lead a quiet revolution of love that garnered the hatred and admiration of an empire. His name has become a symbol and his life inspired a religion. Today perhaps more people are familiar with the traditions and peculiarities of Christianity than the life and teachings of the one they called "the Nazarene." Jesus, in his own terms, was a teacher, a prophet, and a messiah—one who was awake to divine realities and sought to be a light for others.

Was the message Gandhi heard the essential gospel of Jesus or a Christian gospel that appealed to the sensibilities of wealthy Europeans in the nineteenth century? In the introduction to his collection of anecdotes about the life of Jesus, Mark wrote that "Jesus went into Galilee proclaiming the good news of God" (1:14). *Gospel* means "good news." We are invited to wonder, "What is the good news of God for people like us living in the twenty-first century?" In the chapters included in Part One of this book I hope we can begin to explore this question. I am suggesting that:

- Good news is negotiable and must connect with the real needs, demands, and concerns of our daily lives.
- It takes courage and work to investigate the message of Jesus beyond the hype of an overly religious culture.
- Jesus saw himself as both a savior and teacher for life who took on apprentices who would learn from his words and example.
- The message of Jesus was equally about the future and the present.
- We search for what it means to be human and how to connect with our Creator in the context of our relationships with one another.

You can be surprised by the chill of cold or the heat of summer, or the pleasant warmth of the unexpected. The good news that Jesus proclaimed was probably bigger and better than what anyone anticipated—and it may take a lifetime to discover what it might mean to pursue making a life in the Way of Jesus.

A note about the flow and structure of chapters: This book is divided into four parts that correspond to four phrases from the introduction to the Gospel of Mark:

"Jesus went into Galilee, proclaiming the good news of God. 'The time has come,' he said. 'The kingdom of God is near. Repent and believe the good news!'"

Part One explores the context from which we encounter Jesus as a messenger. Part Two addresses issues about how we relate the "good news of God" to our time and place. Part Three investigates how the sacrifice of Jesus is related to the message of God's reign. And Part Four discusses how we might respond to the invitation to "repent and believe the good news." The chapters may best be read sequentially since an internal language is developed as the parts progress. Each part also includes a chapter on praxis inspired by four themes I find evident in the life of Jesus: companion, artist, healer, and mystic. *Conversation* questions and *experiments* are included at the end of each chapter to foster further exploration for either groups or individuals.

CONVERSATION

Experiments in truth.   How comfortable are you with the idea that learning to live life with God is an experiment? Explain your response. Can you think of an experiment or practice you have tried in an effort to honor God in your daily life?

Christians and Christ.   How would you explain Gandhi's observation that the Christians he met were so unlike Christ? Do you think the disparity between Christ and Christians is inevitable, or could a better way be learned?

Adaptive good news.   From what you know of the development and history of Christianity, how has the message of Jesus been applied to life and society in various times and places? Describe. What accounts for the differences? How do you think we begin to figure out how to relate the message of Jesus to our lives today?

EXPERIMENTS

Listening to outsiders.   We often choose the voices we allow to speak into our lives rather selectively. Yet there may be a lot we can learn from the perspective of those who see things differently than we do. Spend some time listening to what people are saying about Jesus and Christianity from outside of your own faith background—by searching Web sites, reading a book, watching a program, or attending a meeting. What surprises you?

Exit interviews.   Most people in the Western world have had some exposure to Christianity. For every person who is finding faith in the message of Jesus, there is someone else struggling to keep their faith. (This may even describe you.) Initiate a conversation with someone who has exited organized religion and ask them to share how they now see God and view the message of Jesus. How were their questions or doubts similar to yours?

CHAPTER ONE

CURIOSITY AND THE
GHOSTS OF THE PAST

On Mission Street, near where I live, are many shops scattered with images of the one called Jesus. Images of Jesus appear on heavily lacquered wall plaques, candles, velvet wall hangings, plaster bobble-head toys, and even liquor flasks—not to mention the many jewelry shops filled with cross pendants, cross necklaces, and cross earrings. When I walk by the store windows I am particularly intrigued by the men's silk shirts, decorated with scenes of the suffering Jesus wearing a crown of thorns. These shirts, available in red and blue, are worn by Latin gang members as they roll toward retaliation drive-bys. Around the subway stations, particularly on weekends, dueling Evangelistas scream the name "Jesus" at pedestrians through portable microphones. The streets are littered with pamphlets full of words about a savior and more pictures of the crucifixion. Even in one of the most post-Christian cities in America you cannot escape the ghost of Christ-consciousness.

On Monday afternoon a shirtless man holding a tall can of malt liquor sits down next to me on the park bench to ask a favor. He pulls out a Gideon New Testament and opens it to find the number of a woman he wants to call on my mobile phone. Sandwiched between Gospel books is a rear-view picture of a naked woman with a phone number scrawled underneath.

"Now that's a piece of ass I'd like to have," he says as he hands me the picture. Slurping his beer, he begins to lecture me on the apocalyptic prophecies of the Bible. "You had better believe me when I say, that the end is near and Jesus is coming back real soon."

Whether Jesus is coming back soon or not, it is clear that in Western societies Jesus is overexposed—like an "it" girl in Hollywood who takes every role she's offered without discretion—only Jesus plays these parts involuntarily. It is often said that when you become a public figure you are no longer in charge of your image; you become a cultural commodity. And so the carpenter from Nazareth has been fashioned into a brand name—his likeness now employed to fuel and justify varied and competing agendas. Governments and gangs invoke his name as they go to war, even while concerned protesters march the streets with painted signs, countering their prayers, quoting his words: "Love your enemies and do good to them."

TOXIC CHRISTIANITY

Waiting to board a plane to Montreal, I listened to the frustrated Francophone voices in front of me grumbling, "Tabernac!" as I tried to decipher their conversation using my rusty college French. Later I discovered that in Quebec the most offensive words are not familiar four-letter profanities, but religious words with specific references to the Catholic Church. When someone is truly angry, you are likely to hear the French word for tabernacle, communion chalice, or the wafer host of the Eucharist. This inventive use of language relates to deep resentment toward the church because of its past dominance and the monolithic role it once played in the public life of Quebec. At one time all the land in Quebec was owned and managed by the church. New immigrants were required to attend Mass, observe the sacraments, and follow the dictates of local priests under the duress that their land grants might be revoked. During "The Quiet Revolution" of the 1960s cathedrals were torn down as an act of liberation.

It is difficult for someone raised under the shadow of these ghosts to find good news in anything associated with the Jesus of Christianity.

For many people in the global West, Jesus of Nazareth is too familiar to be captivating in any sense other than the amusement of taboo humor or in the mockery of "provincial" religious affections. Our familiarity with the one called Jesus has bred both cynicism and sentimentality. My sense, however, is that what most of us know about Jesus we know somewhat vicariously through the later development of the religion that we now call Christianity. Many of us, understandably, are suspicious of organized, institutional religion. Calling to mind the inquisitions, religious wars, and slavery justified by scriptures, we may often feel that religion is the problem—not the solution to our deepest longings as people. And we are invited to wonder whether it was ever Jesus' intention to found a religion at all.

A subterranean narrative stands in contrast to the dominant histories of Christianity, a quieter story of people who did not hold on to power, but attempted to surrender themselves to the energy and teachings of the master in the way of love. In each generation people continue to explore the meaning of Jesus' message and work for their time.

I have become increasingly hesitant to identify myself as "Christian," because when I say the word I notice people clicking over to their default images and stereotypes and responding to me out of those negative constructs. They make assumptions about how I think and feel about various political and social issues. It is as if I had inherited someone else's bad reputation.

In San Francisco I often see a bumper sticker that reads, "Jesus, please save me... from your followers." For many, the disparity between Jesus and those who claim to follow him creates cognitive dissonance, ambivalence, and hostility. At my children's soccer practice a Jewish friend asked me, "Did Jesus hate the Jews?" She went on to explain that her parents, who are holocaust survivors, grew up in Eastern Europe, where "Christian" families often told their children that the Jews chop up little Christian kids and put them in their matzo ball soup at Passover. The generational distance, antagonism, and pain ran so deep in her family that my friend was never told that Jesus was actually Jewish.

Fragile creatures we are, and not always good or reliable containers for divine wisdom and goodness. Leslie, a woman I once worked with, was devastated by her "Christian" sister's response to her coming out lesbian. After listening to the details of the story, I suggested to Leslie that her sister's history of mental instability may have influenced her reaction more than the fact that she was a Christian. The loudest voices among us are not always the most reliable nor credible. Crazy people have always been drawn to religious figures and communities, with predictable results. Conversion experiences, though emotionally powerful, often parallel childlike awkwardness or the extreme behaviors of adolescents. This speaks more to human sociology and psychology than to the relative validity of a given spiritual path. The irony here is that many spiritual communities unintentionally mar their reputations by graciously including unstable and marginalized people who are scorned by the general society. It is often the poor and broken among us who are most willing to become students of the master.

We often spend so much time reacting to religious traditions or a religious culture that we have little energy left to cultivate a proactive spiritual path. Even among "believing" people, there is often more critique and conversation about "the church" or parochial issues than honest engagement with the ways of the master—how Jesus lived and what he taught. Perhaps we have been too easily pleased by our overeducated ability to analyze and deconstruct. Rather than being skeptical, why couldn't our collective sense of unrest about religion and spiritual community motivate us to be more curious and engaged?

PERPLEXED BY CHURCH

In the story of my own spiritual path, I'm told that I was no ordinary child. I don't mean to imply that I was exceptional, only peculiar. I was not a "gold star" student in the Sunday School program I attended, nor was I a particularly noble or sensitive child. But when I was twelve I had a powerful spiritual renaissance—which also happened to coincide with my sexual awakening. I became increasingly aware of the force of my will and was searching for wisdom about how to live. In a rare moment of silence, I contemplated that, if there was a God, and if Jesus had come to show us the way to God, then it made sense for me to surrender myself to whatever God's wishes might be. I recognized my life as a gift and sacred trust and whispered a prayer in which I promised that I would obey whatever I discovered by reading the scriptures.

From a copy of the New Testament, in plain language, decorated throughout with simple line drawings, I read the four Gospels like a magazine, reading the stories that interested me and skipping the parts I found boring. I was drawn to the teachings of Jesus and the accounts of his life. Soon I felt that I wanted to be one of his disciples and imagined myself becoming part of his revolution.

My primitive fidelity to Jesus gave me no love for attending church services or Sunday School. Early on Sunday mornings my family frantically rushed to get ready for church. I pulled on ill-fitting polyester pants, a button-up shirt, and uncomfortable dress shoes in dreaded anticipation of a morning spent sitting in a formal building singing hymns and listening to sermons. As I think about it now, there is more than a little irony in the fact that we sat passively in a regal sanctuary listening to messages based on the adventures of a homeless bearded prophet who wandered the cities and countryside caring for the poor and healing the sick and inviting people to follow his example. How exactly were we seeking his kingdom by gathering like this? For me these environments functioned like museums displaying spiritual realities as exotic specimens in a cabinet of curiosities—removed from life in the here and now. The context conveyed more about the dogmas of tradition and region than the revolutionary life of the master.

Walking down the street in my neighborhood one day, I noticed that the ornate building that once housed St. John's Evangelical Lutheran Church was now painted red and had been converted into the Hua Zang Si Buddhist temple—a major west coast destination for the practice of traditional Chinese Buddhism. The crosses and pews were replaced with impressively large statues of the Buddha, and the parish residence was now a monastery compound housing two dozen nuns. The smiling nuns, sporting shaved heads and wearing bright orange robes, eagerly greet visitors at the door. As I toured the new facility I wondered what the working-class German immigrants, who financed and built this edifice in the late nineteenth century, would think if they knew of the building's new use. It reminded me of the many historic stone-block churches I saw along Lake Street in Aberdeen, Scotland—none of which are used anymore for worship. One was converted to a high-end restaurant, another was an art studio, and a third church building housed a darkly gothic dance club.

Some would think that a church building becoming a Buddhist temple or a night club is an ominous "sign of the times." But people move away, kinship bonds loosen, and buildings fall out of use, becoming standing mausoleums of a spiritual community. The fact that property remains while a community dwindles poses some interesting dilemmas—like the church in our neighborhood with fewer than ten members that owns $10 million in real estate.

Recently a friend told our daughter Hailey about a church burning down. Confused, she furrowed her brow and asked, "If a church is not an event or a building, but a group of people, how can you burn down a church?" To those prone to religious fetishes and rituals, Paul of Tarsus once announced, "The God who made the world and everything in it is the Lord of heaven and earth and does not live in temples built by hands" (Acts 17:24). Jesus taught that God lives inside of people and that our bodies are the temple of God.

Perhaps the reality of the good news proclaimed by Jesus only becomes real to us when we see it manifest through the lives of others. If my interest in spiritual matters depended solely on my experience with church meetings, I would have quickly dismissed the message of Jesus, as many of my friends did in early adolescence. Yet throughout my childhood there was energy and goodness at work in my family that attested to spiritual realities. My parents' faith in Jesus was expressed through an intentional way of life. We lived in a diverse urban neighborhood where I watched them offer care and hospitality. A neighbor my father found lying drunk in a ditch one winter day became our "Uncle Leroy" and joined us for Sunday dinners and holidays. We knew a man in a wheelchair who wore makeup and dresses. I played with kids in smoke-filled apartments on the Native American reservation while my mom chatted with their mothers. We visited people in prison and welcomed travelers. My parents became "Mom" and "Dad" to many of our schoolmates who were neglected or abused. Occasionally my father would say, "We don't need to go to church today; we are the church." Every day my family prayed or read the Bible together, and we sang spiritual songs and discussed our ponderings about what it might mean for us to walk in the ways of Jesus in the times we were living in.

As a teenager my spiritual pursuits became fanatical. I carried a Bible with me, studying and meditating for hours each day. I lived as a self-styled ascetic, without music, movies, or television. Beginning when I was thirteen, I spent the summers traveling and "preaching the gospel" in children's clubs and city parks. By age nineteen I was the director of a Christian nonprofit working with children and families in government housing projects and traveling and speaking to churches.

BETWEEN SENTIMENTALITY AND CYNICISM

As a teenager I often felt stretched between two worlds and still, in fact, feel suspended between the sentimentality of folk religion and the cynicism of a secularized culture.

For those who inherit a sentimental view of religion, Jesus often functions as a ghost or lucky charm. In junior high I was known as "the preacher" among the working-class Catholic and Lutheran kids in my neighborhood, who came to me with their moral dilemmas, prayer requests, and theological musings about heaven and hell, God and Satan. They didn't question the existence of God, nor did they feel captivated by the opportunity to live in the revolution of the kingdom. They were, it seems, haunted by God and by "the church" and wished to do whatever it took to simply be left alone.

In some Christian traditions, children are hurried along to embrace Jesus as a personal savior without space for genuine curiosity: "You love Jesus, don't you Johnny—oh yes you do. Johnny loves Jesus, yes he does," a mother coos in a sing-song voice to her three-year-old. People raised in such practices are often robbed of a genuine inquisitiveness about Jesus—because they know too much too soon. The knowledge that "Jesus is the savior of the world and you're going to hell if you don't believe it" doesn't leave much room for curiosity.

In the accounts of Jesus' life, people had a chance to explore whether or not the message of Jesus was good news for them. Even his closest companions went through cycles of attraction, curiosity, trust, and doubt—and we know that for some of them, this process continued for the rest of their lives.

In other families children learn to despise Jesus as the war-mongering Christmas tree icon of America, a fairy-tale god only believed in by the simple, uneducated, or politically conservative.

In high school I was transferred to a magnet school where my spiritual sincerity was met with predictable antagonism by the children of left-leaning upper-class intellectuals. In a snarky voice my friends would ask, "Does Jesus still love me?" after telling me about a decadent weekend party at one of their parents' mansions along the river. Among my peers at school we debated the existence of God and discussed metaphysics and epistemology. My explanations of belief were consistently answered with default skepticism. Although they prided themselves on being open minded, my classmates were nevertheless blinded by the intolerance of inbred cynicism. Sometimes my only answer to their jeering was to assert that there must be something unique about the only figure among the world's religions whose name is employed as an expletive.

How did Jesus respond to sentimentalists and skeptics? One day a maudlin old woman shouted from the crowd, "Blessed is the woman who gave you birth and nursed you." Jesus countered her syrupy words with the pronouncement, "Blessed rather are those who hear the word of God and obey it" (Luke 11:27–28). And to skeptics who questioned his credibility, Jesus replied, "If anyone chooses to do God's will, he will find out whether my teaching comes from God or whether I speak on my own" (John 7:17). To both the sentimental and the cynical Jesus had one reply: "Walk with me."

After two thousand years, the name of Jesus is still a lightning rod of controversy, bringing out the best and worst of humanity. Haunted by the religious ghosts of our past and the social pressure to accept or reject, we are robbed of the opportunity to be genuinely curious about the one called "the Nazarene." I believe we are invited to move beyond sentimentality and cynicism toward an engaged curiosity about the real Jesus who plays hide and seek with us behind the icons, bobble-head toys, and kitschy liquor flasks. We may find a figure who is far more compelling and mysterious.

CONVERSATION

Jesus and culture.   What cultural associations and images come to mind when you hear the name "Jesus"? How do you think familiarity affects our ability to hear what Jesus had to say?

Who was Jesus and what was his message?   Is this an open or interesting question for you? Why or why not? Jesus confounded even his closest friends, provoking them to ask, "Who is this man?"

Jesus and the church.   Do your experiences with organized religion give you a more or less favorable impression of Jesus and his message? How would you explain the similarities and differences between who Jesus was and how he is culturally appropriated?

EXPERIMENTS

Sentimental or skeptical?   In regard to Jesus, we often lean toward either sentimentality or cynicism. Which tendency is more characteristic of your current posture? You might become more curious about Jesus by talking with someone whose view differs from yours. If you consider yourself a "true believer," find someone to talk with who is skeptical. If you are cynical about Jesus or organized religion, ask someone who is Jesus-positive to explain their enthusiasm.

From critique to creativity.   Most of us have looked around the religious landscape and wondered, Why can't it be different than it is? On a sheet of paper, brainstorm ten words you would use to describe your dream faith community. If you can imagine it, maybe it can happen. What can you do to take the first step to initiate it?

CHAPTER TWO

RABBI AND
REVOLUTIONARY

Despite recent controversy about performance-enhancing drugs, I still find it awe inspiring to watch Barry Bonds swinging at a pitch and hitting the ball out of the park. Once or twice a year my son and I are offered tickets to see the San Francisco Giants play. Not being a well-seasoned sports fan, I'm often mystified by the terminology, rules, and customs of the game—and the ritual of being a spectator. Everyone around us seems to know exactly what the players and coaches should do—though I'm pretty sure the coaches and players can't hear the instructions they yell from up in the bleachers. Avid baseball fans arrive at the stadium hours before the game, carrying coolers and wearing team shirts and hats. Many of these fans look as if they haven't played sports themselves since high school. From what I can observe, watching professional sports requires a lot of eating and standing in lines for the bathrooms. Occasionally something exciting happens on the field, and I see people spilling their beer as they stand to cheer the player who has just scored one for the team.

Were we made to be spectators or players? Everywhere that Jesus went he attracted crowds of fans. They came to see the young rabbi who could perform miracles and who challenged the authority of the religious establishment. Some were hungry for bread and others were curious about the wise and strange things he said. It was a public spectacle. Many hoped that Jesus, and his band of disciples, would bring about a political revolution, overthrowing the Romans and restoring the Jews to their rightful place of power and autonomy. Others measured Jesus' words and actions against propriety and tradition.

It is evident that Jesus saw the crowds as incidental to his real purpose. We are told that he did not entrust himself to his fans because he knew of their mixed motives. Crowds are easily impressed but can quickly become disgruntled. His real purpose, it seems, was to identify people from the crowd who might have the courage to play in the ways of the kingdom, to walk with him.

Being a fan of Jesus is not the same as being a follower. You and I are also invited to step up from the crowd of the curious to join the team of the committed. Jesus invited people who were wealthy and people who were poor, people who were involved in organized crime and people who were piously religious. All of them had to move beyond the norms of their social status into the better way of love.

JESUS THE REVOLUTIONARY

At the tattoo parlor, my friend worked with needle and ink applying a design to the skin on his client's back, as the three of us sat discussing our spiritual desires and ambivalence about religion. In the midst of our conversation, the man under the needle turned and said, "Jesus is cool, it's just that they have f***ed with Jesus. I mean, Christianity was at its best when it was secret and hidden and you could die for it." This profound, if crass, statement recognizes that the power of the gospel lay in its ability to be a counter-cultural and revolutionary force—not only a story to believe, but a distinctive way of life. The man's comment prompted me to consider the question: Am I in some measure complicit in the domestication of Jesus? Has my desire to maintain social status or a standard of living forced me to disregard the revolutionary nature of the life and teachings of the master?

I remember how, as a spiritually sensitive teenager, I felt an increasing dissonance between the vision of life expressed in the Gospels and the culture and traditions that typify Western Christianity. I wasn't satisfied with the explanation that the radical teachings of Jesus on money, material possessions, reconciliation, and community weren't intended to be taken literally. I had a sneaking suspicion that following the Way of Jesus might require more than having "orthodox" beliefs and attending religious services. What if Jesus actually intended for us to grapple with how to follow his instructions for life, instructions like:

"Sell your possessions and give to the poor." (Luke 12:33)

"Love your enemies and do good to them." (Luke 6:35)

"Do not resist an evil person. If someone strikes you on the right cheek, turn to him the other also." (Matthew 5:39)

"Do not worry about your life, what you will eat or drink. . . . Seek first the kingdom of God." (Matthew 6:25,33)

"Whoever welcomes this little child in my name welcomes me; and whoever welcomes me welcomes the one who sent me. For he who is least among you all—he is the greatest." (Luke 9:48)

In his time, Jesus of Nazareth was a trickster, a provocateur, and a revolutionary. He was a disturber of assumptions and cultural norms. With the signature phrase "You have heard that it was said. . . , but I tell you," he broke prevalent myths about what it meant to seek God. His actions and teachings were dangerous, a threat to the religious establishment and political empire. And he promised that anyone with the courage to follow his path of radical love would encounter similar resistance.

People went to see Jesus in hopes that he offered a better way of life. If he had simply affirmed how people already lived and believed, there would have been nothing to see. And yet Jesus was not the revolutionary people expected him to be. Many anticipated that a messiah would bring an externalized political or social revolution by force. Instead Jesus invited an internal transformation of the person that would change the world from the inside out.

TAKING THE RISK TO BE OFFENDED BY JESUS AND HIS TEACHINGS

In our time, Jesus is regularly made protector of the establishment and empire, or he is reduced to a saccharine savior. The words of Jesus are so familiar as to be passé. We may have to adjust our expectations about the kind of character he was in order to understand his message more clearly. Jesus came proclaiming "good news" that would challenge the status quo. His words were intended to provoke us to think and act in new ways—to dismantle and sabotage our long-held assumptions and habits so that we might be released into a better way of life.

Against the backdrop of the city skyline, Gary, a prominent Christian leader, began to address the group with surprising vulnerability: "At fifty-five years old I have been a pastor for nearly thirty years. And as the son of missionaries I have been familiar with Christianity my whole life. And yet I feel like I am going through a kind of conversion. In the past six months I've begun to wrestle with the social implications of the teachings of Christ. I wonder sometimes how I could have read the Bible all these years and missed this." He suddenly paused, red-faced, and began to weep bitterly. "I have tried to love God without really loving people. Now I am wondering whether my values are influenced more by the teachings of Christ or by the biases of my privilege as a white middle-class male. For instance, by what values did I choose to live in a safe and affluent community? And how did I not see that the teaching of Jesus has something to say about our responsibility to the oppressed? I am afraid that, by disregarding Jesus as a teacher, I have been guilty of perpetuating unbridled nationalism and racial and economic injustice."

Gary is experiencing the painful and liberating process of hearing Jesus as the spiritual and social revolutionary that he was. Wrestling with what good news might mean for us in the here and now may require a willingness to risk being disturbed, provoked, and offended by Jesus. We can become so certain of the propriety of our understanding of God that we disallow the work of the Spirit in our lives. Is there space in our imaginations for the voice of God to speak?

For those of us who read the Bible, we often look to the pages of scripture to confirm what we already think or how we currently live. We may be tempted to assume a posture of certainty and arrogance: "I know what this text is about." It may be more appropriate to view the scriptures as something *that reads us*— intending to subvert our thinking, confront our way of life, and produce a change of heart and action.

It may actually be more healthy to be disturbed, confused, or searching than confident, certain, and secure. We are reminded that his companions were constantly being surprised by what Jesus said and did. They struggled to understand and inhabit the fuller implications of his life and message for the rest of their lives. And why should it be any different for us? A posture of humility allows the words of Jesus to speak to the deepest parts of our being, where we can hear the voice inviting us to leave the shadows within ourselves to come more fully into the light of our Creator.

JESUS THE TEACHER

I was thirteen when I became the apprentice of Marvin Bentfield, a simple fundamentalist children's evangelist from rural North Dakota. Every weekday for three summers Marvin picked me up at 7 a.m., and we traveled hundreds of miles in his station wagon to "preach the gospel" to children in inner city parks and suburban backyards. At four or five locations each day, I followed Marvin as he bounded out of the car, quickly greeting the hostess and rallying the kids to sit down for our hour-long program of songs, Bible stories, and games. (If this sounds weird to you, I admit that even back then this was a strange way for a teenaged boy to spend the summer.) I watched Marvin as he labored to captivate the children's attention with exaggerated facial expressions and hand motions, singing out in his loud clear voice. Out of professional decorum, Marvin never took off his blue polyester suit jacket or loosened his tie, despite the Midwest heat and humidity that baked his pudgy frame—soaking the underarms of his jacket and torn white shirt.

Then it was my turn. Shy, self-conscious, covered in pimples, and somewhat embarrassed to be wearing dress clothes outside in

July, I stood up to tell a story, sing a song, or give the invitation for the kids to ask Jesus into their hearts. During lunch I listened to Marvin chat graciously with suburban housewives or urban church ladies. On the way home he would give me feedback on my technique or we would listen to Christian radio and talk about theology, breathing in the rush-hour exhaust fumes in the old rusty car without air conditioning. Gradually, by the sheer force of time and our common work, I adopted Marvin's cheerful enthusiasm, conversational manners, and simple fearless courage. Marvin taught me a lot about loving people and treating them with dignity. Minus the suit jacket and receding hairline of his sweaty brow, in his best qualities, I became like him.

Jesus also was a rabbi—a traveling spiritual teacher who took on student-apprentices. The rabbi would present not only knowledge but a comprehensive agenda for the life of an apprentice. In the contract between rabbi and student, the student was expected to do whatever the master assigned—to become like the teacher. Students would literally entrust their lives to the wisdom of the master. Jesus once said, "A student is not above his teacher, but everyone who is fully trained will be like his teacher" (Luke 6:40). Jesus articulated and modeled a way of life so that people could learn to be like him and collaborate in the agenda of God's reign. In effect Jesus continues to invite people to be his apprentices and learn to walk in his ways.

SURRENDERING TO APPRENTICESHIP

As a child I thought of myself as something of a prodigy in the visual arts. I won awards in school and was encouraged by teachers who marveled at my abilities with drawing, painting, and sculpture. Seeing myself as an artist was a significant part of my identity.

Though my interest in the arts had diminished somewhat as I grew older, in college I took a drawing class. It was taught by an older professor, a small angry man known for his impatience with students, whom he knew took his classes not for the love of art but only to fulfill credit requirements. When a freshman complained that she had gotten India ink on her pink cashmere sweater, he dumped the entire bottle of ink on her and said, "This is an art class, not a Junior League tea party. You should have come prepared with the proper attire.'' Every Friday the professor had us pin our drawings to a wall for his examination. In front of the class, he would critique our work using a razor knife to cut away the parts of the drawings he disliked. People regularly left his classes in tears. When someone commented about how hard they had worked on a piece, he replied, ''You haven't really learned to work on your art until you have spent eight hours staring at a blank canvas.'' He wanted us to love art-making and take it as seriously as he did.

The professor liked my drawings and collected several of my pieces to show other classes as examples. Toward the end of the semester, upon his recommendation, I received honors in the arts by the faculty of the university. When we were alone in an elevator one day, he turned to me and said, ''You are a very good art student.'' I knew this was a great compliment, especially considering his high standards. Yet inside I resentfully thought, ''Good art student? Am I not a good artist?'' Only later did I realize how right he was. He recognized the potential I had to become an artist, but I had not surrendered myself to the discipline, training, and apprenticeship required to become a true artist.

It can feel naked and agonizing when you realize that your sense of identity is not matched by action. We may be quite captivated by Jesus, without actually surrendering ourselves to the discipline and endurance necessary to becoming an apprentice of his ways.

Are we apprentices of Jesus when we say we are, or when we begin to do the things he taught? Are we willing to take Jesus seriously as the kind of teacher he intended to be? Hearing the message of Jesus in a way that can be good news for us in the here and now begins with an appreciation for the fact that he spoke with authority. Very simply, Jesus expected to be obeyed. He did not present an esoteric theory of God or the afterlife merely to stimulate the intellect. He believed he held the words of eternal life and that people would ignore his teachings at their own peril. And yet Jesus did not exercise the kind of power that would force people to obey him against their will. His teachings could only take root in the lives of free people—people liberated to surrender themselves to his authority and the reign of God.

Apprenticeship to Jesus requires a posture that is unfamiliar to many of us. We are not of a generation that easily follows instructions or submits to authority. Culturally speaking, we are reticent about making commitments, taking vows, or pledging ourselves to anything or anyone outside ourselves.

Anyone can be an apprentice of the master, but all of us are not willing to submit to the authority of Jesus as teacher. Does this sound like some kind of elitism? Jesus once said, "Small is the gate and narrow the road that leads to life, and only a few find it" (Matthew 7:14). We resist this teaching and do not want it to apply to us. Perhaps in our time it has become too easy to claim to be a follower of Jesus. The narrow way has been made wide and shallow, so that many people can come in, but what do they come into?

THE POSTURE OF AN APPRENTICE

It is actually a terrifying thing to be invited to be an apprentice of Jesus. Perhaps we should not so easily presume that it is a way we want to follow. John the Baptizer, the desert-dwelling, locust-eating prophet, said that he was not even worthy to untie the sandals on Jesus' feet (Mark 1:7). Jesus told the crowds of spectators, "If anyone wants to follow me, they must deny themselves, take up their cross and follow me. Whoever wants to save their life will lose it, but whoever loses their life for me will find it" (Mark 8:33–35). And when Jesus invited Peter the fisherman to follow him, Peter, understanding the cost, pleaded, "Go away from me, Lord, I am a sinful [person]" (Luke 5:8).

An Ivy League-educated former congressional aide, entrepreneur, and executive, Caroline is gradually working her way down and off the corporate ladder. Serving at-risk youth through an agency that does job training and mentoring, she is deeply admired for her kindness, character, and the conscious choices she makes. So it sounds strange to hear Caroline say, "I feel like such a beginner at following the ways of Jesus, with so much to learn." After dinner one night at our house she offered to share a prayer that she prays at home each evening. "It was written by Metropolitan of Philaret of Moscow," she explained, "and comes from the Orthodox tradition." Quietly and with great feeling Caroline recited from memory:

Lord, I know not what to ask of You.
You alone know what my true needs are.
You love me more than I myself know how to love.
Help me to see my real needs, which may be hidden from me.
I dare not ask for either a cross or a consolation.
I can only wait upon You; my heart is open to You.
Visit and help me in Your steadfast love.
Strike me and heal me; cast me down and raise me up.
I worship in silence Your holy will.
I offer myself to You as a living sacrifice.
I put all my trust in You.
I have no other desire than to fulfill Your will.
Teach me to pray. Pray Yourself in me. Amen.

For a moment after Caroline finished praying, no one spoke. We were mesmerized—both by the wording of the prayer and by the reverence and sincerity evident in her voice. Perhaps we are most open to transformation when we assume the humble posture of an amateur in our approach to Jesus—unsure of our own abilities but confident in the care of the master.

LIVING INTO WHAT WE ALREADY KNOW

On a recent trip to London I noticed the prominent warnings on tobacco products, bold-faced statements in large print covering most of the packaging: "SMOKING KILLS"; "SMOKING SERIOUSLY HARMS YOU AND OTHERS AROUND YOU"; or "SMOKING CAUSES SEXUAL IMPOTENCE." Despite these dramatic warnings, everywhere I went I saw people smoking.

Safety warnings, diet and nutritional recommendations, articles on relationships and money management—we are overwhelmed with good information about how to live a healthy life. Yet we frequently assume that the healthful changes that elude us will come through the additional data we lack—and we bring this assumption to our spiritual ambitions as well, presuming that even more advice and greater understanding will automatically lead to transformation. But does it?

It is likely that we have more collective data about Jesus and the scriptures than anyone did in the first century. If what was needed was more information, we should expect radical transformation of individuals and communities—because in a literate society we have unprecedented access to the sacred texts and interpretive resources. Most of us could close the scriptures and simply spend the rest of our lives trying actually to obey the wisdom we can remember.

In Western society we are also culturally conditioned to assume that intellectual assent to a set of propositions is an adequate substitute for obedience. If the progeny of those who kill the prophets build their shrines, then perhaps it is those who refuse to obey the teacher who immortalize his words.

Seek. Sell. Give. Be reconciled. There is an existential quality to the teaching of Jesus—a call for an immediate, visceral, and bodily response. Jesus cautioned his audience, "Consider carefully how you listen" (Luke 8:18). And he often finished a teaching by saying, "If anyone has ears to hear, let him hear" (Mark 4:23). In a story that he often repeated, Jesus gave a warning about how we listen. A wise man builds his house on rock. A foolish man builds his house on sand. When the storm comes only the wise man's house is left standing. Jesus made his point obvious: "Everyone who hears these words of mine and puts them into practice is like a wise man who built his house on the rock" (Matthew 7:24). The $64,000 question is, How, exactly, do we put the teachings of Jesus into practice? The short answer is that we try. Just do something. As you look at what Jesus said and how he lived, what immediate implications do you see for your own life? Begin with those hunches. In college I began experimenting with the teachings of Jesus, struggling with their meaning and possibilities. I volunteered at a mental hospital. I stopped to help strangers along the highway. I cleaned out my closet and gave my extra clothes away. What may have been juvenile attempts at obedience somehow propelled me toward a more mature dedication to the ways of the master. Sometimes we learn to do things well by first having the courage to do them badly.

JESUS THE EXAMPLE

One night our family read from a section of the book of Matthew, where Jesus pronounced seven "woes" against religious leaders. Together we wondered why Jesus pronounced these seven woes, speaking so sternly and even calling them "white washed tombs" (Matthew 23:27). In our discussion I speculated that the dynamic equivalent of "woe" in colloquial language might be "Damn you teachers of the law and Pharisees.... You do not practice what you teach." The problem, it seemed, was that they had knowledge without practicing the way of love. Our nine-year-old son Isaiah said, "What's the sense of that, Dad? That's like playing Ping-Pong with a baseball bat."

We live in a time of apparent crisis between what a person teaches and how he or she actually lives. We are familiar with the medical doctor who smokes cigarettes, the financial planner who carries large personal debt, or the spiritual teacher, priest, or pastor who lives a hurried, angry, or undisciplined life. In each case "experts" live in direct contradiction to their message.

It is an ominous task to aspire to be a teacher in the ways of the kingdom. Anyone who attempts to teach places themselves under great scrutiny. Jesus, as teacher, did not merely provide information or motivation, but also inspiration through how he lived in his body, time, resources, and relationships. Later teachers would be measured by his example: "Remember your leaders, who spoke the word of God to you. Consider the outcome of their way of life and imitate their faith" (Hebrews 13:7). The true value of a teacher can be measured by their inhabited example. Paul of Tarsus taught with the recognition that how he lived was as important as the words he spoke: "Whatever you have learned or received or heard from me, *or seen in me*—put it into practice" (Philippians 4:9).

Jesus, as a teacher, embodied a total pattern of behavior including habits, disciplines, and learned responses to circumstances. The early followers of Jesus understood that Jesus was significant as a savior but also as a teacher who demonstrated a new way of life. There were distinctive lifestyle habits adopted by devout disciples. "Join with others in following my example,... and take note of those who live according to the pattern we gave you"(Philippians 3:17).

The skill of these early spiritual teachers was their ability to imitate and model the kind of life Jesus lived: "Therefore I urge you to *imitate me.* For this reason I am sending to you Timothy, my son whom I love, who is faithful in the Lord. He will remind you of *my way of life* in Christ Jesus..." (I Corinthians 4:16–17). These early teachers were so convinced of the necessity of modeling that they urged their apprentices, "Follow my example, as I follow the example of Christ" (I Corinthians 11:1). We can get clues about making a life in the way of Jesus by spending time with people we admire for how they live a life of radical love.

When I met Andrew and Debbie Jones they were living on the corner of Haight and Ashbury in a flat they shared with their three children and seven other adults. They called this little commune "the Celtic Christian House" and spent their time caring for the needs of homeless kids who lived on the streets or in Golden Gate Park. Thirty kids a day would stop by their apartment for food or a shower. Andrew took me on a walk around the neighborhood and introduced me to the gutter punks and hippie kids he knew. I watched Debbie, with a baby on her back, prepare food for a free grocery program they organized. The four hours I spent with them completely altered my view of what it means to follow God in the Way of Jesus.

A TASTE FOR ELOQUENCE

It may be important to think about the reasons behind our attraction to certain teachers and personalities. Do we choose to listen merely because they speak well or because they teach and live so that their words and actions are consistent? Our loquacious tendencies as a culture may inhibit us from directly facing Jesus' call to transformational action. As a society, we are fascinated with attractive and charismatic figures who can entertain us with their vaudevillian humor, dramatic storytelling, or sophisticated intellectual "insights." We often make a teacher popular not because we are eager to submit ourselves to a contract of apprenticeship, but simply because that person amuses us. This tendency was predicted in ancient times: "They will gather around them a great number of teachers to say what their itching ears want to hear" (II Timothy 4:3). Paul of Tarsus, knowing how easily people are drawn to the profound, said, "I came to you in weakness and fear, and with much trembling. My message and my preaching were not with wise and persuasive words, but with a demonstration of the Spirit's power'' (I Corinthians 2:3–4).

As someone who spends a good bit of time speaking to groups, I am often confronted by my desire, or the expectation, to entertain. How will I make people laugh? Or what evocative story should I tell? Or even worse, what can I say that will leave people feeling impressed with me? Sometimes the relative size of the crowd dictates the need to be larger than life. The epitome of this tension comes on occasions when I have been asked to speak to large groups of teenagers after two hours of comedy sketches, audience contests, dance music, streaming video, and people dressed up in gorilla suits. When the light show, loud music, screaming, and applause have ceased, I am left alone on an empty stage to talk about the simple ways of an ancient rabbi. It is a challenge to match the energy of a crowd hyped on amusements and caffeine.

I think this is why Jesus, though he told stories and spoke to large crowds, was most interested in the minority of people who would hear the message and decide to become students of his Way. Jesus knew that his real influence was with the few who persisted beyond the crowds. His public message served as an advertisement to come closer, to learn the ways of the master in more intimate settings.

''Now when he saw the crowds, he went up on a mountainside and sat down. *His disciples came to him, and he began to teach them...*'' (Matthew 5:1–2).

We often imagine that Jesus went up on a mountainside to speak to a crowd of thousands of people. A closer look at this introduction to the ''Sermon on the Mount'' suggests that Jesus went up on the mountain to get away from the crowds so that he could teach his disciples. Perhaps his fans and spectators followed at a distance, watching Jesus speak and whispering about what he might have said to his apprentices.

Where do we stand in relation to Jesus the teacher? Are we in the crowd, drawn in by the spectacle, by bread and miracles, but scared by the demands of a revolutionary? Or do we wish to come closer, to become apprentices of the master, to surrender ourselves to authority and obedience, to move from spectators to players in the ways of the kingdom?

CONVERSATION

Fan or follower?   How would you describe the similarities and differences between a fan of Jesus and someone who has surrendered to apprenticeship?

Wild or tame?   How does the tendency to make Jesus safe and domesticated affect our ability to hear what he had to say?

An A for effort.   Describe an early experience you had trying to live with moral or spiritual courage. Do you still have the humility to try new things, to make bold statements about your intentions?

EXPERIMENTS

Be disturbed.   Read the Gospel of Luke, and notice the way Jesus took on disciples and taught them to obey his teachings. Underline all the instructions or statements Jesus made that you find confusing or disturbing.

Follow an example.   Whom do you know who you think most resembles how Jesus lived and what he taught? Make an appointment to spend time with that person, asking questions about what has shaped their life and character. What can you learn from their example? Consider spending regular time with them.

CHAPTER THREE

COMMUNITY: THE PATH OF A COMPANION

In London I awoke and left my hotel in the early morning darkness to wander the streets of the sleeping city. I walked north through Kensington Gardens and Notting Hill, past the gypsies setting up their wares along the Portobello Market in the chill of a December dawn. There is nothing I love more than exploring an unknown place on foot. Two hours into my walk I found a bakery and sat down to enjoy a pastry and café au lait among Portuguese immigrants speaking in their native tongue. On my first visit back to Europe as an adult, the leisure of this trip afforded me the opportunity to reflect on where I have been and where I am going.

Travel, I believe, is an apt metaphor for the spiritual life. The Apostle Paul showed himself to be a restless soul and vagabond when he wrote, "Not that I have already obtained all this, or have already been made perfect, but I press on to take hold of that for which Christ Jesus took hold of me. . . . I do not consider myself yet to have taken hold of it. But one thing I do: Forgetting what is behind and straining toward what is ahead, I press on. . ."

(Philippians 3:12–14). If life is a ceaseless journey, then you are always on the threshold of new beginnings and possibilities.

A few days later my friend Andrew and I and three other friends left an apartment in South London and took the subway to Kings Cross Station to catch the train to meet a shuttle that would take us to Gatwick Airport—where we slept for two hours on the tile concourse floor before boarding the plane to Aberdeen. There we took a taxi downtown for a Scottish pub breakfast. "I'm taking you this way," Andrew explained between bites of blood sausage, "to give the trip a sense of pilgrimage. We are traveling together like companions on a quest—and going slow enough to notice our surroundings."

In Aberdeen we boarded a ferry for the turbulent seven-hour voyage across the North Sea to Kirkwall, and then rode in a van over bumpy roads the last nineteen miles to the port of Stromness on Orkney Island.

Orkney Island is so far north and the winter days so short that the sun rises at nine and sets before three. After a porridge breakfast the next morning, Andrew and his wife Debbie took us to the site of a fifth-century Celtic monastery. "The Celtic Christians embodied the metaphor of pilgrimage and saw their lives as an unending quest to know and follow the will of God," Andrew told us as we stood shivering by the edge of the sea. "They were apt to launch themselves in boats to drift in these waters trusting that God would lead them to the next place on their journey."

He then took us to Skara Brae, a Neolithic human settlement of stone huts dating from 5500 BC. The fate of the people who abandoned this settlement remains a mystery. From the earliest times people in search of God have wandered the Earth. The patriarch Noah spent 120 years building a boat for travel. Sarai and Abram left their home when they heard a voice calling, not knowing where they should go. In the exodus from Egypt to the Babylonian captivity, the Israelites were most awake to the Maker in times of journey and instability. It was the settled times that brought on indulgence and complacency. We too can see ourselves as either settled and waiting or searching and wanting.

Thinking of the Celts and of my own longings, I was reminded of the psalm that exclaims, "Blessed are those... who have set their hearts on pilgrimage" (84:5). In our journey, we discover how we can walk in harmony with Creator and creation, exploring what "the good news of God" is in our time. Perhaps it is in the journey, not the destination, where we will unearth our vital connection with God and one another. And surely this is a quest we were made to embark on together.

ROBUST CONVERSATION

I had traveled to the United Kingdom to make friends with other people trying to follow God in the Way of Jesus amidst the complexities of contemporary urban society. Our conversations, if nothing else, were animated, taking place over dinner tables, inside of smoky pubs, outside waiting for the train, on long walks along the Thames, or late at night in the curry shops on Brick Lane.

Pilgrims always have a lot to talk about. There are stories to tell, advice to exchange, and plans to make about the best way to reach the next vista. Revolutions are often planned in cafés and begin with talks among friends. Great social and spiritual movements germinate when a few isolated people find one other, share deeply, and dream out loud about a different and better future. Through generative friendship a collective voice becomes stronger, and what was once timidly whispered in private emerges to become the topic of public discourse and reform. Dialogue creates resonance that fosters grass-roots energy and initiative. Conversation at its best is never just talk; it is the means by which we kindle imagination and gain the courage to take action together.

Through dialogue over meals, along the road, and out at sea Jesus invited his disciples into deeper understanding and collaboration. He spoke *to* the crowds but talked *with* his disciples. If we really intend to be followers of the master, and not merely spectators, then conversation is indispensable. Through conversation we learn to integrate the force of love into our daily lives and discover what it means to seek the reign of love in our time.

In the Tanakh (the Hebrew scriptures), the ancient Israelites were commanded to talk perpetually about what had been revealed to them. Moses recorded the instruction: "Talk... when you sit at home and when you walk along the road, when you lie down and when you get up" (Deuteronomy 6:7). We learn how to live the way of love by talking about what has been revealed and how it relates to our current circumstances.

For twenty centuries each generation has asked, "What does the gospel of Jesus mean for us?" And "How is the message of Jesus good news for our time?" (And for much longer people have asked, "What does it mean to love God and my neighbor?") A casual reading of Christian history reveals that people bring the nuance of time and place to their exploration of the significance of Jesus' life and teachings. To talk, search, and ask questions together is integral to being God-seekers in any age.

My friend Anne once told me that she has struggled for years to maintain a connection to her church tradition: "All the changes in society and new discoveries in the sciences and technology have great spiritual implications, but my church seems unwilling to discuss these things." I believe part of our society's frustration with organized religion stems from a lack of discourse and question-asking. The one-way communication from pastor or priest to congregants that is so prevalent maintains awe, authority, and distance, but does not invite fully engaged participation, ownership, or collective action. If our goal is generative loving activity, rather than mere indoctrination, then candid dialogue must be encouraged. We need casual cooperative contexts in which we can ask questions and navigate how to live and travel well together. Perhaps this is one of the reasons why early followers of the Way so often ate together in their homes and met from house to house.

After dinner one night on our visit to Orkney Island, Andrew speculated about a contemporary resurgence in the ancient tradition of wandering pilgrims who travel from place to place in search of guidance. In our time many people are desperate for conversation about spiritual matters and will go to great lengths to find someone to talk with—like Nick, who had recently found our organization's Web site and began e-mailing to ask if he could come visit our small intentional community. When he arrived by plane three weeks later, he told me that he was having a hard time finding people locally who were asking questions similar to his. During the week of Nick's visit he shared meals and lived with various families and volunteered with our neighborhood projects.

He went home encouraged that there were other people asking questions similar to his and working things out together—and he resolved to find people in his local area to journey with.

Toward the end of Luke's Gospel account, we read about two friends who walked along the road to Emmaus together talking about the significance of recent events. During their conversation they were approached by a stranger who asked, "What are you discussing...?" They told him about what had happened to Jesus of Nazareth, that he had been crucified and how he had disappeared from his tomb. The stranger engaged them in more discussion about Jesus and later accompanied them to dinner. As he broke the bread, they recognized the stranger as Jesus himself (Luke 24:13–33). These two companions met Jesus in the context of their conversation and later they would say, "Were not our hearts burning within us as he talked with us?" Like these early seekers, might we discover the presence of Jesus in our conversations with one another?

WHO IS MY COMMUNITY?

Just before sunset Andrew took us to the ring of Brodgar, an ancient circle of twenty-seven massive standing stones once used for ceremonies and tribal gatherings. The wind howled under a stormy sky and the dewy grass soaked our feet as we stood reminiscing about the enduring gregarious nature of human existence. We humans have always searched together for meaning and for our connection to God.

Jesus lived his life and fulfilled his purposes as a companion—sojourning in the caravan of his relationships with family, neighbors, friends, strangers, and enemies. We can learn a lot about being a companion through the way he lived and what he said. By his words and example he invites us to see ourselves not merely as individuals, but as part of a community of people yearning for wholeness and completion. This is evident in the way he taught his disciples to pray using the plural, "*Our* father in heaven ... give *us* this day *our* daily bread.... Forgive *us our* sins" and "lead *us* not into temptation" (Matthew 6:9–13). We are invited to see our lives and our destiny as interwoven with one other.

Our interconnectedness should seem obvious—except for the fact that many of us have been groomed by a society that celebrates the success of the individual apart from the community. Traveling alone is less complicated but ultimately more lonely. Mobility, global economics, and technology have radically shifted our sense of identity and relationships. Many of us find ourselves socially and geographically stretched, racing between where we live, where we work, and where we feel we most belong. In a time when traditional kinship networks are being redefined, "Who is my community?" is an important question for us to consider.

I frequently hear people use the phrase "my community" to refer to a special group of people they have chosen to relate to. We sometimes speak of "community" as the illusive and idyllic sense of warmth and connectedness that we long for. But perhaps in actuality most of us have all the "community" we need: neighbors, coworkers, relatives, and friends. Our challenge is to learn to embrace, nurture, and cultivate these relationships to their fullest potential—to become the best kind of neighbor, daughter, uncle, colleague, or friend.

My grandmother Mary, a proud daughter of the American Revolution, once told me of a street in London designated by our family surname. My friend Michael walked with me for an entire afternoon searching for it in Wapping, near the Tower of London. At dusk we finally found Scandrett Street by the docks north of the Thames River. In a cemetery across the street from a pub, I paused to imagine the possibility that my ancestors lived in this borough when London was merely a series of smoky medieval villages. I thought of my grandmother, now deceased, standing in this same spot on a trip she took here in the late 1960s. As Michael snapped pictures of me by the street sign, I also thought nostalgically about my parents, sisters, aunts, uncles, and cousins who have carried this name, scattered across the country. With a sudden surge of yearning I also thought of my wife and children. I was in London with the companions I had chosen, while my family stayed behind. "This time," I reasoned, "but next time I will bring the family with me."

Jesus recognized and managed the tension between the chosen community of his disciples and responsibility to his extended family. Even during his crucifixion he was attentive to his mother, saying, "Dear woman, here is your son." And turning to his friend John, he said, "'Here is your mother.' From that time on, this disciple took her into his home" (John 19:26–27). Later Paul of Tarsus urged followers of the Way to remember their families: "If anyone does not provide for his relatives, and especially for his immediate family, he has denied the faith and is worse than an unbeliever" (I Timothy 5:8). Caring for children and aging parents or helping a relative through hard times are important practices of companionship and spiritual formation. The daily life of a household with meals and chores and the cycles of weddings, reunions, and funerals are a rich context for our pilgrimage. We are invited to embrace every person in our relational horizon as having an integral role in our spiritual wayfaring. Whatever can be discovered about life with God in the here and now we will discover together.

GENERATIVE FRIENDSHIP

Jesus had twelve disciples, but a few friends had a more significant role in his life. Mary, Martha, and Lazarus seemed to be kindred spirits of a special quality—as well as Peter, James, and John. He invited these latter three along to share his most ecstatic and vulnerable moments. They were with him on the mountain when he was mystically transfigured and in the garden of Gethsemane, where, in distress and soaked in sweat, he prayed, anticipating his imminent crucifixion. Jesus shared life on a deeper level—with a few trusted confidantes.

Rachael came to me frustrated about her current friendships: "The past couple of years I've become more conscious of the presence of God's kingdom, and I am longing for a more holistic spiritual path. But at my church I have a hard time finding people I resonate with. The teachings of Jesus, for instance, make me want to simplify my life. But when I go out with friends from church, they always choose expensive restaurants and only seem eager to talk about what they own or earn or what they want to buy next. I feel like I don't fit. Where can I find people more like me to walk with?"

We naturally gravitate toward people in a similar life stage or with whom we share common background or experiences. But what we really need, more than relationships that are convenient or homogenous, are friends who support and resonate with our highest aspirations. A good friend is a positive force in your spiritual formation who will help you take your next step toward wholeness. A generative friendship doesn't happen accidentally, but requires consciousness goals and intentionality.

"I'm tired of going to farewell parties," Darren said, in a lamenting voice that conveyed the frustration of living in a place where 20 percent of the population moves away each year. "In fact I refuse to go to any more farewell parties." He added, "We should have a party exclusively for people who are staying in this city." Out of our conversation we made a commitment to develop our friendship. With a social calendar full of so many transient acquaintances, we both needed companionship that could be generative and enduring. Darren and I didn't enjoy the same music or have the same hobbies, but we had common aspirations about our values and goals—and we lived close enough to one other to make our relationship sustainable. We began eating meals together with our families once a week. Through the past nine years, as other friends have come and gone, we are cultivating a legacy of shared memories and milestones: the birth and growth of children, career changes, the challenges of becoming, and even creative collaborations birthed from our camaraderie. We are learning that there is no instant recipe for generative friendship. Having quality companionship takes time and intent.

COMMUNITY AND VULNERABILITY

After Jesus was baptized in the Jordan River, two disciples of John the Baptizer approached him with timid curiosity. Flustered, and not knowing what to say, they asked, "Rabbi, where are you staying?" He replied, "Come and you will see" (John 1:37–39). He brought them home and spent the rest of the day with them. By welcoming them into his home Jesus also welcomed them into his life, allowing them to see the private side of a very public life.

After two nights in a hotel in London, our new friend, Si, invited us to stay at his modest flat. Now it takes a certain degree of vulnerability to welcome someone into your home to use your toilet, towels, pillows, and beds. Stepping into Si's home, we found out whether he keeps his clothes picked up, if he could cook, his tastes in music and books, and how thoroughly he cleans the bathroom.

You follow the path of a companion by welcoming people to come see where you live and who you really are. Sometimes we fear that if people really knew us they would respect us less, or worse, reject us. And so often we create elaborate public personae and pretensions to hide behind. Or we simply limit how close we allow people to get to our true selves. By keeping people at arm's length you protect yourself from embarrassment and accountability but also prevent true intimacy. Revealing where you live and who you really are is an act of courageous trust. John said, "There is no fear in love. But perfect love drives out fear" (I John 4:18). By inviting people into his private life, Jesus modeled the kind of fearless vulnerability that fosters true companionship and love.

One of the greatest gifts my parents gave me was their vulnerability. They were able to admit the places where they struggled in life and weren't afraid to say, "I was wrong, please forgive me." Their honesty and openness allowed me to feel close to them and helped me realize that seeking God is a messy process that intersects with the most personal aspects of our humanity. We need places where we can be known as we really are and still be nurtured and loved.

Chris had a secret from childhood that he tried to hard to forget, memories of the sexual acts the teenage boys next door forced him to perform while his mom was away at work. Once as an adult he took the risk to tell someone and was shut down, so from then on he kept the wounds and confusion to himself, except that the pain was still leaking out in panic attacks, attention deficit disorder, and persistent struggles with pornography. The quiet moments were the most difficult. If he kept himself distracted and busy, he thought, the memories would fade. But eventually his normal coping strategies failed. When other people could see the cracks and inconsistencies, he realized he needed to tell somebody. At forty-three years old, he is learning to be vulnerable and is finally finding help and healing.

I have coffee with the same group of friends every Thursday morning. For five years we have shared life together, talked about our marriages, careers, successes, struggles, indiscretions, aging bodies, and intestinal problems (well, that's usually just me). Our group began when one of us had the courage to reveal a place of critical need in his life. That kind of honesty begs to be reciprocated, and gradually other people began to speak more openly about their own issues, doubts, and ponderings. Meeting consistently over time and negotiating a contract of safety and confidentiality provided space for our companionship to grow. We have invited each other to speak into our lives, wading through our places of woundedness and insecurity. These friends know me too well, actually—and yet still believe in me. It is a great gift to be completely honest with others and reminded that there is a force at work in us greater than ourselves.

RADICAL OPENNESS AND HOSPITALITY

I suspect that riding a bus across the country may be the closest modern equivalent to ancient travel by caravan, which would have been common in Jesus' time. I once rode a bus from Minnesota to Alabama, on a cold January day. It was a twenty-four-hour trip through cities like Milwaukee, Chicago, Louisville, and Memphis, with frequent stops at bus stations and greasy fast food restaurants along the way. The landscape revealed itself incrementally and, looking out through the window, I noticed the subtle shifts in climate, flora, and terrain. If you have ever ridden the bus cross-country you know that the scenery inside the bus is as interesting and colorful as the views outside. There is plenty of time to listen and observe, overhearing the tales of other travelers. You become all too familiar with each other's smells and the sounds of people arguing and babies crying.

At 2 a.m. in Louisville, a tall man who had just been sick on himself sat down next to me. Chain-smoking, with his arm wrapped around me, he regaled me with vividly traumatic tales that transported him back to the jungle warfare of Vietnam. That ride on the bus provided a far richer experience than any three-hour plane ride could afford.

Not many of us travel by bus anymore. Aside from the fact that it takes too long, you would likely be in the company of strangers of a different class and sort. For many of us, our relative prosperity allows us to avoid the discomfort of such situations. If Jesus lived in our day, I think he would take the bus. Perhaps the example of Jesus can inspire us to travel by new paths.

Jesus demonstrated a radical openness to people. He was a companion to the poor and marginalized, to tax collectors and "sinners." He ate with criminals, prostitutes, and religious extremists. He approached people with leprosy and spoke with people whom we might call crazy. He violated the cultural conventions of his time, speaking with women and even asking a scorned Samaritan woman of questionable morals for a cup of water when he was thirsty. Jesus gave to outcast people, but he also recognized their dignity and equality by receiving help from them. He crossed boundaries of social class, lifestyle, and ethnicity, and we are invited to follow his example.

Darin and Meeghan are two friends who come to mind when I think of radical openness and hospitality. Heads turn at parties when their ragamuffin family arrives. Meeghan leads the entourage, carrying their infant son, Justice, followed by Darin, who walks arm in arm with Guinn, an eighty-six-year-old woman with Alzheimer's who is both sweet and sassy. She has lived with them the past four years. Darin patiently answers Guinn's questions about where they are, and once accustomed to her surroundings, she eagerly greets the young men present with hello kisses and flattery. Shyly standing behind Guinn, Irma follows, carrying the diaper bag. She is a middle-aged Eritrean refugee living with Darin and Meeghan while they help her obtain a work visa and greater emotional stability. Then Meeghan quickly introduces one more person, Sarah, a twenty-five-year-old neighbor who has been staying with them the past few months. Sarah ran into financial trouble when she broke up with an abusive boyfriend and needed a place to stay until she could get back on her feet. Simply by being friends with Darin and Meeghan, all who know and encounter them are swept up in the current of their radical hospitality.

The best traveling companions help us see and connect with everyone around us, knowing that we learn more about the good news of God by sharing our lives with an ever-widening cast of characters. This kind of hospitality isn't about cooking a delicious and elegant meal for friends or entertaining with style and panache. It is what Jesus was talking about when said, "But when you give a banquet, invite the poor, the crippled, the lame, the blind and you will be blessed" (Luke 14:13). Through the practice of radical hospitality we welcome the stranger into our lives and communities. "Do not forget to entertain strangers," the Hebrew pilgrims were told, "for by so doing some people have entertained angels without knowing it" (Hebrews 13:2).

Like any new skill, you can learn to offer this kind of hospitality by small incremental steps.

COMMON ACTION

On our last night in London Si took us to the red light district of SoHo, where actual red lights glowed in the second story windows along the narrow streets. Si explained that many of the girls who work in these upstairs brothels, from Eastern Europe, Asia, and Africa, are victims of human trafficking. Si and a group of friends have channeled their outrage at this injustice into positive action, organizing a campaign to liberate women from their slave masters and advocating for changes in public policy.

Generative friendship, at its best, leads to positive action and societal transformation. Jesus invited his companions into his revolutionary enterprise and a common rhythm of life. Together they traveled and shared the good news of God among the poor. He sent them out to other towns and villages in groups of two to proclaim the message and heal the sick. Jesus took them along when he prayed. They also went to weddings and feasts and even vacationed together. To be a disciple and companion of Jesus implied a distinctive call to a common life of action.

As important as conversation is, it is stillborn if it doesn't eventually lead to common action. In our fragmented society it is too easy to have discussions about problems and how we wish things could be different without making a commitment to work together to see change occur. Through the example of Jesus and the disciples we are invited to move from passive speculation to creative action—from talking about prayer to practicing spiritual disciplines, from debating social issues to engaging affected peoples, from discussing justice and poverty to eating with the forgotten and hungry. It is not enough for us to have conversations about how we want to live. Most of us do not have the momentum or persistence to act alone. We need to find ways to move forward together, adopting common habits, rhythms, and experiments in obedience.

After my trip to England and Scotland, a trickle of visitors began arriving on our doorstep from various small communities in the United Kingdom. Many of these guests had begun to describe themselves as being part of a monastic movement—meaning a group of people intentionally committed to a set of vows and common practices. These kinds of groups are popping up all over the globe and in the press have been described as "the new monastics." Similar to our community in San Francisco, these friends were realizing that to get momentum in their ambitions to follow the Way of Jesus, they needed concrete actions to take together. Some groups live in co-housing, other groups share a common rhythm of prayer and hospitality, or work together to address local or global needs. There is an element of monastic practice present whenever a group of people make a commitment to act on the example and teachings of Jesus together. What we are all learning from our various experiments with a common life is that the message of Jesus takes on more urgency and vibrancy as we interact with it communally in the details of our daily lives.

If we can imagine a world that is different, together we can make it happen.

CONVERSATION

Traveling companions?   All the people in your proximity are the companions for your spiritual journey. Make a list of the communities that you are a part of. Consider what your next step might be—moving from independence to greater solidarity.

Generative friendships.   Think of people you know who might resonate with your desire to explore the message of Jesus more concretely. Consider how you might cultivate more intentional conversations and generative friendships.

EXPERIMENTS

Transforming conversation.   You may find it helpful to participate in discussion in which you can share aspirations and ask honest questions about integrating the message of Jesus into life in the here and now. Robust conversations can also help you develop intentional traveling companions. Consider starting a group with friends and acquaintances that would meet monthly or weekly six to eight times over a meal in someone's home. You may want to identify topics together ahead of time and rotate facilitation among participants. This book, or one like it, might be a useful tool for your discussion. Have two people facilitate together. The conversation will have more forward energy if you avoid criticism and negativity. Encourage one another to move from talking to action by committing to a common practice between meetings.

Who can you be real with?   How comfortable are you inviting people to see where you live and who you really are? Take the next step to reveal yourself more fully to a friend or small group.

New boundaries of friendship.   Each person has something to teach us about God and ourselves. There are lessons in life you may only learn with people who are different from you. Identify someone in your workplace, neighborhood, or city that you can begin to cultivate a new friendship with.

CHAPTER FOUR

EXPERIMENTS IN TRUTH

It is bittersweet to recall the first few years that our family lived in San Francisco. We had moved to the city with a dream: to form a community of people who would take Jesus seriously as the teacher and revolutionary he intended to be. Our new neighbors and acquaintances were quick to point out that people who called themselves "Christians" were responsible for the inquisitions, religious wars, and homophobia—not to mention the historic use of scripture to justify slavery, the massacre of native peoples, aggressive foreign policy, and the destruction of the Earth's resources. I had to agree that there was tremendous dissonance between the dominant reputation of Christianity and the life of Christ and the early church. We desperately wanted to be people who embodied the revolution of the kingdom of love—offering an apologetic for the authenticity of the Way of Jesus as an alternative to mainstream Christianity.

A small group of us began meeting together to study the gospel accounts and the documents of the early church. We were drawn to the communal nature of the primitive church and the power, solidarity, and compassion followers of Jesus exhibited under persecution during the Roman Empire. Our faith community, which at the time we called a house church, attracted zealous idealists as well as people who had been hurt or marginalized through their experiences with organized religion. For a while we felt criticized and misunderstood, both by the culture and by the mainstream church. It took some time to move beyond critical deconstruction—to define ourselves more by what we were for than what we were against.

Gradually we learned to channel our group energy toward experimenting with how to imitate the path of Jesus and the early disciples. Some things we took quite literally. We tried fasting and praying for forty days. I grew a beard and long hair. We began living communally. And we hosted parties for neighbors and offered hospitality and friendship to people battling addictions, personality disorders, and depression. It was, in retrospect, a fertile and chaotic period for our family. We were being formed through these experiences with great intensity. One thing we try to preserve from that time is a sense of humility and risk taking.

We found that one of the best ways for our group to learn the Way of Jesus was by trying to imitate his example through some tangible exercise or activity. Mahatma Gandhi described this kind of intentional pursuit as an "experiment in truth." Experiments are always successful on some level, because by taking a risk you learn both from your failures and accomplishments. And there is a depth of understanding that can only be achieved through conscious activity.

It is my hope with this book not only to explore ideas about making a life in the Way of Jesus, but also to share some of our family and community "experiments in truth."

EMPEROR ARCADIA

After reading about the kind of companion Jesus was, and knowing what he taught about love for neighbors, my friend Joseph and I decided to try some experiments in radical openness to people. We began by making a daily practice of picking up trash on our block. In the evenings, along with my kids, we walked around the block with trash sticks and plastic bags greeting neighbors and collecting debris. The sidewalks in our neighborhood were notoriously dirty, strewn with household garbage, old couches, bed frames, and broken TVs. People's reactions to our nightly trash walks varied. One person offered us cold beers. Another asked us to pray for his family. One neighbor thanked us for our kindness and another cussed us out because he thought our clean-up was a manifestation of privilege and gentrification. What we hoped would be a sign of neighborly affection was interpreted ambiguously.

After a few months of picking up garbage we prayed that God would bring someone into our path that we could care for more deeply. Riding the bus home from work one night, Joseph met an elderly man who seemed lonely and in need of a friend. He invited Joseph to visit and the next day Joseph took me along to see him.

"Come on in, boys. Will you smoke a joint with me?" the old man said as Joseph and I climbed the steps of the rusty old school bus, searching for a place to sit. The bus, parked in a vacant lot on Potrero Hill, was painted in bold letters that read: "I HAVE BEEN CONDUCTING EXPERIMENTS ON MYSELF FOR 30 YEARS—EXPLORING THE MYSTERIES OF CHEMISTRY AND HEALTH. MY PRESCRIPTION: EAT A CLOVE OF GARLIC AND DRINK YOUR OWN URINE AND SEMEN TWICE A DAY." Joseph and I glanced at each other and wondered what we were getting ourselves into. Shaking my hand, the small old man, wearing a black evening gown, took a bow saying, "You may call me Emperor Arcadia." Seated again, his arthritic hands struggled to roll a joint while he spoke. "I've been taking speed for thirty years, medicating myself. The combination of speed and special topical chemicals is curing me of all human diseases." As he continued we stole glances around the crowded old bus containing soiled clothes, salvaged computer monitors, and buckets of urine. A mix of curious smells strained my nose for recognition.

"The government has lied to us! It's a conspiracy to extermi-nate the planet! If I were in charge I would burn all the money and declare the planet monetary and class free. We will all be equal and wealthy."

I attempted to break into his monologue with a question: "Emperor, how long have you lived in San Francisco?"

He quickly replied, "Too long. Do you have an estate in the country where you would like me to be the caretaker?"

I tried again: "How old are you?"

He quickly answered, "I'm not old, I'm as young as they come."

I persisted. "Where did you grow up?"

"Grow up? I haven't grown up. . . ." He then returned to his speech, "Boys, I advise you to drink your own urine twice a day, those golden showers will cure what ails' ya." When he could sense that we were only listening to be polite, he became defensive. "I can see you don't believe me. But you had better. I am a messenger from God."

Joseph spoke up. "What a coincidence. We are also followers of God's messenger, Jesus." That was the wrong thing to say, for the emperor grew agitated and exclaimed, "I'm #$%! Jesus Christ, the G——n messiah, Jesus isn't coming back so you had better listen to me! If you don't believe me, then get out my bus!"

We groped for a diplomatic way to end our visit. "It was good to meet you, Emperor!" I said, as we exited the bus, befuddled by this strange encounter.

I turned to Joseph. "Well, I guess that attempt to be intentional about having relationships with people on the margins failed," I said.

"We can't make someone be our friend," Joseph said, "if they don't want a relationship."

A few months later I ran into the emperor at the plaza downtown. Slumped over, sunburned and haggard and sitting in a wheelchair, he was hardly recognizable. Yet he was dressed impeccably, decked out in a costume crown and bright gold jewelry, wielding a royal amulet in his jittering hand. When I greeted him, he smiled, saying, "I'm doing better than ever, can't you see? I was just going to get something to eat, would you like to join me?" Recalling our first encounter, I was taken aback by his friendliness. He insisted on buying me a strawberry shake. As he went up to pay, several tablets of methamphetamines fell out of his wallet onto the counter. Sitting in a booth across from me, he repeated, verbatim, the monologue from our first visit. I looked at him intently—his hands brown with filth, dirt caught in the creases of his worn skin. That mouth!—grotesque, toothless, and rotting, wildly chomping a chicken sandwich. My stomach turned. Sputtering incoherently now, he was desperately trying to get through to me, as his spit and chicken sandwich landed on my face. I stared into his hazel-green eyes, wondering what he was thinking and feeling inside. "Emperor Arcadia, what has it been like living by yourself in that bus all these years?"

He paused dramatically. "It feels ... lonely sometimes."

I pressed for more. "What do you do when you are lonely?"

Subdued for a moment, he answered, "I lock myself in my bus for three or four days, or come down to this corner." And then he quickly changed the subject. "I need to get a shower.... Hey! Look at him, I'd like to have him on a chain to dominate...."

I racked my conflicted brain and heart to understand. I wondered, "Am I wasting my time with this man, or is he teaching me something about the compassion of Jesus?" When I told Joseph about my encounter with the emperor, we debated about engaging him further. We had previously written him off because we didn't see much hope for change in his life. He also didn't make us feel rewarded for our efforts. "Is an act of love only significant because of the change it produces? Or, can the meaning be in the act itself?" I pondered aloud. It seemed like God had brought the emperor back into our lives. While Joseph and I were discussing what to do, we thought of Jesus' teachings about giving to others without expecting anything in return and the fact that God is kind, even to the ungrateful (Luke 6:35). We realized that, as followers of the Way, we were being invited to love the emperor despite his prickly hostility and highly unusual personal habits.

A few days later Joseph and I stopped by the emperor's bus. More sedated, he expressed that he was glad to see us, and explained that he had just completed one of his "cycles of treatment," which involved covering his entire body with menthol vapor rub followed by petroleum jelly, then taking a hit of methamphetamines. "We all have these bugs living in our bodies that are killing us. I'm slowly sweating them out," he said. "This treatment forces the bugs from deep within the body to surface where they drown." He explained how he then washes in a solution of vinegar, bleach, dish soap, and urine. "The whole process takes three days. Look at how young and fresh my skin looks now. Pretty good for being sixty-three years old."

"Emperor, is there anything we can do for you?" I asked.

"Well, I'm hungry and I haven't eaten for days. My legs aren't working too good so I can't get to the store." Handing us some money, he asked us to buy him an Italian sausage sandwich. "Make sure you get it with mayonnaise and provolone cheese—and buy yourselves sandwiches with my money too. They are very delicious."

As we ate the sandwiches together, two young men approached the bus. Dressed in leather pants and jackets, with their faces covered in sores and their hands black with grease, they looked like survivors of a nuclear holocaust. He handed these men, his drug suppliers, a wad of cash. "Keep the change, honey, for a personal favor I might ask of you later," he said with a wink.

Along with other friends from our community we began visiting the emperor several times a week, bringing groceries, helping to cut his hair or clip his toenails, and cleaning up around his camp. Gradually he began to trust our friendship and revealed more about himself. His real name was Robert. Estranged from his family after years in mental institutions, he had moved west from Wisconsin. During the sexual revolution of the 1970s he was something of a celebrity in San Francisco's gay club scene, hosting "naked pool" on Sunday afternoons at a popular bar South of Market where he would prance nude around the pool table exchanging fiery jabs with patrons. The club owner let him live in the basement of the building for many years. We learned that Emperor Arcadia was locally famous for crashing society balls, civic celebrations, and parades, announcing himself swathed in a velvet cape and crown and accompanied by his matching miniature poodles on leashes. As he got older and more peculiar, he lost his social currency and became more isolated.

The emperor's health continued to deteriorate and by December he was confined to a wheelchair. In addition to this trouble, the owner of the property where he was squatting was taking legal action to have him removed. We advocated for the emperor with the health department and social services and pleaded with him to move into an assisted living facility. He pessimistically predicted that the apocalypse would come by the first of the year. "I'm going to kill myself on New Year's Eve," he told us, by mixing vodka with a fatal dose of phenobarbital.

"I would be really sad if you chose to kill yourself," I told him.

"Why should you care if I live or die?" he asked indignantly.

"Emperor, you are valuable to God and to the people who love you. We would miss you."

"Nobody has ever cared about me," he replied bitterly.

"I'm really sorry you feel that way. After all the time we've spent together the past few months, I hoped that you might consider Joseph and me to be your friends."

At Christmas we decided to throw a party for the emperor, including his favorite foods and a birthday cake. I told him that I was going to bring my family along, so he would need to be on his best behavior. We could never predict what the emperor would say or do.

There was a full moon on that December evening when I knocked at the door to the emperor's bus. He came out wearing an elegant purple bonnet, with freshly painted fingernails. A thin young woman, who we knew worked as a prostitute, lived in a trailer on the street nearby, joined us, along with one of her "clients." We ate by candlelight serenaded by music from a transistor radio. The emperor declared that the food—a collection of favorite dishes he requested—was delicious. After dinner my wife Lisa put candles on a cake. "Let's sing Happy Birthday to someone who hasn't celebrated their birthday in awhile," I said. "Who could we sing Happy Birthday to?"

Just then, beaming, our three-year-old son Noah blurted, "It's Christmas, let's sing Happy Birthday to Jesus!"

I panicked. The name "Jesus" was the worst thing I could imagine mentioning in front of the emperor, and I waited to see how he would react. Slowly, with a big toothless grin, he said, "Yes, let's sing Happy Birthday to Jesus." Under a clear and starry night the eight of us sang together—Lisa and me, a streetwalker and her john, a sixty-three-year-old transvestite, and three small blond children with red cheeks. As I helped the emperor back into his bus, he turned to me and said, "This was the best night of my life. Thank you!"

We told the emperor that the following Sunday we would stop by with some friends to help move the bus and his belongings off the property to comply with the owner's injunction. When we arrived Sunday morning Joseph and I knocked at the door of the bus. There was no response, but we heard a faint groaning from inside. We broke down the door and found the emperor collapsed on the floor, lying in a pool of his own waste. He tried to talk, and through his slurred speech, I deciphered that he wanted water. We sat him up, though he was semiconscious and weak, and gave him a drink. As we began to change his clothes and wash his body, what had happened slowly dawned on us—he had taken the phenobarbital as planned. Searching quickly we found a few of the tablets scattered across the floor by a bottle of vodka. The rest of our group had just arrived when we called for an ambulance.

As the paramedics lifted him onto the gurney he pleaded for me to stay beside him. I rode along to the hospital in the back of the ambulance holding his hand.

At the emergency room after he was stabilized, a nurse invited me into the examining room where I stood alone by his side. "Emperor," I said, "it's Mark." With his eyes still shut he murmured, "I wanted to die. Why did you save my life?"

I hesitated for a moment, searching for words. "You are my friend and I care about you."

Agitated, with speech still slurred, he asked, "But why do you care about me?" And then louder and more desperately he repeated, "Why do you care about me?"

Slowly I lifted my hand and began to caress his bald head. "Emperor, we are all loved," I said. Then I heard him snoring and watched his chest rise and fall with each belabored breath.

I stood there for a long time, praying, and thinking about this man who felt so isolated and lonely that it was impossible for him to imagine that anyone would care. Perhaps he was a living caricature of the feelings we all share—doubts about our worth.

When Joseph and I arrived at the hospital the next day he was wide awake and smiling. With hugs he greeted us like long-lost sons. He quickly handed Joseph some money and told him to go out and buy each of us a prime rib dinner to eat together. The hospital psychologist was anxious to meet me and discreetly invited me into her office. I held the keys to his bus and kept all his legal and personal papers and gave her as much of his life story as I had pieced together through our conversations. As I shared what I knew I had the strange realization that, although I had only known the emperor for six months, I was closer to him now than anyone else alive.

After the interview the doctor curiously asked, "What exactly is your role in the neighborhood?" I explained that Joseph and I were part of a small church community trying to imitate the example of Jesus by making friends with lonely people. "That sounds like the kind of church I would love to join," she replied.

Even now as I retell this story I am drawn back into the sights and smells and complicated emotions I felt during that time. I realize there is unique absurdity to the characters and situation—two idealistic young men and their experiment in friendship with an eccentric old man with a death wish. By telling this story I'm not suggesting that everyone could or should make friends with someone like the emperor. What I do know is that I feel alive when I am testing the limits of my own boundaries—finding a source of love that is greater than my own and discovering beauty in unexpected places.

CONVERSATION

Credibility.   What kind of reputation does the Way of Jesus have with the people in your community? How might this be changed or improved by people who take Jesus more seriously as an example and guide?

An experiment in friendship.   What were your feelings or thoughts as you read about the emperor? What did the details and ambiguities of the story provoke in you?

EXPERIMENTS

Be open to the peculiar.   There is likely someone in the periphery of your relationships who is lonely or peculiar. Quite often the public services and support offered to people living with mental illness are inadequate. In the Gospels these kinds of people were often drawn toward encounters with Jesus and his disciples. Go out of your way to cultivate a friendship with such a person—in partnership with a friend who can help you navigate the relationship.

Teach a child to care.   You may wonder if it is safe for children to be around unstable or addicted people. If there is adequate guidance and supervision, it can be helpful to introduce children to the more sobering realities of our society—and they may be less likely to have an unhealthy fascination with illicit activities if they learn to care about people who have been damaged by them. Take a child with you to visit a shelter, prison, soup kitchen, or assisted living facility. Kids learn to be compassionate by watching their parents and elders care for the needs of others.

PART TWO

EMBRACING LIFE AS A GIFT AND SACRED TRUST

ARE YOU FEELIN' ME?

The time has come....
MARK 1:15A

On Saturday morning I walk outside to empty the trash and find my neighbor Ron-Ron cheerfully sitting on the front steps. He greets me warmly as he takes a sip of cheap vodka from a small bottle. It has been a good morning for my neighbor. Reaching into his pocket, with a glad smile, he produces a handful of wadded bills and a few small bags of yellowed crystals. The money has come from transactions earlier that morning involving those little bags of crack cocaine, which some of my neighbors smoke each day.

Ron-Ron is a simple man who pretends to be a street hustler more than he is one—like a young child pretends to be a superhero. Sometimes when I see him and know his name, he runs toward me, hugs me tight, and repeatedly kisses my cheek saying, "You remembered me, bro. You remembered me." After each sentence of our conversation he turns to me and says, "Are you feelin' me? Are you feelin' me?" If you are not familiar with his question, this is an Ebonics phrase meaning, "Are you listening? Do you understand what I am saying?" And I reply, "I'm feelin' you, Ron-Ron. I'm feelin' you."

"Are you feelin' me?" Perhaps it is the heart cry of all of us as we ponder our situation as citizens of planet Earth, struggling with the meaning and moments of our lives. Is there someone or something out there or behind all this who understands what we go through, who knows what it is like to be a human being, who can show us the best way through?

Jesus said, "The time has come." Those who first heard these words found it hard to believe their age was the time of the Maker's presence and care. At that moment they were an oppressed people, occupied by a foreign power. On their backs they carried the packs of Roman soldiers. They were forced to pay taxes to Caesar. Their temple had previously been desecrated. Patriot insurgents were being executed. For hundreds of years no prophet had spoken. Where had Yahweh gone? Was Adonai asleep? A crazy man in camel's hair was somewhere out in the desert shouting, "People get ready! Something is about to happen!" This they sincerely doubted.

For hope they looked to the past. In the chronicles of their history they identified the hand of God. Perhaps they recalled their creation story, the covenant with Abraham, the exodus from Egypt, Moses leading their ancestors to the promised land. Or they thought of the golden age of the warrior poet David, the kingdom of Solomon, or the epic songs of the prophets. "Was it not better even when we were children?" they asked.

And for hope they looked to the future. The prophecies spoke of a time when they would be delivered from all their enemies. A time would come when Elohim would bring lasting peace and prosperity. But this was surely not that time.

With his first line, Jesus awakens their expectancy about the present moment. This is the moment of the Creator's care and activity. If you look you will see. If you listen you will hear. If you sniff you will smell that God is on the move.

We often struggle, as they did, to recognize the care and activity of God in the present moment. It is often more convenient to make conjectures about signs of goodness in the past or in the future. We may think of the years that Jesus walked the earth, or the radical love of the early followers of the Way. We may long for another time or place that appeals enviously to our sensibilities. Or we might reminisce about another year or an earlier decade when life was better or we felt closer to the heartbeat of God. Some of us dwell perpetually in the psychic past—grounded there by disappointment, failures, or regret.

Faced with the trials, ambiguities, and routine of life in the present, we may be tempted to wager our satisfaction on preferred scenarios for the future (when I graduate, get promoted, get married, get pregnant, buy a home, retire). I suspect that our society's enduring fascination with apocalyptic prophecies and speculations about how and when the world will end have something to do with our frustrations with life here in the present. We are perplexed with how to interpret and act heroically in the here and now.

Can we be optimistic about the future? What about the prediction that things will get worse before they get better? Is our obligation simply to hold on as the world collapses around us? What if we are invited to trust that God is at work in our time and that, even if we can't see whether the world is getting better or worse, we can cooperate with our Creator's agenda that we become better people who live out a legacy of love in a world desperate for healing?

These are exciting times to be living in, with unprecedented opportunities! Some have called the changes we have experienced in our lifetime a virtual collapse of space and time. Our mobility allows us to be increasingly aware and connected to global friendships and concerns. The diversity and pluralism of our world allows us to explore and struggle together with how to move beyond the social and cultural fragmentation that has characterized past decades. We can either approach the changes we perceive with fear and skepticism or embrace change with a sense of hope and expectancy.

The acceleration of our society can make us feel disoriented—grasping for some kind of equilibrium. And you may feel pulled in one of three directions. The traditionalist in us longs for the mythic past, an illusive golden age that really never existed. Another part of us may wish to be passive consumers of the present. And something inside of us wants to become culture makers: people who imagine and work toward a better future for all people.

Jesus speaks into our situation with existential words of hope and possibility. For us the time has come and the time is now. This is the anticipated moment when we recognize the presence and care of the Creator and act to fulfill our eternal destiny. If we listen we will hear. If we look we will see. If we inhale we will smell the invitation and presence of God in our time and our place.

The chapters in Part Two explore what it might mean for us to embrace our lives and our times as a gift and sacred trust. I think there are several key concerns to address that will help us embrace life with God in the here and now:

- The message of Jesus was as much about the present as about the future.
- Our window on the world either inhibits or encourages us to live generatively in the here and now.
- It might take some conscious searching to make the connection between the epic story of creation and the specific stories of our lives.
- We were made to be artists, collaborating with our Maker to dream and work toward a better future.

When you think about God or ask a question like, "Are you feelin' me?" you want to know that there is someone who listens and understands you, remembers you, and knows you by name. Making a life in the Way of Jesus is about our journey to trust that we are truly cared for and loved.

CONVERSATION

Are you feelin' me?   Do you think God is aware of or concerned about the details in your everyday life? Do you tend to see God as close by or far away?

Better or worse?   Where do you see evidence that human society is getting better or worse? How do you think your perception of history and destiny affect your daily choices? Do you think this is an exciting and important time to be alive? Why or why not?

Traditionalist, consumer, or culture maker? Do you tend to be a traditionalist, a consumer, or a culture maker? What is one thing about the world we live in that you would like to see change in your lifetime? How can you begin to instigate that change?

EXPERIMENTS

Turn off the TV. Our attitudes are shaped by our influences. The sensationalism of the media can give the impression that life is better or worse than it actually is. Go on a media fast for one week, avoiding television, movies, web surfing, magazines, and radio (and maybe even books). Is this a challenging exercise for you? After the experiment reflect on how this experience affected you.

Who are you and where are you going? Take an hour this week to journal about who you are and where you are headed in life. Do you tend to dwell on the mistakes or glory days of the past, or wager satisfaction on what could be in the future? Process how you can receive this time in life as a gift and seize upon immediate opportunities to be vital in the lives of others.

CHAPTER FIVE

DARKNESS AND LIGHT: THE SCANDAL OF ETERNITY

A fine French champagne is uncorked and poured as more guests arrive, shedding umbrellas and raincoats on a cold and rainy winter night. Some are beckoned to help with preparations for potato latkes while others mingle and nibble on crackers, salad, and noodle kugel. We are clustered in the kitchen between the counter where the bottles of wine are set to breathe and the stove where soups simmer and latkes sizzle in the pan. Excited children run in and out of the room with handfuls of golden plastic dreidel coins. Our host, Michael, collects fascinating friends, and at this party we are all on display: artists, photographers, horticulturists, writers, an attorney, an expert in the classics, a screenwriter and opera singer, an offshore accounts portfolio manager, and the production designer from a major film studio. As I scan the familiar faces in the room I notice: this is a Hanukkah party mostly for and by Jewish atheists who married gentiles and relocated from New York to California.

Conversations at Michael's parties are always interesting, smart, and spirited. It is not long before someone brings up religion, a sore point with many because of the current political administration's aggressive foreign policies and alliances with religious conservatives. The expert in the classics, raised in the Dutch Reformed tradition in Grand Rapids, Michigan, opens the discussion with a merry declaration, "The only religion I'm against is Christianity!" He holds up a tumbler of whiskey and provides a detailed and mocking elucidation of the five points of Calvinism. One woman warns the group to be nice because she is a devout Catholic. With panache the opera singer exclaims, "Just don't talk to me about intelligent design. I can't stand to hear that crap," he says with a teasing smile. "Evolution is a scientific fact."

Perhaps taking our conversation a little more seriously, I suggest that evolutionary process doesn't negate the possibility of divine origins. "The greater question," I add, "is whether life comes from chaos or some benevolent force."

"Well, the only thing I hate more than Christians is agnostics," the opera singer retorts with a sly laugh. "I mean, get off the fence. Make a decision. Either God exists or doesn't."

I quietly interject, "Some would say that atheists have the most courage—because of the terrorizing implication that life is without meaning or purpose."

"Well, if there is anything I hate more than Christians or agnostics, it's nihilists. I can't stand nihilism and drab talk about how everything is meaningless," the opera singer says, feigning melancholy. Someone else proposes that it may actually take more courage to believe that God does exist—because of the haunting possibility that how we choose to live really matters. I add, "Even if we try to avoid the tensions and debate about the existence of God, we are still faced with the persistent question: Is there a meaning and purpose to our existence? And if so, what is it?" There is an awkward pause.

"More latkes anyone?" Michael asks.

We drift off to refill soup bowls and wine glasses, mixing into more intimate side conversations. The classics professor continues to monologue about total depravity, unconditional election, and limited atonement, but by now no one is listening.

When I get involved in the same conversation over and over, I start to wonder whether we are having an honest exchange or simply talking past one another to affirm what we already believe or doubt. Early impressions of spiritual beliefs can be enduring, even while they may be simplistic or misinformed, and can serve to vaccinate us from further spiritual curiosity. The limits of childhood understanding often continue to inhibit our adult imaginations—and we frequently resist information that would challenge our embryonic assumptions. Real spiritual investigation sometimes requires overcoming or undoing our earlier impressions, including notions about the message of Jesus.

SCARY JESUS

I can still see my daughter Hailey's big blue eyes welling up with tears, her soft face grimacing with pain as she began to cry. I was telling her about Jesus and showing her a book of pictures. They were the usual images: Jesus as a baby nestled in a feed trough; Jesus bleeding and hanging on a cross; Jesus lying dead in a tomb; and Jesus sitting on a golden throne. Generally I don't show pictures of bloody dead people to children—but this was an exception, it was Jesus. The morbidity of these brightly colored pictures did not occur to me—since I had seen them all of my life. As I turned the pages I told her an abbreviated version of the story, finishing with the phrase, "Jesus died on the cross so that someday we can go to a wonderful placed called heaven." That was when Hailey burst into tears. Sobbing, she murmured, "Daddy, I don't want to go to heaven! I want to stay here with you and Mommy." I took her in my arms, attempting to comfort and explain, but my words were no help. For the next few weeks Hailey cried every time she saw the book cover. We hid the book, promising we would not show her any more scary pictures of that man Jesus.

JESUS THE SADOMASOCHIST

My ill-fated telling of the story to Hailey reminded me of my earliest impressions of Jesus and his message. These recollections play in my mind like film noir, with heightened contrasts between shadows and light—juxtapositions between the warmth I felt when my family held hands and prayed to Jesus at meals and bedtime and the cold mildew of the church basement where we sat in rusty folding chairs listening to old ladies teach us songs and use paper cutouts stuck to flannel boards to tell us stories about Jesus. In the pictures and porcelain figurines, Jesus was a white man with soft brown hair sitting with children like me on his lap, or carrying a lamb on his shoulders, or bleeding on a cross, or knocking on a metaphorical door—the "door" to my heart.

When I was three I heard a man on the radio describe the fiery flames and torment of eternal damnation as we bumped along in the old green Pontiac one summer afternoon. The backs of my preschool legs were sweating against the hot vinyl seats as I heard the preacher say, "Believe or burn! Believe that you have sinned and that Jesus died in your place." "If this is true," I thought, "then I would be a fool not to pray 'the sinner's prayer.'" And I prayed it: "Jesus, forgive my sins and come into my heart." And in some soothing strange haunting and intangible way Jesus became my savior and I was going to heaven someday when I died.

In my child-mind the story, as I heard it, had sadomasochistic qualities. The world I enjoyed (ice cream, toys, zoos, and movies) was, unbeknownst to me, a dark wasteland that would ultimately be destroyed. God had me tied down and dangling over the flames of hell, demonstrating his love by offering to release me, but only if I would beg for mercy. Love, pain, and intimacy commingled. God was obviously powerful, but was God truly good? And could this God be trusted? I would have to move from fear to trust and unlearn what I knew in order to embrace a life with God more fully.

I later realized that the story was told to me in such a dire manner and with cataclysmic effect in order to bring me to a point of singular decision. Who wouldn't want to believe when the stakes were so high? My decision was a matter of life or death, heaven or hell. I had to choose now. Telling the story in terms of eternal destiny might have expedited my decision, but it offered little incentive for me to keep seeking or believing. High-pressure sales tactics had forced the deal but did not produce a satisfied repeat customer. I had done my business with God and was now glad to have God off my back.

If my early impression of the gospel of Jesus seems distorted or peculiar, you don't have to look far to hear the same story being told today. It is probably the version of the message familiar to the most people. At home I have a growing collection of gospel tracts that are handed to me by well-meaning Evangelistas when I walk down Mission Street. They all contain a message similar to the one I heard and told Hailey—that the message about Jesus should drive you toward one decision, motivated by fear of punishment that will determine your eternal destiny.

As I grew older it didn't take me long to begin wondering about whether what I was told was really the whole story. Does someone have to become fixated on death and damnation before the life of Jesus makes any sense? Is the message of Jesus only about a distant God and the future in another world? Is fear of eternal punishment the healthiest or most enduring reason to seek your Maker? And, is choosing the path of life really as simple as saying "the sinner's prayer"?

OBSESSED WITH ETERNITY

On my third helping of latkes Kendall sits down next to me. We chat about our kids (my son Isaiah and her son are best buddies) and then about our families and work responsibilities. She is a production designer at a major film studio. I was fascinated to learn more about the intricacies involved in creating big-budget animated movies. When she eventually asked about my work, I found myself hesitating. People have so many preconceived ideas about ministers, churches, and religious organizations. If I sound too excited about what I do, will she think I'm proselytizing?

Once I searched for the word *pastor* in an online thesaurus and found the following synonyms suggested: "Holy Joe, Glory roader, Sin Hound, Harp Polisher, and Sky Pilot." The definitions assumed that someone with my vocation is singularly interested, even obsessed, with preparing people to die and meet their Maker. God and eternity are often conceived as being far away and disconnected from our current reality. Sometimes people who are deeply interested in eternity have the tendency to dismiss the significance of life in the here and now—as if a person has to choose between concern about their eternal destiny and caring for the immediate needs in our world. If this world is destined for the wrecking ball, as the logic goes, why seek personal or social transformation? The only thing that matters is spreading the apocalyptic message so that others might believe and be airlifted away from the here and now. It is not surprising, then, that so many people who think that the message of Jesus is primarily about another world struggle to find a meaningful and integrated spiritual path in the here and now. If good news is about another time and place, you may be ready for heaven, but feel unprepared for life on Earth.

Our understanding of the time dimension of the message of Jesus can either limit or expand our creativity and imagination for life here and now. Even if we suspect that an extended version of the Jesus story might reveal a more holistic, nuanced, and tangible message, the fact remains that the collapsed version familiar to the most people is biased toward the apocalypse. Perhaps we see the otherworldly ramifications of the story because this is what we were first invited to observe, and we tend to only notice what we are expecting.

In psychology class at my university a professor asked us to count how many times a basketball was passed between players on a video recording. We watched the ball dutifully. At the conclusion of the five-minute video clip he asked how many times the ball had been passed. Our numbers varied just slightly. "And class, how many of you saw a woman walk across the court through the players holding a rainbow-colored umbrella?" Huh? We didn't see any woman carrying a rainbow-colored umbrella. When the professor replayed the video clip, there she was. Some of the players had to move out of the way to avoid being hit by her large bright umbrella. Most of us hadn't noticed her because we were looking for something else: basketballs.

If we are invited to look at the significance of Jesus' message solely in terms of the afterlife, that is all we are likely to find. In groups, when I have asked, "What is the message of the gospel?" most people predictably respond with a statement like, "Jesus died for our sins so we can be forgiven and go to heaven when we die." I then ask, "Where, exactly, did Jesus state this as his message?" Awkward silence. There is little evidence within the gospel accounts to suggest that Jesus' message was primarily about another world or the afterlife. We should wonder about the difference between what Jesus proclaimed as "good news" and what is now commonly thought of as "the gospel."

Is the message of Jesus primarily about another world or about life in the here and now? The Gospel writer Mark wrote that Jesus came to proclaim the "good news of God"—to illuminate or remind us of the fact that there has always been and will always be a source of life who is present, caring, and active in our world. In context, Jesus spoke as an ambassador of hope for the future *and* for the present. According to Mark's Gospel, he traveled throughout Galilee announcing, "The time has come, the kingdom of God is at hand" (Mark 1:15). When asked by what power he performed miraculous signs he explained that it was because "the kingdom of God has come to you" (Luke 11:20). When people misunderstood and thought that he was only speaking about the future reign of God he clarified, "The kingdom of God does not come with your careful observations, nor will people say, 'Here it is,' or 'There it is,' *because the kingdom of God is within you"* (Luke 17:21).

Maybe there isn't such a clear distinction between our world and eternity. Jesus described the kingdom of God as a present reality stretching perpetually into the future. He spoke of "eternal life" not as a destination but as an enduring quality of relationship with our Maker. He once prayed, "Now this is eternal life: that they may know you, the only true God, and Jesus Christ, whom you have sent" (John 17:3). Eternal life is the reconciled connection to our source that is made available through the sacrifice of Jesus. God is not far off and eternity is not in another world. If we find a connection to the eternal life of God in the present, the future will take care of itself.

What difference do these clarifications make? I believe we are more ready to embrace our lives in the here and now when we are able to recognize the continuity between the immanence of God in our world and eternity. Rather than simply waiting to be liberated to another time or place, we are being invited to collaborate in the healing and redemption of our world.

EXPLORING THE ESSENCE OF JESUS' MESSAGE

After we finish the latkes and soup and refill our glasses, it's time for the lighting of the menorah. Excited children gather around to light the candles. "Remind me again of the historical background for this holiday," one adult asks. It takes several of us brainstorming together to assemble an answer. Something about the Maccabean wars and an oil lamp that miraculously stayed lit for eight days without fuel. "Really a minor Jewish holiday that took on inflated significance as an alternative to Christmas," someone adds. The lights in the room are switched off, and with gusto Michael leads us in a Hanukkah song, sung in Hebrew; those of us who know it sing along. In the dark room under the glow of candles Michael says, "Hanukkah, it's the festival of lights," and concludes with a toast: "L' chaim! To Life!"

Light and *life* were two of the favorite words the disciple John used to describe the message of Jesus. Toward the end of his life John was sequestered on the Island of Patmos. As the last of the original disciples, he made an attempt to summarize the essential message of Jesus—and he did it in three words. In the preface to his first general letter he wrote, "That which was from the beginning, which we have heard, which we have seen with our eyes, which we have looked at and our hands have touched—this we proclaim concerning the Word of life." Here John reminded his readers that he was intimately acquainted with Jesus. He goes on to say, "The life appeared. We have seen it and testify to it. And we proclaim to you the eternal life which was with the father and has appeared to us." In John's mind, eternal life was less a destination and more an immediate personal connection. Then John described the essence of Jesus' teaching: "This is the message we have heard from him and declare to you: *God is light,* in him there is no darkness at all" (I John 1:1–5). Three words: "God is light." Light here implies warmth and illumination, and the clarity to move without fear. John is saying that we can walk confidently in the awareness that the source of all life is good, and that everything Jesus said and did simply confirms that our Creator is good and can be trusted.

Imagine someone asking, "John, what was the message of Jesus about?" And John answering, "Well, it's really simple: God is light." I can't help but notice how different John's summary of the gospel was from what I heard as a child, or what I told Hailey, or the impression many people have. If I could start over to explain the message of Jesus to Hailey, I would begin in a different place, maybe starting with something like, "Hailey, God is light. Jesus came to remind us that our Maker is good and can be fully trusted. Jesus taught people how to trust the ways of their Maker again. Some people didn't want to remember that God is good, so they had Jesus killed. But love is stronger than hate. And light is brighter than darkness. And Jesus came back from the dead to keep reminding us that God is light.''

The evidence for a good God can seem ambiguous at times. Life doesn't always feel good. We can easily look out on our world or within ourselves with eyes that see more darkness than light. Perhaps this is why Jesus said, ''The eye is the lamp of the body. If your eyes are good, your whole body will be full of light. But if your eyes are bad, your whole body will be full of darkness'' (Matthew 6:22–23). We are invited to have eyes that recognize the essential goodness of the Creator and creation—to read the narrative of history and the narratives of our own lives searching for signs of life and noting the ways that God can be trusted.

THE CHOICES WE MAKE

At the break during a lecture a young man approached me and asked a familiar question: ''Do you think gay people can go to heaven?''

I replied, ''I didn't know I was in charge of deciding who goes to heaven.''

It is commonly assumed that it is our responsibility to assess who is ''in'' and who is ''out'' of God's plan. One day a friend asked my wife Lisa a similar but more personal question: ''I need to know if you think our family is going to hell—since we are not Christian. Because if you believe we are going to hell then I don't think we can stay friends.'' Historically, emphasis on a singular spiritual decision has been motivated by an attempt by an institution or community to judge who is ''saved'' and who is not. Jesus described the way to life as a metaphorical road that we may travel down (Matthew 7:14). Perhaps we should be more concerned about our own pace and direction on that road than someone else's. Certainly we will each end up at the destination in the direction we are heading toward: either life or death.

I've notice that people suddenly become more generous in their assessments about eternal destiny when someone is experiencing loss. My friend Brad was fifteen when he and some friends got drunk and drove a car up a hill on the wrong side of the road and smashed into an oncoming truck at 80 miles an hour. His parents rushed to the scene and held his hand as he took his last breaths trapped in the back seat of the mangled vehicle. I recall standing with his parents in front of the casket, his body patched with embalmer's putty and heavy makeup, searching for words to console them. At the funeral the minister comforted the family with the hope that Brad had said "the sinner's prayer" earlier in life. The family clung to any evidence that Brad had chosen the road to life.

At the Hanukkah dinner, the first pangs of flu come over me just as I finish the strudel we have for dessert. I am talking with a professional photographer I just met when my stomach begins to rumble violently. "Excuse me for a moment," I say as I rush to the upstairs bathroom. When I am finished, I quickly collect our coats and weakly say, "Good-bye," and "Thanks for the nice evening." We walk out the door into the darkness of a winter night to begin the mile-and-a-half walk home over the hill in the rain.

It is later than I thought, and we have to walk slowly because of the trembling aftershocks in my intestines. We follow the path of streetlights past the dim doorways where groups of men lurk in the shadows to conduct nocturnal business. We are usually asleep before this cast of characters appears on the streets. "What series of choices would lead a person out into this cold darkness?" I wondered. My mother-in-law always says that nothing good ever happens after midnight, and I believe she is mostly right. The disciple John concluded that in contrast to the fact that "God is light," we tend to choose darkness when our deeds are evil. Every choice we make seems to be either a step into darkness or a step toward the light. John concluded that our greatest choice is between remaining in the darkness and learning to walk in the light of God's love (I John 1:5–7).

Is belief in God one epic decision or a series of choices in the same direction? As a child I was pressed to make a singular decision to believe. The assumption was that this epic decision, once made, endures for all time. Practically we know this is not the case with the other decisions we make. When two people, for instance, decide to get married, they must confirm their choice in daily care and fidelity. Marriage is a persistent series of choices in the same direction.

Spiritual belief functions similarly. Each day we decide whether or not to trust that our Maker is good and has our best interests in mind. We see this in the ancient contracts of the Tanakh: "This *day* I call heaven and earth as witnesses against you that I have set before you life and death, blessings and curses. Now choose life" (Deuteronomy 30:19). Each day and each moment we are choosing a path toward life or death. All of our choices matter and function cumulatively to express faith or doubt in the goodness of our Maker.

For three days after the Hanukkah party I lay sick in bed, hoping that I hadn't given anyone else the flu. For some reason when I'm sick I think more about God. Maybe it's the altered state brought on by nausea and dehydration or the feeling I have that I am dying. I don't think it is necessarily a bad thing, on occasion, to consider one's mortality. There is a certain reverence that comes by contemplating this finality. Lying on my bed with the blinds drawn, I am the little boy again in the back seat of the green Pontiac with sweating legs, except that now I am less afraid and more entranced by the chance to seek a God that can be found, to find my place in the greater scheme of a good creation. I find comfort in the whisper of words I once memorized: "You will seek me and find me when you seek me with all your heart" (Jeremiah 29:13).

Jesus declared, "The time has come."

The time has come for us to see the thin space between our lives and eternity.

The time has come for us to imagine again that God is light and that we are cared for by a Maker who is good.

The time has come for us to seek light over darkness and to perpetually choose life over death.

CONVERSATION

The present? The future? Or both?   What effect do you think it has that so many people believe the message of Jesus is primarily or exclusively about the future? How would a here-and-now orientation affect your perception of the message of Jesus?

Good news about what?   If heaven or eternity were not the primary concerns of first-century people who heard the message of Jesus, what else was compelling to them about his message? Why was his message so controversial?

God as light.   Does the suggestion that the message of Jesus can be summarized with the statement "God is light" seem attractively simple or fuzzily disturbing?

EXPERIMENTS

Reminiscing.   Write a journal entry exploring how your view of God has evolved and changed as you have grown and experienced more of life. Include a few interesting anecdotes that illustrate the shifts in your perceptions. What are the critical decisions, to seek, ignore, or reject God, that have shaped your current reality and direction?

Choosing life today.   If eternal life is something we access now and in the future, this implies that we are continually choosing whether or not to walk in the light of God's presence. Consider what tangible trust in God implies for you today. Try spending the day in conscious awareness of the Maker's presence. Some people find it helpful to use a method called "breath prayer" as an aid in doing this. As you go about the day, whisper a phrase (such as "Lord Jesus have mercy on me," or "Your love endures forever"). Repeat the phrase under your breath as you go about daily tasks. See if this helps you stay more aware of God's care and presence.

CHAPTER SIX

OUR EYES AS WINDOWS ON THE WORLD

On Saturday morning my two sons and I jump on our bikes and race past the sailboats harbored in the marina toward the farmers' market at the old Ferry Building by the bay. My wife Lisa had arrived earlier to help sell greens, heirloom tomatoes, and lavender products for the community-supported agriculture farm that delivers weekly boxes of fruits and vegetables to our neighborhood. Locking up our bikes, we walk toward the produce stand to surprise her—but stop momentarily to observe Lisa while she is still unaware of our presence. A street musician plays an old-time song in the background as I recall how fitting it is to see Lisa here working along side the farmer. Lisa grew up on a family farm where their table was supplied through the labor of their hands and the mystery of photosynthesis.

The boys rush ahead wrapping their arms around their mother. We buy cups of coffee and pain-au-chocolat and wander together among the vendors selling organic fruits and vegetables, fresh meats and fish. We sample locally grown citrus, nuts, cheeses, olives, fruit jams, and chipotle sauces. The market is alive with the best of what the Earth produces: radiant flowers, figs, grass-fed meats, artisan breads, stone fruits, and Asian pears. Week by week we observe the changes in what is harvested: strawberries in spring, pomegranates in the late summer, and Swiss chard in winter. As we make our way through the crowds, I think, "Coming to the market is one of our spiritual practices—it reminds us that we live in a good world of abundant provision. Here we taste and see that God is good."

TASTING A WORLD THAT IS ALIVE WITH THE ENERGY OF GOD

One of the ways we learn to trust the presence and care of God is through the awakening of our senses: tasting, touching, seeing, hearing, and smelling. What really moves you? The sight of a newborn baby? The taste of fresh orange juice? Symphony music? The exhilaration of sexual release? The smell of spring? All these teach us something about the character of our Maker. The wonder we feel for the things of Earth is the pleasure of God. Learning to love and enjoy the creation is a doorway to restoring our trust in the message that "God is light."

I hear spiritual leaders mourn the increasing absence of people who worship in churches. Where are they? After a week spent in long commutes to work with machines inside offices or industrial buildings, they are hiking the hills, surfing and playing on beaches, riding in boats, or enjoying gardens, parks, and museums in search of a connection to the goodness of God. They are outside gazing, tasting, smelling, and touching the beauty of creation, and the Earth is their sanctuary. Collectively we are increasingly concerned about how we manage our natural resources because it is our most direct source of life. And our rapid divorce from the natural world has led some to embrace creation as the object of, rather than the inspiration for, worship.

The situation was quite different, I believe, a hundred years ago when my Grandfather Onas was born onto a farm in rural South Dakota. His family lived close to the land, working with crops and animals, dependent on the forces of nature. On Sundays after barn chores, they arrived at a building with mud on their feet to give thanks to God, seated next to neighbors with whom they had worked in fields during the week. Perhaps as they sang, "Praise God from whom all blessings flow," they called to mind a good heavy spring rain or the fruit of their fields set on their tables. "Praise him all creatures here below"—those were the chickens and cows they knew by name and cared for with gentle husbandry. I have seen my relatives work those fields and sing that song amid the cornfields of the Iowa plains. Though I run the risk of painting an overly nostalgic picture, their lifestyle lent itself more easily to the awareness of God's essential goodness and nature's unpredictability.

I once stood with a friend on the beach at sunset. We had built a fire, and our children played and laughed in the waves. He talked about his work, as he continually looked down for messages on his mobile phone, occasionally answering a call. As the sky climaxed over the horizon in pink, orange, and purple brilliance, he stood with his back to the ocean. "Turn around and look, my friend," I said. "Be here now and pay attention. This moment is a gift."

In the hurried and technological society in which we live, we may have to be more intentional about practices that help us recognize the goodness of God revealed in creation. Many of us live and work in contexts that are divorced from the rhythms of the natural world. We have lost our connection to the soil, our food sources, and the skill of making things with our hands. We rarely notice the rising or setting of the sun. We gulp food without tasting. We rarely pause to look at the flowers or into the eyes of a child. Our pace of life affects our capacity to appreciate the goodness of God. We may simply be too busy or distracted to notice and receive the bounty that surrounds us. The demands of a hurried life and the dominance of technology cloud our awareness. Slowing down and learning to pay attention to the moment may be a path to affirming God's essential goodness and presence.

LEARNING TO BE LIKE THE BIRDS OF THE AIR

When Jesus came announcing, "The time has come, the kingdom of God is at hand," he was reminding us of the enduring presence and care of God manifest in our world. We know that we are at home in the universe and that we are loved by the signs we discover in creation. Jesus taught his disciples that they did not need to worry about their lives because God takes care of all creatures: "Look at the birds of the air" and how "your heavenly father feeds them. Are you not much more valuable than they?" (Matthew 6:25–26).

The Earth is a self-renewing ecosystem that provides for our sustenance. Rain falls. The sun shines. And the Earth produces all that we need and more. With every breath we inhale the spirit of life and affirm that we are part of a good creation. Through his life and message Jesus sought to remind us that God can be trusted—by bringing into focus what we already know from our own experiences and what our ancestors have taught us about embracing the abundant goodness and beauty of creation: "One generation will commend your works to another; they will tell of your mighty acts. They will celebrate your abundant goodness and joyfully sing of your righteousness. The LORD is good to all; he has compassion on all he has made" (Psalm 145:4,7,9).

In our society each generation seems compelled to discover its own window view of God, the Earth, and humanity. Yet our gaze on the world and ourselves is significantly influenced by parents, grandparents, and kinship affiliations. Even the quest for an independent window is shaped within the continuity of the perspective we seek to resist, reject, or improve upon. We build our windows on the world from the views passed down to us. What have you learned from your elders and the past generations of your family about embracing life as a gift and sacred trust?

SEARCHING AMONG THE BONES AND DECAY

My grandfather, Ray Clow, was a figure out of the old American West. With a deep voice and tanned leathery skin, he wore western shirts, a big gold belt buckle, and rings studded with turquoise and rubies. A simple man who, for thirty-eight years, worked in a factory loading sacks of cement, he taught me to see the world with eyes bright with wonder and curiosity.

Though he left school in the eighth grade, Grandpa Ray read voraciously—books about geology, astronomy, and biblical archeology. He sat in his rocking chair studying from an old and worn King James Bible, with maps of the ancient Middle East in the back, which he pored over alongside his collection of mail order replicas of the Dead Sea scrolls. In Grandpa's mind the stories of the Bible were directly connected to the land, to dinosaur bones, to old coins and pottery fragments.

There was a secret room in my grandfather's basement, a tiny museum full of mysteries and specimens. He collected Native American arrowheads, fossils, minerals, and prairie antiques. Most of these he found wandering in the deserted ghost towns and barren wilderness of the South Dakota Badlands. Hundreds of framed arrowheads lined the walls along with glass cabinets displaying jars of agates, hematite, turquoise, antique guns, original Thomas Edison light bulbs, and a small vial of gold dust. Other cabinets contained jars of minerals, shells, petrified wood, and larger pieces of dinosaur bones.

Grandpa Ray meticulously reassembled the fractured remains of a wooly mastodon jawbone, which he preserved with heavy shellac and displayed under glass. When I was five, I was captivated by these prehistoric creatures, and Grandpa Ray gave me my own collection of fossils, which I kept in a shoebox underneath my bed. Touching those bones, I was fascinated by the mystery that these massive extinct creatures were once alive.

Today Grandpa Ray's own bones lay buried in the land he loved, and I am reminded of the tension between the essential goodness of creation and the fact that we suffer, die, and feel pain. Are we part of a good creation that went bad—a failed experiment, broken beyond repair? Or are we part of a good creation that is incomplete? Did God make a mistake? Was Yahweh an amateur at creating worlds who might do better if given another opportunity? Would version 2.0 or 3.0 improve on the Creator's original design, eliminating the "flaws" we find? Perhaps we confuse goodness with our notions of perfection. And from where we stand in the universe, who are we to say whether this world is good or bad?

It is often assumed that, through original sin, Adam and Eve destroyed God's dream for our world, making this world an ugly shadow of what it might have been. And yet contrary to this sentiment, the Apostle Paul noted that our world is unfinished, not as a result of Adam and Eve's choices, but because of the will of the Maker: "The creation waits in eager expectation for the sons of God to be revealed. For the creation was subjected to frustration, *not by its own choice, but by the will of the one who subjected it*, in hope that the creation itself will be liberated from its bondage to decay and brought into the glorious freedom of the children of God" (Romans 8:19–21). Perhaps we are living in the best possible world.

We are invited to trust, though we experience the inconvenience of living in an unfinished world, that we are part of a good creation becoming more fully realized. We hold in tension our sense of frustration and the hope of progress and completion. We embrace life by affirming that we are living in a world where God is at work, patiently bringing all things to their ultimate destiny.

On my hand I wear a ruby ring that belonged to my Grandpa Ray. This ring, now a family relic, will be passed down through generations as a reminder that we are anxiously waiting for a time when there will be no more death or decay.

"We know that the whole creation has been groaning as in the pains of childbirth right up to the present time. Not only so, but we ourselves, who have the first fruits of the Spirit, groan inwardly as we wait eagerly for our adoption as sons, the redemption of our bodies" (Romans 8:22–23).

EMBRACING HUMANITY AND SENSUALITY

My other grandfather, Onas Cudley Scandrette, could not have been more different from Grandpa Ray Clow. He and my grandmother Mary lived in a college town near Chicago where my grandfather was a professor of psychology. Their home, instead of being decorated with church craft-bazaar knick-knacks, knitted Kleenex box cozies, and dinosaur bones, was furnished with 1950s modern furniture, shelves of art and psychology books, and walls hung with black and white art prints and paintings—including signed lithographs by Marc Chagall, Pablo Picasso, and Thomas Hart Benton.

Grandpa Onas looked the part of an eccentric college professor, wearing thick glasses, suit jackets, and a derby hat as he drove his red MG convertible through campus. He dabbled in mountaineering, experimented with Pop Art, and was an accomplished photographer who corresponded with Ansel Adams. In his basement there was a darkroom where he perfected experimental print techniques that he documented for publication in photographic society journals. I rarely saw my grandfather without an SLR camera around his neck.

He also wrote down and told stories about his childhood experiences and wrote romantic and philosophical poetry exploring the human psyche. Academically and personally, Grandpa Onas was interested in the intersection of faith and humanity—particularly the psychological dimensions of human spirituality. He was a lifelong fan of the Hebrew Psalms because of their resonance with subjective human moods and motivations. Raised in a religious tradition that regarded the arts and culture as "worldly" and the cravings of the body as shameful, he sought to find God in the pleasures of human creativity.

Always a bit of a hipster, Grandpa Onas wore the latest running shoes, was the first person I knew to own a personal computer, and gave me recommendations about his favorite rock music. For birthdays and Christmas he and my grandmother gave me art supplies and books. They took me to museums and galleries where I recall seeing Andy Warhol's car crash sculptures, the photographs of Robert Mapplethorpe, and the assemblage sculptures of horses by Deborah Butterfield. From Grandpa Onas I learned to explore the goodness and beauty of God revealed in humanity—through the arts, philosophy, literature, history, and the study of cultures.

An integrative spiritual path recognizes and appreciates the sacred in all of life. Yet, like my Grandfather Onas, many of us were conditioned to see sensual experiences, bodily or sexual pleasure, and the appreciation of aesthetics and cultural artifacts as opposed to the pursuit of the sacred. We may feel that we should look beyond what is earthy or sensual for confirmation of God's care—as if intangible esoteric notions and mystical experiences are more reliable signs of the Creator's love. Because we are continually surrounded by human creativity and the wonders of the natural world, we may be tempted to take these immediate signs of God's care for granted, hoping instead for a "special" revelation of God's love.

Phenomenological approaches to spirituality often deny or minimize the goodness revealed in the natural world, relying instead on ecstatic experiences and emotional peaks as confirmation of God's love. While heightened religious experiences need not be opposed, they are often sought when we fail to embrace all of life as sacred. An unhealthy fascination with the supernatural can be a sign of spiritual fragmentation, a falsetto spirituality that strains to reach beyond the normal. Some would argue that, to the extent that we set aside certain times, places, and rituals as more sacred than others, we deny the essential goodness and sacredness found in all of life. We were made for this world, a world already full of the wonder, mystery, and immanence of God.

OUR EYES AS WINDOWS

On rue de St. Catherine in Montreal I am seated in a café frequented by students from McGill. I'm in the French-speaking province by invitation of David Brazeal, a musician and curator of Curieux: une communauté de foi (a community of faith). Friends from this artist's collective trickle in one by one, shedding winter coats to join our afternoon discussion over soup, bread, and frothy pints of beer. We talk for a while about what various people study (literature, photography, musical composition) and discuss favorite philosophers and writers and their contribution to the quest for integrative spirituality.

The central theme for our afternoon conversation is "navigating faith in post-Christendom contexts." Many of these artists and students grew up in devout households and are now dubious about the relevance of their religious tradition to their current life as cultural creative urbanites. Daniel describes his experience of this tension: "In my studies and through friendships at the university I've come to recognize and appreciate the presence of God in many different cultures and religions. In particular I'm fascinated by Eastern thought and Zen practice because of a friend who meditates regularly—he is a truly beautiful and peaceful person." I respond to Daniel's comment with an observation: "In our generation, we seem hungry for a spiritual path and practices that are more grounded in our experiences in the here and now."

Monique interjects, "It seems as though the mystics or contemplative traditions of each religion share common practices and experiences." With excitement Daniel adds, "I wonder then if 'the way of God' is progressively revealed in all of the world's religions—and if each religion is the revelation of God for a particular time or culture. Perhaps all of the religions share a common core." I see that Daniel's comment makes some of the other students listening squirm uncomfortably, so I offer, "The sentiment that all beliefs are equal is an attractive proposition—particularly in places where religion has divided people and caused conflict—but it rarely compels anyone to be earnest in their spiritual pursuits. I wonder if there is a way to respectfully acknowledge the common threads and practices among religions without diminishing the uniqueness of Jesus and his claim of authority."

Standing outside on the street after our meeting, Daniel lights a hand-rolled cigarette. Taking me aside he confides, "I guess because I was raised in the church, it is difficult for me to find God there. I am now looking for God outside the windows of the church."

Our quest to see God as light and to trust the goodness of God is complicated by the windows through which we view the world. Sometimes the windows we inherited are dirty, distorted, foggy, or scratched. When someone says, "I don't believe anymore," what they often mean is that the window they shared with their family, culture, or religious tradition has been smashed—or they can no longer see God, the world, or themselves through the same limited perspective. Because our windows are small, crude, and tentative, we should be open to looking through many windows from different angles.

Many of our problems with God are actually the problems we have with one another when we aren't looking at God through the same window. If a person's yearnings or doubts lead her to look at God and her world from another window, she is often given a subtle or not so subtle message that she is out of bounds. Sometimes it only takes looking out the same window from a slightly different angle to get this reaction.

Some friends who were looking through new windows once told me, "We have three years of funding to start a church, but we aren't sure that we will even be Christians a year from now." What made them make such a brash statement? They were waking up to the social ethics of Jesus, and a desire for more integrative bodily spiritual practices—two things that had not been emphasized in their family or religious background. Their instinctual reaction was to assume that because these explorations were incompatible with their inherited window of "orthodox belief," they were losing faith. "Are you losing faith," I asked, "or just learning to enlarge your perspective on God and to practice your faith more holistically?"

New information and experiences can make it necessary to adjust our view of God and ourselves. Accommodating to a more complex view from other angels can be a tumultuous process—especially if your doubts or questions make you feel like the glass in your window has shattered. Sometimes our mental categories are the problem. We have a tendency toward an either/or rationale in regard to our beliefs about God and our world, often assuming that rather than being complimentary or paradoxical the different windows are in opposition to one another:

- *Either* the Earth is perfectly whole and human nature is completely good *or* the world is totally wrecked and human nature is entirely evil.
- Truth is revealed *either* through nature and personal experience *or* exclusively through scripture.
- Jesus was *either* a moral and ethical teacher *or* a messiah and savior.
- *Either* the message of Jesus is about social transformation in our world *or* about future salvation in another world.
- *Either* God's grace is received without effort *or* we work to inhabit grace through practices, bodily actions, and discipline.
- Faith is rooted *either* in action, awareness, and experience *or* the propositions of scripture.

These are just a few examples of where the windows of our categories can create problems. When the finite mind uncovers its limited ability to resolve paradox, it is often our tendency to choose one side of a truth over another. And yet it is entirely possible that two statements can be true or partially true at the same time. Human nature could be both noble *and* evil. Jesus might both be a wise ethical teacher *and* a savior. We could pursue a faith that is both rooted in propositional revelation *and* in action, awareness, and experience.

DISCOVERING CONNECTIONS BETWEEN EARTH AND ETERNITY

Twenty-five years after leaving the church, Thom was beginning to have the courage to look for God again. A colleague of my friend John, Thom invited both of us over to his apartment for tea and spiritual talk. He greeted us in the dark front hallway lined with books on German literary criticism (Thom's academic avocation). He seemed a bit anxious and tired, which made sense when I learned that he was on a six-week leave of absence from his job (at a wine label print house) for depression. After greeting us each with a weak handshake he invited us to sit down, in a living room that was obviously designed around the needs of one man. After enough chairs were brought in and the tea was poured, Thom explained his current predicament.

Like many highly intelligent, eccentric people, Thom enjoyed his books and the companionship of his beloved dog more than he did the company of most people. "But my dog died two months ago—he was fourteen years old," Thom explained sadly. "In fact his ashes are on the shelf there by your chair," he said, pointing toward me. "I've never felt this lonely," he explained, "and lately I've wondered if what I'm missing is belief in God."

"I stopped believing in God twenty-five years ago because I couldn't reconcile my views with the church." John asked him to explain. "Back then I felt like I needed a daily practice to help me stay centered, so I took a class and started meditating. It really helped with my anxiety, but I was told that it was incompatible with the teachings of the church."

"It surprises me that you didn't feel supported," John said, "since meditation has long been a practice in both Jewish and Christian traditions." We talked philosophically for a while about the nuances, similarities, and distinctions between Buddhist and Judeo-Christian meditation.

"Another reason I stopped believing or praying was that I gradually saw God differently from what I had been taught. I'm attracted to what I know about Native American spirituality—because they see God as present in nature. I remember a profound experience I had hiking out in the Marin Headlands. When I looked at the mountains descending into the ocean I was moved very deeply. I felt God more there than I ever had in a church. It made me wonder if God is not far off somewhere up in the sky, but actually right here with us—and in the water, trees, and rocks."

As Thom shared this memory he became more alive and I could see the delight in his green-blue eyes. "Thom," I said, "it sounds like you were experiencing the glory of God in creation. I know that same feeling. It reminds me of a place in the book of Romans where Saint Paul wrote, 'For since the creation of the world— God's invisible qualities—God's eternal power and divine nature—have been clearly seen, being understood from what has been made.' My understanding is that the Earth is infused with the voice of God speaking to us. This was a theme in many of the ancient poems preserved in the Bible. One that I especially like says:

> The voice of Adonai is over the waters;
> the God of glory thunders,
> Adonai thunders over the rushing waters.

Thom looked surprised and said, "The church always gave me the impression that God is far away from Earth because physical existence is essentially evil."

John interjected, "Wow, that's curious because in the Genesis narrative God calls everything that has been made 'good.'" Thom's eyes brightened and he seemed to be making a connection between his experiences and the reality of God.

"If there is a difference between the Native American and Judeo-Christian understanding of God," I added, "it might be that creation is seen as referential to the unseen and permeating reality of God. The Earth is not an end to itself, as something to be worshiped, but it is the muse that inspires our reverence for God."

After more conversation, Thom suddenly spoke up with tears in his eyes. "I think I'm ready to pray." Standing up from his chair he asked, "Will you pray with me?" We each took one of Thom's hands as he stammered and then began, asking God to help him in his loneliness and grief.

The discontinuity between Tom's inherited window of God and the new angle of his experiences created a long and frustrating journey back to embracing God as good and trustworthy. What

I'm trying to illustrate throughout this book (and in the particular examples of this chapter) is a quest for continuity: between what we have been taught about God and what we may have yet to learn; and between what we say we believe and how we actually live. By examining our windows to God and by learning to embrace all of life as a gift and sacred trust, we take steps to navigate making a life in the Way of Jesus.

CONVERSATION

What kind of world do we live in?   Do you find it easier to believe that we live in a good world gone bad or a good world that is getting better (even if it is frustrated and incomplete)? Were you raised to embrace or fear your humanity and the sensual aspects of life?

Windows and paradox.   Your spiritual path has a lot to do with how you handle paradox. If you see every issue as an either/or, some facet of reality or truth will lose out in the end. How do you think we are helped in overcoming our either/or thinking—learning to see the world through multiple window panes?

EXPERIMENTS

Telling the next generation.   What have you learned from your elders and the past generations of your family about embracing life on Earth as a gift and sacred trust? Write a tribute to a parent or grandparent about how they helped you see the beauty and goodness of creation. If the person is still living, you could give it to them on a holiday.

Tasting the goodness of God.   Since ancient times, feasting has been an important rhythm of the spiritual life. The Israelite people were commanded to use a tenth of their yearly income for a weeklong feast. King Solomon said that the ability to enjoy food with gratefulness is a sign of living in harmony with the Creator. Together with family or friends, throw an extravagant feast of abundance including new and favorite foods. Eat slowly, savoring the flavors, giving thanks for the goodness of life on Earth. How might being intentional about enjoying food help you trust God more?

City walk of awareness.   Take a walk around your neighbor-hood or nearby city as practice for recognizing God's care and activity. If it is helpful use the phrase: "God show me where your beauty and glory are displayed in this place and among these people." Notice the creativity revealed in what you see (clothing, architecture, facial features) and in what you hear (music, conver-sation, children's laughter, or the syncopation of hammering at a construction site). In some places you may have to look hard for a sign of God's presence that registers with you. Remember that even a blade of grass poking out of cracked concrete is a sign of the Creator's generative presence.

Nature walk of awareness.   In the ancient Psalms, the beauty of creation was often used as inspiration for giving praise to God. Psalms 29 and 104 are good examples of this. Take a walk in the woods, the wilderness, or a botanical garden noticing the beauty of God revealed in the natural world. Write your own psalm of praise to God.

Slowing down.   Reserve a day soon to do nothing. Shut off the TV, cell phone, or computer and head to a natural place for a picnic and maybe a nap. Notice whether slowing down to enjoy the small things helps you connect with the presence and goodness of God. How can you incorporate this kind of Sabbath keeping into your regular practice?

CHAPTER SEVEN

LIVING AND TELLING THE STORY OF YOUR LIFE

In late afternoon, my son Noah and I climb Bernal Hill, a grassy mount south of our house. Our breathing becomes heavy as our legs strain to ascend the steep incline. Views from the top of the hill are vertigo inducing and we feel as though we are flying, suspended above the city. Directly below us are miles of Victorian apartments that survived the earthquakes, followed by larger industrial buildings and the skyscrapers of the financial district. To the north we see the rust-colored spires of the Golden Gate Bridge silhouetted against the green hills of the Marin Headlands. To the east we see Treasure Island and the spans of the Bay Bridge over shimmering waves. Across the water, where cargo ships from Asia make their way toward the Port of Oakland, we see the orange sunset light reflecting off homes in the Berkeley hills. On clear days Mt. Diablo towers over the horizon further off in the distance.

From up here I can imagine a time long ago, when the voice of the Creator spoke all of this into existence, carving out this spectacular bay and depositing gold and silver in the hills of the

Sierras. Destiny would have this become a place where millions of people from every nation and tribe would come to live—captivated by the hope of a better life, attracted by the promises of riches, beauty, liberty, or sanctuary—and now millions of us are here seeking our dreams and paying outrageously to live in small congested spaces.

On this windswept, rocky crag I call to mind the words of Paul of Tarsus in Athens as he stood atop the jagged rocks of the Aeropagus: "God determined the times set for us and the exact places where we should live. God did this so that [people] would seek [God] and find [God] though [God] is not far from each one of us. For in [God] we live and move and have our being" (Acts 17:26–28).

The announcement by Jesus that "the time has come" was partly an invitation to recognize the connection between the epic story of creation and the particulars of our lives in the here and now. Where we live and the times we live in are the place from which we will seek the God that can be found. We are not here by accident. We were made for this time and place. And our lives are pregnant with meaning and purpose.

TRYING TO GAIN PERSPECTIVE

From the top of Bernal Hill I always look for the tiny speck of our house in the maze of streets and buildings below. Up here, at least geographically speaking, I can get my bearings. As impossible as it is to get an objective view on everything that goes on in the world or even a city, it is equally daunting to fully grasp the meaning and significance of your individual existence. But we are invited to look within ourselves for the presence and activity of God in the stories of our lives.

Some children are taught the simple song, "Jesus loves me this I know, for the Bible tells me so." But for many the words of this song fall flat because they fail to recognize how they are being loved in the present moment. It's one thing to say that you are loved but quite another to know that you are loved. This is why it is important to search for the presence and activity of God in your own story. To fully embrace the message of Jesus (that God can be trusted), we have to connect the particulars of our lives to the reality that we are being loved. We must seek to discover how we are being loved through every moment in our lives.

EMBRACING YOUR OWN CELEBRITY

Noah and I give each other knowing looks when we pass a group of tourists with a cam recorder trying to film themselves against the backdrop of the skyline. We think it's funny to step out of our house and see tourists from Europe or Asia filming the tacky mural of dancing burritos painted on the Taqueria wall next door. Yet we are secretly proud that we live in such a popular tourist destination. I always wonder, though, what people miss by spending their whole vacation looking through the screen of a digital camera. And who has to watch all those hours of recordings? Or do they just get stored and then thrown away?

Our society's preoccupation with celebrity can often make us feel as though the best of life is happening somewhere else—for people more famous, fortunate, wealthy, well traveled, or attractive than we are. It can be tempting to live vicariously through the experiences of others. On television you can watch other people exercise, cook food, make love, make war, go on vacation, remodel their homes, lose weight, argue with their children, or even clean out their messy rooms and closets. In a media-drenched culture you run the risk of knowing more about someone you've never met than someone you live with, or the somebody that you are.

Sometimes we become paralyzed by thinking of what might have been. We wonder what life would be like if we had had different parents, gone to better schools, chose different companions, or had been born taller or smaller, richer or poorer. Would I be happier if I were not me? We are haunted by the original deception that our world is not enough—that something is being withheld from us. A sense of scarcity fuels our jealousies and insecurities, and inhibits us from receiving the gifts of creation with gratefulness. I've seen the ruin of children, tormented because their piece of cake was smaller than the rest. How are we to know whether we have been cursed or blessed? The journey back to God involves recovery of our sense of abundance and trust in the Creator's provision. We choose whether to be ruled by wanting or thankfulness.

We can become so adept at envying the interesting memoirs of others that we forget to live and tell our own stories. My self-described "literati" friend, Audrey, often spoke about herself in regretful self-depreciating tones. "My life has been rather boring and uneventful," she would say. "There is not much to tell. I mostly remember things from when I was three or four years old—before my parents got divorced and I started getting shuffled between Portland and L.A." You can talk about yourself in many ways. You might tell the story of your life a thousand times, and each time it could sound like the memoir of a different person—weaving a tale of abandonment, tragedy, or triumph—depending on the lens you choose to view your life through. Through persistence and the support of friends, Audrey is gradually learning to change the themes of her story. When she saw herself as boring, lonely, and abandoned, she lived and told that story. What if the real story of Audrey's life is about a vibrant and adventurous person who is discovering who she was made to be and learning to care for others out of that abundance?

WHO IS WELL OFF?

On a dirt trail going down the hill, Noah and I walk past a homeless encampment just a stone's throw from designer hillside homes with million-dollar views. In this study in contrasts, each party plays their role dutifully—the victimized homeless person chronically down on his luck, and the wealthy person made depressed and guilty by her relative privilege.

In our community we regularly dialogue about how we navigate the inequities in our global society. I recall one such conversation in which Lisa shared about her experiences living in Mexico City: "I went there to help people I thought were poor and disadvantaged. The children wore worn clothes, had no toys, and lived in cinder block houses without windows. And yet they were so generous—offering me their food and few possessions. I had to be careful not to notice the things they had, because if they saw that I liked it, they would offer it to me. I realized that, even if they didn't live well by our standards, in other ways they were happier than most Americans—they had loving families and enjoyed the simple pleasures of life together."

Ryan adds, "I've heard that when Mother Teresa once visited San Francisco, she commented that there is a level of poverty here that they do not have in Calcutta—a soul or spiritual poverty. One culture starves for food, clean water, or healing medicine, while another starves for time, relationships, and meaning. Who are we to say whether we are better or worse off than others? I am reminded of a proverb by a wise sage who wrote, 'Each heart knows its own bitterness, and no one else can share its joy' (Proverbs 14:10). Maybe we should avoid the temptation to compare."

"May I add something about poverty?" Jason asked, and then paused pensively to collect his thoughts. "I am tempted to be offended when I hear people talk about 'the poor.' Growing up Hispanic in one of the more violent neighborhoods in Southern California, we were often visited by affluent people from the suburbs who wanted to practice their 'charity' on us. From their perspective we were disadvantaged. I have a good deal of lingering resentment about being labeled 'poor.' We were not poor. And yet we thought of ourselves as poor and acted poor because of their patronizing. I once heard a statement suggesting that 'if the imaginations of the poor are awakened, they will liberate themselves.'"

CITY WALKING EXERCISE

As Noah and I descend back down into our neighborhood, we trade the relative silence of the mountain for the bustle of the city, the low rumble of traffic noise, the siren howl of fire engines, and the laughter of children.

Walking past the housing projects and the corner liquor store, I'm reminded of the way I used to tell the story of our neighborhood. For years I have taken visitors on guided walks through various San Francisco neighborhoods. Many of the people who came on these walks saw the city as a dangerous, exotic, or evil place—usually in sharp contrast to the safe and clean suburbs or small towns where they lived. Regretfully, I played the role of the sensationalist tour guide, tantalizing and shocking them with sordid tales of aberrance, indecency, drugs, guns, gang violence, and homicide. Not surprisingly, on our walk they noticed the things that confirmed these themes—and ignored all signs of health, safety, beauty, and vitality.

Eventually I learned to tell the story of our neighborhood and city more evenly. I talked about amazing cultural diversity, cooperation, creativity, and a dedicated and heroic citizenry. I invited people to look for signs of God's glory, goodness, and beauty in the things that they could hear, taste, touch, see, and smell—even if it was only a blade of grass growing out of a crack in the sidewalk. They still noticed differences, but they also found reasons to love and embrace the place where we live.

How we tell a story depends on the themes we choose, and applies as much to the stories of our lives as to the story of a city. If we look at ourselves through the themes of weakness, failure, or disappointment, these are the tales we are likely to tell. Sometimes we become fixated on the most dramatic parts of our personal narratives, failing to notice the small and enduring themes of beauty. We may have to keep retelling our stories until they have more resonance with the grander narratives of creation and redemption. This may not be something we naturally do, but we can cultivate that kind of habit through our conversations with one another.

READING AND WRITING YOUR LIFE STORY

Many of us struggle to see the provision of God in the narrative of our own lives. If we are part of a good creation, living in a world where God is present and active, then this truth can be reflected in how we tell our stories. Once during a group exercise I asked people to share stories about themselves that revealed something about the goodness and care of God. At first my suggestion was met with blank stares that begged to ask, "A good story about me?" But gradually people began to speak.

Luke, a handsome and well-liked young man, spoke quietly, "Frankly, so far I have a hard time finding much good in my life story." Listening and knowing something about Luke's family, his talents and affluence, I wondered why he couldn't see good things. When I asked him to say more, he offered, "Well, I guess I felt misunderstood by my family and I didn't feel loved by my dad in the way I needed."

"Luke," Michael responded, "I'm sad that you are having a hard time finding good in your life story. I think the people who know you well see a lot of goodness and beauty in your life. It seems like many of us were hindered by the dominant messages we received from our families. Yet I don't think we can expect another person to see us exactly as God sees us. Only God is entitled to put a title on your life.''

Elizabeth offered, ''The feeling you shared about your dad reminds me of a psalm I once read that says, 'God sets the lonely in families.' We often assume that our love needs have to be met in a particular way, or by a particular person. What if instead you ask, 'Who did God place in my life to demonstrate love in the ways I needed?' There were probably other people, many fathers and mothers, who affirmed and supported you in ways that were helpful.''

Michael, a hyperactive musician with arms covered in tattoos, sat fidgeting in the corner waiting to speak: ''It's not hard for me to see the hand of God in my life. I've been sober for eighteen months now, and my life is better than ever because of the grace of God.''

Michael's girlfriend, Elizabeth, chimed in: ''The story of my life is a real drama. I was homeless as a teenager, then an addict and alcoholic. There have been so many times when I should have been dead—it's a miracle that I'm alive and sitting here. Even if I wasn't aware of God at the time, I think God was there loving and protecting me.''

During a lull in the conversation I made a suggestion. ''Maybe it would help some of you if we try telling our stories in the third person.'' I offered, ''You can pretend that the story is about someone else. It doesn't have to be the whole story of your life. Maybe just explore one anecdote that illustrates a pivotal moment. You could start off by saying, 'There once was a girl or a boy named....'''

''I think I can go,'' Damien offered. ''There once was a boy named Damien who loved solving problems. One day his parents gave him a complicated computer game and for months he spent all his spare time trying to solve its riddle. One day he finally solved the game and rushed to tell his parents. That night they ate a special meal as a family to celebrate.''

''Good job,'' Michael said. ''What do you think that story reveals about the goodness of God in your life?'' Elizabeth asked.

"When I was telling the story I realized how that childhood event illustrates something key to my personality. I think I was made to solve problems. I guess that explains how I ended up working as a computer programmer."

"I think I could try next," said Christine. "This is a story about a girl who had two names. First her name was Ming Lee. Her mother called her Ming Lee and her sisters called her Ming Lee and her father called her Ming Lee. Life was very hard for her, but one day she was taken to a safer place where she wouldn't be hurt anymore. The people there said, 'We can't call you Ming Lee here; you need a new name.' So together they chose the name Christine. And Ming Lee, who was now Christine, was very happy."

"That was a beautiful story," Deborah said. Then Christine added, "It is the true story of how I immigrated from China to the United States when I was eleven."

"And what did telling that story help you see about the presence of God in your life?" I asked.

"As I think about my life I realize that the two events I considered to be the hardest things were actually the doorway into what has proved to be the very best experiences of my life. I know this sounds so trite, but I can see how God works out everything for the good of those who love God." Christine's words had weight—she is a courageous survivor of domestic abuse.

FINDING A WAY THROUGH

My neighbor Janice stopped by in the evening to have me sign papers that would give her permission to adopt a Doberman pinscher. (This was shortly after a woman in San Francisco had been mauled to death by a similar animal.) "Perhaps it would be helpful for me to explain why I feel the need to have such an aggressive dog," Janice said. "My life has been full of surprises."

Janice had fallen in love and married a man just before he was sent off to Vietnam. Soon after she discovered that she was pregnant. When he returned she found that her husband had been changed by the war. He drank a lot and was abusive. After three years they divorced and she was left to care for their daughter. To make ends meet Janice worked as a casino cocktail waitress. One cold winter night after work, when her car wouldn't start, she was offered a ride home by a stranger parked nearby. With some hesitation Janice consented to his offer. But instead of taking her home, he drove to a remote place in the woods and raped her repeatedly at knifepoint.

At that moment I interrupted Janice to offer my sympathy. "I'm not done yet," she said. "Then he tried to kill me! He began stabbing me in the chest. All I could think of was that I must stay alive to care for my daughter. While he continued to plunge the knife into my chest I screamed and struggled and eventually seized the knife and cut his leg badly. He hobbled off into the woods. I woke up in the snow several hours later and dragged myself out to the highway. I was weak and had lost a lot of blood. I lay by the side of the road and managed to wave an arm when cars passed by. Eventually someone saw me lying there and brought me to the hospital. That man stabbed me a total of forty times and I spent six months in intensive care getting strong enough to see my daughter again."

Janice tells me this story with little emotion, and I want to ask a million questions. She is a petite, elegant, and fashionable middle-aged woman. It is hard to fathom that beneath her clothes she bears the scars of attempted murder. I want to know if justice came to the man who did this and how Janice has managed the trauma over the years. I want to do or say something that will bring Janice a bit of healing. We talk for a long time, and then she glances at her watch saying, "I didn't mean to stay so long, but I wanted to give you some explanation for why I want such an aggressive dog. Ever since that night I've always felt safer with a big animal around."

"I understand why you wish to have this dog," I said, signing the papers. "What has helped you the most dealing with the pain of this trauma?" I asked. Wiping her eyes, Janice replied, "It's been difficult, but my family and a few friends have helped a lot. I've tried to be aware of God, and like you, I have my spiritual practice that helps me stayed centered. I guess I'm finding a way through."

Many of us carry painful wounds, either physical or emotional, and we are searching for signs of goodness in a world that feels dangerous and hostile. The encouragement to read and write our lives differently does not imply that we gloss over injustice and tragedy. We hold in tension the fact that we are part of a good creation that is frustrated and groaning in the pangs of labor. We feel the pain of being part of a world that is still being made. King Solomon of Israel captured the irritation of living in this cosmic construction site when he wrote, "I have seen the burden God has laid on people. [God] has made everything beautiful in its time. [God] has set eternity in the hearts of [people], yet they cannot fathom what God has done from beginning to end" (Ecclesiastes 3:10–12). We struggle to make sense of the hurt and to stay hopeful about where this is all going.

We are not alone with our questions. Jesus the teacher and Messiah also endured loneliness, public disgrace, abandonment, physical torture, and rejection. We know that he was misunderstood by his family. His brothers did not believe his message and, for a time, even his own mother thought he was crazy. Then his relatives wondered why Jesus didn't take better advantage of his popularity. Religious leaders accused him of being demon possessed and taunted him with accusations. Eventually they sought his public humiliation and execution, and all of his companions abandoned him. Jesus endured these trials with great humility. Even as he was being crucified, he prayed, "Father, forgive them for they do not know what they are doing" (Luke 23:34). At the climax of his suffering he cried out with the words of an ancient psalm: "My God, my God, why have you forsaken me? Why are you so far from saving me, so far from the words of my groaning?" (Psalm 22:1).

We are invited to wrestle with God to negotiate how we are being loved through every moment of our lives. You will find a way through affliction by giving yourself permission to complain. People of faith in various times have struggled with God in the midst of their sorrow and disappointments. The Sons of Korah composed a song that the Israelite community used to cry out to God, expressing their misgivings: "Awake, O LORD! Why do you sleep? Rouse yourself! Do not reject us forever. Why do you hide your face and forget our misery and oppression?" (Psalm 44:23–24).

David, the poet-warrior king of ancient Israel, grumbled and negotiated with the confidence of someone who knew he was loved by God: "How long, O LORD? Will you forget me forever? How long will you hide your face from me? How long must I wrestle with my thoughts and every day have sorrow in my heart?" (Psalm 13:1–2a). David's songs often expressed a struggle to reconcile pain and suffering with God's benevolence. In essence he was saying, "God, where the hell are you? I know you love me, but in my situation, I do not feel loved, I feel abandoned—so we have some negotiating to do." Perhaps the question we should ask is not "Have I been loved?" but "*How* have I been loved through every circumstance in my life?" David was tenacious in his attempts to find solace for his sufferings: "I am worn out calling for help; my throat is parched. My eyes fail, looking for my God" (Psalm 69:3). The alternative to complaining and negotiating is simply giving up on God altogether. We honor our Maker by aggressively negotiating for a good story about our lives.

How does all this relate to making a life in the Way of Jesus? We can only trust Jesus as teacher and Messiah, to the extent that, despite our wounds, we believe we are deeply loved. The path of faith is a gradual process of learning to trust in the benevolence of God again.

I walked into Rod's apartment and found him lying under a blanket on the floor. He was too weak to attend the board meeting for ReIMAGINE, an organization we founded together. Rod was recovering from his fifty-third surgery for abdominal cancer. Propped up on a pillow, with a legal pad in hand, he was jotting out a business plan for a new socially responsible company.

Rod asked about my family and then showed me his notes on a development strategy for our organization. Then he played me a song from the solo album he had just finished recording. Amazed, I thought, "Rod accomplishes more lying sick on the floor than most healthy people do on their best days."

I could hardly keep pace with his long strides on the days when Rod and I would run together early in the morning. Before his cancer diagnosis he was a college track star. "I decided," Rod said, "that if I ever got well enough to run again I would finish a marathon." (He had just completed his third race.) On a good day Rod could run ten or fifteen miles. Some days it was difficult for him to run three blocks. Other days he struggled just to stand and not throw up. "How do you exercise with the cancer still active in your body?" I asked, as we sprinted up a steep hill. Confidently he replied, "I made a promise to myself that every day I would put on my running shoes and walk out the door."

Rod learned to endure early in life. His mother had a self-induced abortion and miraculously, Rod survived—rescued by a nurse who found him lying in a bucket in the hospital hallway. A grandmother took care of him until he was eight, when his parents regained custody and moved him into their apartment in a large government housing project in Birmingham, Alabama. At age eleven Rod began bagging groceries at a neighborhood store to earn the money to feed and clothe his sisters. His parents spent the family's resources on their drug addictions, eventually selling their daughters into prostitution.

College was Rod's escape from the trials of his home life. On scholarship to a university in another state, Rod excelled in sports and academics and was the first African American initiated into a historically segregated fraternity. He went on to become a pastor, an accomplished musician, technology company CEO, and successful nonprofit organizational consultant.

"I've spent my entire adult life trying to do two things," he says, "stay alive and leave a legacy." Beyond his professional achievements, Rod's greatest legacy is his family. Ten years ago Rod helped his sister flee from an abusive marriage, moving her family to California where he serves as a surrogate father to five nieces and nephews. Still battling cancer, Rod is currently completing a PhD in Social Entrepreneurship at Columbia University in New York City, where he devotes his spare time to racial reconciliation projects and the empowerment of at-risk youth.

Once, when I asked Rod about what kept him motivated, despite so many obstacles, he said, "Cancer has taught me to value each day. Every moment I am alive I have the opportunity to extend the boundaries of love in the world."

Instead of being paralyzed by anger or regret Rod has learned to embrace each day as a sacred gift.

ON THE STAGE OF YOUR LIFE

At the end of the day I kiss my daughter Hailey good night. Hailey is an actress who loves Shakespeare; she recently appeared in a film honored at the Cannes International Film Festival. On the stage or in front of the camera she comes alive with her best self. In the Jekyll and Hyde of adolescent emotions she experiences rapturous days of unnatural exuberance and other days battling the hormonally induced poison of negativity. In an effort to calm the storm I sometimes ask, "On the stage of your life, is this the character you want to play?" Hailey understands the art of character development, in books and film, and knows that my question hints at the truth that we choose what we make of each situation in our lives.

We are each in the process of discovering our unique role in the grand narrative of creation and the reign of God. The good news is that there is a place in the story for every one of us and we are not obligated to stick to a minor role we thought we had to play. We are invited to embrace our own celebrity on the stage of our lives. We were made to collaborate with the eternal voice of love, fulfilling our unique contribution to a good story. And so we are learning to search for clues that lead us to connect the vision of our destiny with the details of everyday life, asking, "Who was I uniquely made to be?" and, "How can I cooperate with the voice of God in my life?"

> Spring blossoms cling
> Delicately to trees
> Against the blue sky of an April afternoon.
> Sun-kissed faces
> Greet and grimace
> At the passing of winter's mildew.
> The air smells of sweet perfumes never bottled.
> The chocolate on my breath
> Reminds me of your abundance,
> traded and shipped across oceans,
> harvested from fields cultivated by hands
> who know the sacred mystery
> of solar, water, and dirt mixed,
> and made tasty pleasure,

by the hands of one who speaks in thunder
Smoky bites of burrito mojado
Set our mouths on fire
Quickly quenched by sweet milky
Cinnamon horchata just acquired
Our inheritance spills
Out onto city streets:
Once read books,
An extra coat,
Three pairs of pants
5 pairs of shoes, gently worn
And doggy bags of our unfinished plates
From the finest epicurean temples
This world has ever known.
Our streets are littered with gold
And we hardly glance at the treasures at our feet
I now walk by a loaf of bread
And because I merely look down
Find a twenty-dollar bill and a collection of Elvis songs
Recorded by Vegas impersonators
Cigarettes are shared
Change is dropped in cups
Money is loaned
Advice and wisdom unsolicited
are freely given
Every city block is an ecosystem of
Friendships, trust and neighborly affections.
Nay one of us falls to the ground
In drunken stupor, trip or cranial torture,
Than six friends rush to help her.
Canes are given to those who limp.
And at the first flush of want or need
Provision comes to lavish and please.
The pulse of hip-hop on the
boom box
reminds us we are alive—
and it is time to go out and make something of our lives.

This garden is well tended
And we are well cared for
—even as we roll and sit in ditches of briars and thorns
that tear our skin and make us howl in terror.
Pink is still the color of bubble gum,
still the color of little girls' dresses.
We are tortured by the memory
That we live in a good story
Which we try to forget to be like gods
—knowing good and evil,
striving as if the sun does not shine
and we are not the beloved of creation.
"I said I gotch you."
He says leaning toward her.
"I said I gotch you."
He says as they walk along together.
"Yeah, I said, I gotch you."

CONVERSATION

Embracing your own celebrity.   Do you find it easy or difficult to embrace the beauty and significance of your life? Explore why.

Learning to trust again.   How do the difficulties and disappointments you have faced influence your ability to trust in the goodness of God? Explain.

Who is well off?   Did you grow up feeling privileged or disadvantaged? How did this influence your decision making? Do you think we could redefine success and prosperity in a more holistic way? How might we begin doing this?

EXPERIMENTS

Wrestling with God.   We are invited to "negotiate" with God for how we are being loved through every moment of our lives. Read Psalm 13 or 27 or 44 and then write your own song complaint.

Tell your story.   If we are the beloved of God and part of a good creation and a good story, then we can learn to tell the stories of our lives as good stories. Using the third person, write a creative short story of your personal narrative, exploring God's care and provision in your life. What are the key turning points or scenes in the story that reveal who you are becoming?

Thanking your mothers and fathers.   In addition to your biological parents, who are the people who have played the role of supportive and guiding influences in your life? Write a letter to one person who fulfilled a parenting role, thanking them for the way they were used to meet a love need in your life.

CHAPTER EIGHT

CREATIVITY: THE PATH OF AN ARTIST

When I was in grade school I loved sketching pictures of monsters, faces, trees, and mountains, filling many sketchbooks with my drawings. I have watched my own children express themselves with similar uninhibited exuberance. My oldest daughter Hailey began telling elaborate stories when she was two or three, "reading" her tales from scribbles on a piece of paper—about a girl who wore pink dresses and lived in a pink house. Noah, a born naturalist, spent hours sketching hundreds of detailed pictures of birds. And our youngest son Isaiah creates epic comic book adventures that he illustrates with happy stick figures.

You too may have had some way of expressing your own creativity through dancing, singing, building or inventing, telling stories or pretending. But maybe you stopped doing that as you grew older. Most of us, at some point, began to stall in our creativity as we became more self-conscious. The expectation to conform to established standards of precision or beauty caused us to hesitate, weakening our courage to create. I remember when this happened for me, and, with anguish, I am watching my children enter the doldrums of self-critique.

On a Tuesday I visited Vincent Jackson, a local artist whose prolific works in oil pastels demonstrate a rare combination of primitive expressiveness and technical skill. I tell Vincent that it is an honor to meet him because I am a big fan of his work. "In fact," I say, "I have one of your pieces in my collection at home." He eagerly explains his technique and philosophy of art-making, as he continues to sketch casually: "My art is a part of me. It comes from within. It brings up a whole identity of myself. Instead of thinking it's a blunder—it's what we are." Creativity Explored, where Vincent exhibits, is a studio and gallery space in San Francisco's Mission District that is dedicated to artists with developmental disabilities. My friend Paul, who introduced me to Vincent, is on the teaching staff at the studio. Vincent's paintings, reminiscent of Picasso, call to mind the unencumbered freedom of childlike creativity. Perhaps the popularity of this gallery, and works like Vincent's, can be explained by the capacity of developmentally disabled artists to remind us of the lucidity we have lost.

The loss of creativity is where many of us most feel our spiritual need. Visit an art museum in any large city and you will see that it has become a temple where the artists are saints and deities and their collected works are objects of ritualized ceremony. We envy the unbridled liberty of the "rock star" artist, who is able to channel inspiration like an epiphany. I wouldn't be the first to suggest that the quest for artistic freedom is a veiled hunger for God because, as an imprint on our being, creativity is closely linked to spirituality.

The ancient narrative of Genesis affirms that we were created in the image of God, who is the ultimate artist (Genesis 1:27). We were made for creativity and freedom, to be collaborators with God in the ongoing work of creation. Our creativity and freedom are often blocked by dark imaginations and the shadows of selfish will. If we were made to work on the open canvas of creation, we have too often exchanged that canvas for a coloring book, assuming that it all comes down to whether we color inside or outside the lines. What if our true destiny is to flow with the freedom of the Creator, painting a life of goodness and beauty on the canvas of Earth and eternity? Paul of Tarsus wrote, "Where the Spirit of the Lord is, there is freedom'' (II Corinthians 3:17). We are invited to tap into the Spirit of Yahweh for the recovery of our creative potential.

Some would say that the highest form of creative expression is the capacity to live artfully. Through the freedom of his being, Jesus shows us the generative path of an artist, as one who approached life with sensitivity, compassion, and imagination. An artist, in the broad sense used here, is someone who, with acute skill and ingenuity, uses the tools of language and symbol to express and explore meaning and identity within a community. Employing the raw materials of Earth, humanity, and culture, Jesus collaborated with the creative and redemptive energy of the reign of God. We can learn to follow the path of an artist by adopting practices inspired by his example.

A GROWING APPETITE FOR BEAUTY

One of the more surprising, if not overlooked, aspects of the life of Jesus is the sensual and bodily nature of his existence. Despite the mythology about his superhuman strength, Jesus lived in his body much as we do: he got tired, thirsty, and hungry. We can only surmise that he did love food and drink by this response to his critics: "The Son of Man came eating and drinking, and they say, 'Here is a glutton and a drunkard, a friend of tax collectors and "sinners."' But wisdom is proved right by her actions" (Matthew 11:19). Jesus did not follow the path of an austere religious, eating only a crust of bread and a little water. In addition to certain times of fasting in stories of Jesus' life, there were also many episodes of feasting. His first mighty act was turning water into wine at a wedding party. Jesus walked from place to place, noticing the trees, villages, landscapes, and people along the way. Most artists crave the cultivation of the senses to fuel the imagination. We can begin to follow the path of an artist by learning to taste the good gifts of creation.

A former high school football player with a master's degree in mechanical engineering, my friend Adam isn't what most people expect when they think of the word *artist*. By day Adam works as an IT consultant and trains aggressively to compete in triathlons, but he is also a poet, chef, soulful mystic, and street sage. He writes and reads his spoken word poetry at local venues. The words come during his two-hour daily workout sessions, which he seizes as time for meditation and prayer. "I want to taste all of the abundance of God's creation," he says, "without having to conform to conventional categories." Adam blurs the lines in a quest to become a contemporary Renaissance man.

In grade school I was moved by the Renaissance paintings I saw while perusing books about Raphael, Michelangelo, and Leonardo da Vinci. I was impressed by their technical skills and attention to detail. These artists seemed equally comfortable depicting the narratives of biblical stories or rendering the curves of a woman's body. When I was eleven, a school art teacher, John Donais, recognized my passion. A devout French Catholic bachelor, Mr. Donais was a dedicated inner-city public school teacher. He set me up with a "studio" where I spent three hours a day painting and sculpting with a seemingly endless supply of terra-cotta, plaster, and artists' acrylics. We ate lunch together each day and I felt as if I were the son John Donais never had. At the end of the year he gave me his copy of *The Masters of Painting,* and inside the cover of the book he had written: "Artists have recorded man's history and each looked at their world with their own vision. Learn how to see and you too will create your own kind of beauty! Mark, artists are the world's caretakers of nature's beauty. Join them and discover your world."

We are helped in our role as creators by sampling things that inspire and feed our appetites for beauty, responding with conscious receptivity and gratitude. We follow the path of an artist by learning to taste, touch, see, and hear how Yahweh is present and caring in our world.

NAMING

My earliest memories are from a time when my family lived in a small apartment on the fifteenth floor of a city high-rise. Nearly every evening my parents would take my sister and me to a small public zoo where we could run and play. I remember how amazed I was to see the exotic zoo creatures: elephants, giraffes, orangutans, crocodiles, snakes, polar bears, and the mighty lions pacing in their cages. I learned to talk by trying to pronounce their names.

The book of Genesis tells the story of Yahweh inviting Adam to name the animals: "He brought them to the man to see what he would name them and whatever the man called each living creature, that was its name. So the man gave names to all the livestock, the birds of the air and all the beasts of the field" (Genesis 2:19–20). Yahweh made the world, but it has been our job to name it. Naming is one of the essential functions of our humanity—because language allows us to construct a common understanding of reality. We use words and symbols to communicate with each other, developing mutual references and meanings. We designate our thoughts, experiences, and sensations to build community together. And the language and symbols we choose shape our perceptions of ourselves, our world, and our Maker.

Although all of us use language and symbols to explore and express what it means to be human, artists do it with virtuoso skill and intentionality. Similarly, a theologian uses language to explore questions about God and humanity, though likewise, every person is a theologian—because each of us wrestles with how to speak about God and ourselves. You could say that the highest form of theology is art or the best kind of art is deeply theological.

Jesus was an artist *and* a theologian in the sense that with great skill he used language and symbols to explore and express who God is and what it means to be human. He used various names for God (including "my father," which described the Creator as a personal and relational being as opposed to an impersonal force). He employed a variety of names to identify himself that were symbolic and evocative (the Son of Man, the bread of life, the good shepherd). And he used particular language and declarative statements to describe his audiences (salt of the earth, sheep, children, friends, and even brood of vipers).

Jesus understood that how we speak about God and ourselves really matters, because language shapes our perceptions and categories. Our naming either enhances or diminishes dignity. People who are between jobs sometimes call themselves "consultants" because it sounds more promising than being "unemployed." The word *mother* might connote "someone who just stays home with the kids" or "someone investing in a generational legacy." Reading classic books aloud as a family, we notice gender-exclusive references, strict social roles, and unfair racial profiling. The words sound strange because we have now learned to speak more generously. For some, even calling God "father" signals conflict instead of confidence.

Occasionally I will hear someone rhetorically ask, "Why do we need any more books? Hasn't enough already been said?" Language is something that is always evolving, as each generation attempts to name their experiences of the world to make it their own. While our naming is dynamically related to the theologies of other times and places, we still have the task of constructing local theologies. Words by nature are provisional, so it is helpful to take a poet's inventive and experimental posture toward them. We are invited to look for new and fresh words, images, and symbols to communicate what is important to us.

Holly Sharp is an artist who uses painting to explore the external world of people and the interior landscape of the soul. Her husband, Ryan Sharp, is an avid songwriter and traveling performer. Through his music he chronicles his own attempts at naming God and his experience of the world. Ryan refers to their work as creating "cultural artifacts"—documenting common struggles to seek God and understand the world we live in. The letters of the New Testament suggest that songs and poems were circulated among first-century communities to express their aspirations and beliefs. Rather than relying solely on a consumer market, many contemporary faith communities are now trying to cultivate a local culture by writing their own songs, poems, and liturgies—and creating their own aesthetics to express the yearnings of a particular people. If we want to see spiritual renewal in our society, we should remember that, historically, the revolution often begins with the poets, painters, and musicians awakening new vision.

Here is a prayer Adam wrote for our local faith community, which we have used as a daily liturgy:

Abba
As the morning mist rises from the mountain tops,
So may your spirit rise from within us
Your beauty, your majesty, surround us
We give you thanks

Look upon us in your love
Teach us your ways, guide us
May we set ourselves in rhythm with your heart-beat
Sitting in silent peace enjoying the radiance of your presence
May our lives be an enchanting song of praise
emanating our gratitude heavenward
We need you, you are our redeemer, our sustainer, our
    savior, our friend, our comforter, our guide, our creator,
    our muse, our God
Open our eyes to see, our ears to hear, and our hearts to
    obey
Your touch is sweeter than the finest chocolate
Your presence more soothing than the warm summer breeze
As the sun pierces the billowing clouds
May your love pierce our souls
Set us on fire with the breath of your spirit
Teach us to live with unfathomable joy
May we live with blazing intensity and comforting compas-
    sion.
Abba, incline your ear to us that we may tell of your wonders.

DWELLING IN A LOCAL CULTURE

The message of the kingdom of love comes to us in the context of
our culture, and we grasp the message by awareness of its meaning
in our particular time and place. Jesus was a student of his time
and related his message to the concerns and context of people in
a particular place. He spoke Hebrew and Aramaic. As a rabbi he
occupied a distinctive social role in the community. He probably
dressed like other teachers in his society. He used stories and
examples that people in his region could identify with—analogies
to farming, local social customs, Jewish tradition and law, and
current political issues. He knew that his audience was specific:
"I have been sent to the lost sheep of Israel" (Matthew 15:24).
He carried out his mission and pilgrimage within the zeitgeist of
first-century Palestine.

We enter the practice of *dwelling* through conscious engagement with the culture(s) in which we live. I say culture(s) because
so many of us dwell in several cultures simultaneously. My friend

Christine, for example, travels between the cultures of her corporate job, her evangelical church community, and her identity as an Asian American woman (with a prescribed role in a traditional Chinese family). Dwelling has different implications in each of the cultures she is a part of. I would not be the first to suggest that Western culture is becoming increasingly tribal—that we now tend to form community around niche interests and life experiences. Due to the increasingly tribal nature of our society, it can be a complex task to navigate between the culture(s) we inherit and the culture(s) or subculture(s) we choose.

Following the path of the artist means observing and interacting with the artifacts of your particular culture: its media, books, film, fashion, cuisine, politics, economics, advertising. This might sound like simply consuming current news and entertainment, but it can be done as a conscious discipline. I watched the film *Boys Don't Cry* to get a better understanding of my neighbor, now in a same-sex relationship, who, much like the girl in the movie, spent her teenage years in a small town. Discussing the film together opened the door to more intimacy and trust in our friendship. I like to watch movies or read books with other people so that viewing becomes a springboard into conversation about meaning and values. If we find that we don't like what we see in the arts and media, we are invited to transition from culture consumers to culture makers.

I see Susan Cervantes walking down Balmy Alley in her signature beret, horn-rimmed glasses, and paint-splattered pants. Balmy Alley was a dirty street where addicts would go to shoot up until artists like Susan helped transform it into a mural gallery. Susan moved from Texas to San Francisco in the late 1960s. Familiar with the struggles of Latin immigrants and African American residents in the poorer parts of town, she began exploring the power of public murals in Latin America and in New York City during the Harlem Renaissance. Eventually Susan abandoned her personal painting and for thirty years has devoted herself to coordinating community murals: large-scale public artworks that are designed and painted by people from the community to voice their histories, hopes, and dreams.

Dwelling is about connecting your words, symbols, and expressions with the ongoing conversation of meaning in your culture.

I've worked with Susan on community murals in our neighborhood and also dabble in spoken word poetry, drumming, and creative writing—because these are mediums of public discourse in the Latin/artist/activist neighborhood where I live. (If I lived elsewhere I might be folk dancing or writing and performing country western songs.)

You may not think of yourself as an artist or even an art lover, but I suspect you still watch movies, listen to music, or read books. Aside from being entertaining, creative mediums play an important integrative role in our lives. There is a reason why we are moved by a scene from a movie or a lyric from a song or a character in a story. The arts serve to integrate the mind, soul, and body, connecting ideas with tangible realities in ways that inspire and motivate.

Many of us formed our ideas about God in a rather abstract way, seeing spiritual beliefs more like math or science than literature or history. As if it's all about the facts—though by themselves the facts can't motivate us to action if they are divorced from the stuff of life. Creative expression helps us dwell in the integrated space of truth statements grounded in our experiences and humanity.

I asked Pete, an accountant by trade and temperament, to write a prayer expressing his personal longings for the kingdom of God. At first Pete thought this was just a hokey activity for artist types, but later bashfully read what he had written for our group. We were all amazed at the depth of emotion in his prayer. Writing his prayer as a poem helped him make a connection between his factual mind and his feelings.

Sheri, a busy mother of two toddlers, was in a group where I invited everyone to use clay to sculpt an object that embodied something about their unique contribution to our community. We had just read a passage together from the Bible about being parts in the body of Christ. Sheri surprised herself and the rest of us by sculpting a beautiful rendering of human hands. Tears came to her eyes as she tried to explain her process in making this piece: "I've always had a hard time figuring out what I have to offer others. I realize what I have to give are my hands. I like to help people." Making something with clay unlocked an insight that Sheri hadn't been able to get to by just thinking.

STORYTELLING

Storytelling is a universal human phenomenon. Through stories, both fictional and biographical, we search for redemptive analogies. Stories enliven our imaginations and get at the things that cannot be said any other way. The contemporary novel and film, for instance, could be considered works of theology, using characters to explore more universal categories.

Jesus, of course, was a superb storyteller. Matthew the tax collector said that Jesus never appeared publicly without telling a story, fulfilling an ancient prophecy from Psalm 78 about the Messiah: "I will open my mouth in parables, I will utter things hidden since the creation of the world" (Matthew 13:34–35). Jesus used parables as allegories to explore the question, "What is the kingdom of God like?"(Luke 13:8). Not to be taken literally, parables allude to some higher truth. For example, Jesus said that the kingdom of God "is like a treasure hidden in a field. When a man found it, he hid it again, and then in his joy went and sold all he had and bought that field" (Matthew 13:44).

Like the work of any great artist, the parables of Jesus both reveal and conceal. Jesus said that he spoke in parables so that "though seeing, they do not see; though hearing, they do not hear or understand"(Matthew 13:13). The ambiguous and sometimes enigmatic nature of his stories allowed their meaning to be discovered only by those who had "eyes to see." Yet the parables could work into the psychic memory of the listener, since we learn and remember stories much better than facts or statements.

We have a lot to learn about storytelling from the example of Jesus, who told imaginative, personal, and evocative stories. We are not always good storytellers, and are often better at revealing than concealing. Often preoccupied with being literal, factual, or technical, we can come across as dogmatic when we try to speak about God. As evidenced by the enduring popularity of the memoir, what we trust more than anything is the voice of personal narrative. Knowing this, Jesus grounded his message in personal experience. We see this in the way he responded to his critics: "Even if I testify on my own behalf, my testimony is valid, for I know where I came from and where I am going" (John

8:14). A posture of authentic testimony is far more persuasive than badgering or rhetorical arguments.

TRICKERY

Several years ago I helped plan a large national event for faith leaders. Our planning team felt ambivalent about the consumer mindset encouraged by the scale and venue of a convention center. In addition, we had a reputation for being a rather pensive, dark, and deconstructive group and we wanted to subvert those expectations with a bit of hopeful pageantry and humor. We hired circus acrobats to perform and served popcorn and cotton candy as people walked through the doors. I encouraged presenters to wear brightly colored jester hats on stage, explaining that we were "going for the concept of holy fools." One rather dignified speaker politely declined, explaining, "I'm still working on the holy part." I stepped onto the stage wearing a court jester costume to deliver a partly satirical, mostly prophetic poet monologue. As a provocative statement during the music segment, we walked through the audience interrupting ardent worshipers by offering them cotton candy. Was cotton candy a symbol for what they were really looking for: a cotton candy experience of God—unhealthy, sugary, and artificial?

Artists have been known to be tricksters, shamans, seers, troubadours, holy clowns, and prophets who speak the unspeakable to their community. I'm not sure I did this well, but there is, nonetheless, a long historical precedent for provocative performance art in the name of truth and love. From the prophet Ezekiel, who played with toy soldiers and lay on his side cooking his food with excrement, to a dreadlocked John the Baptizer eating grasshoppers and wild honey, to Francis of Assisi stripping naked in front of church leaders, messengers have used trickery to surprise and subvert their audiences.

Jesus used trickery to convey his message of hope and revolution, making inflammatory and symbolic statements. He told the crowds who followed him, "Whoever eats my flesh and drinks my blood has eternal life" (John 6:54). In response to those who questioned his authority, he declared, "Destroy this temple, and I will raise it again in three days" (John 2:19). Jesus made radical reinterpretations of cultural symbols and rituals: declaring forgiveness of sins, riding into Jerusalem like a king on a donkey, and bringing new meaning to the Passover Seder. Jesus also made provocative statements by his actions. We see this in the way he incited his disciples to break local Sabbath laws and on the occasions when he stormed the temple with a whip to overturn the tables of currency traders and merchants.

While recognizing the special role and authority of Jesus, we can still learn from his ability to be subversive by calling commonly held assumptions into question. He did things that people did not expect from a "religious" teacher. And he said things that countered conventional wisdom. If nothing else, the message of Jesus was a gospel of surprise. By the practice of trickery, we follow the path of an artist to be unpredictable, undomesticated, and unexpected. Jesus once told his disciples, "I am sending you out like sheep among wolves. Therefore be as shrewd as snakes and as innocent as doves" (Matthew 10:16).

RISK TAKING

As an integrative exercise I invited the group to draw a picture. Ken said, "I can't do this, I'm not an artist," as if some people are born to be creative and other people aren't. What is an artist? In one sense an artist is simply one who does—a person with the courage to try. The most accomplished and prolific artists are not necessarily the most talented. What they possess is motivation, discipline, and the audacity to take risks. An artist can make creating look easy, but this is only because of great persistence and dedication. Creativity is more about passion and courage than talent. Passion provides the momentum you need to become skillful.

At its core, creativity implies taking risks. When speaking of John, the locust-eating prophet, Jesus said, "The kingdom of heaven has been forcefully advancing, and forceful [people] lay hold of it" (Matthew 11:12). This text speaks to the intensity and unrestrained wildness we are invited to bring to the task of seeking the kingdom of love. Our hesitancy must give way to confident action. Paul of Tarsus once reminded his apprentice Timothy that "God did not give us a spirit of timidity, but a spirit of power, of love and of self-discipline" (II Timothy 2:7).

The path of the artist means adopting an experimental posture toward life, fully aware that what we try may fail. It would be better to risk failure than to be paralyzed by calculation and fear. Once Jesus told a story illustrating the value of risk taking, which I have often used as a *lectio divina* (a guided scripture meditation) for artists' retreats. In the story, Jesus said that God's realm is like a landowner who gave three employees money to invest, "depending on their abilities." Two of these employees invested the money and doubled their assets. "Good work! You did your job well. From now on be my partner," said the landowner. The third employee, intimidated by the risks, buried the money in the ground. When the landowner returned, the employee tried to explain himself: "I know you have high standards and hate careless ways, that you demand the best and make no allowances for error. I was afraid I might disappoint you, so I found a good hiding place and secured your money. Here it is, safe and sound down to the last cent."

Eugene Peterson's translation of this parable in *The Message* makes the landowner's response especially poignant: "[He] was furious. 'That's a terrible way to live! It's criminal to live cautiously like that! If you knew I was after the best, why did you do less than the least? The least you could have done would have been to invest the sum with the bankers, where at least I would have gotten a little interest.' Then the landowner said, 'Take the [money] and give it to the one who risked the most. And get rid of this "play-it-safe" who won't go out on a limb'" (Matthew 25:14–30, The Message Bible).

Jesus said that we enter the kingdom of love by becoming like children again, eager to taste, explore, play, and take risks. I know how happy I am to receive the earnestly scribbled drawings of my children, and I can't help but think that God is equally pleased with our bold and awkward gestures. By the example and sacrifice of Jesus, the childlike creativity we have lost can be found again through the Spirit energy that is now available. Paul of Tarsus once reminded his disciples that "we are God's workmanship created in Christ Jesus to do good works, which God has prepared in advance for us to do" (Ephesians 2:10). Our Creator longs for us to embrace our role as artists and collaborators in the ongoing work of creation. We were made to create goodness and beauty in the world, blurring the line between fine art and artful living.

CONVERSATION

Childlike creativity.   What was your favorite way to express your-self as a child? What has prevented or allowed you to express that creativity as an adult? Are there ways that you long to be more creative in your approach to life?

Words and language.   How do you think the words we use to talk about ourselves and our Maker affect how we perceive reality? Can you think of ways of describing human experience of God that have now fallen out of use? What kind of words do you find helpful for exploring what it means to be human in God's world? Who are people you admire for their creative and insightful use of language to awaken hope and imagination?

Jesus the trickster.   How does it strike you to consider Jesus as a trickster and provocateur? What kind of revolutionary and prophetic statements would he make if he appeared in our time? Who are the holy tricksters of our time?

EXPERIMENTS

Awareness of culture.   Take a friend along to visit an art museum, to listen to live music, or to see a film. Afterward have a conversation about how what you saw or heard together enriched your experience or understanding of life in God's world.

Naming creation.   What is your personal medium for exploring who God is and what it means to be human? Words? Paint-ing? Music? Film? Find examples of ways that others have used your medium to explore and describe your experience of the world—and develop your own project. It could be as simple as writing a song or taking a series of photographs. Taking your questions into a medium that is beyond words will foster greater integration.

Telling stories.   Jesus often used parables to describe the kingdom of God. Read the book of Matthew and note every place where he mentions the kingdom of God or the kingdom of heaven. Beginning with the statement, "The kingdom of God is like...," make up some parables of your own using contemporary situations. What words would you use to describe "the kingdom of God" in language that might be more appropriate for a contemporary audience?

Risk taking.   You stretch your imagination and understanding by trying new things. What is something that you have always wanted to do but have never gotten around to? What keeps you from taking the risks you wish to? Take a risk and try something new this week.

PART THREE

THE GREATER WHOLENESS OF GENESIS-VISION

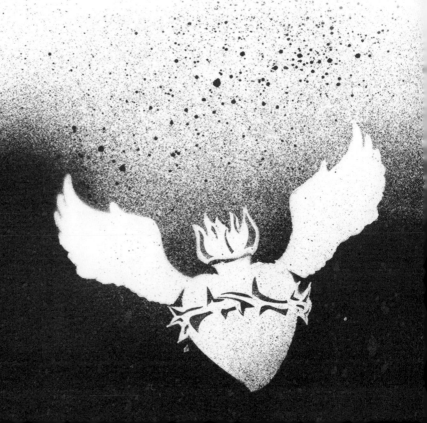

FAT CHANCE
BELLY DANCE

The Kingdom of God is at hand.
MARK 1:15c

During National Dance Week one April, Lisa and I attended a showcase performance of modern dance companies. One of the featured troupes was curiously named Fat Chance Belly Dance. As the tribal drumming began, more than forty women emerged from behind a curtain, moving their bodies in rhythm to the music. The women smiled broadly as they clanged hand cymbals and gyrated their bellies in unison to the beat. We were startled by their joy and exuberance and the variety of body shapes and skin colors—black bellies, brown bellies, tattooed bellies, taut tan bellies, stark white bellies, bellies from fit and skinny to plus-size pudgy. All of the women danced with such strength and confidence. Four dancers sashayed to the center of the stage for their solo performance while the other women continued to sway behind them. "These must be the best dancers," I thought, "and the other women are just here for background." But I was wrong. Eventually every dancer had a chance to perform in the center of the stage. The older and heavier women danced with moxie equal to the young and fit. The women hooted and cheered for each other as each new set of soloists made their debut in the center of the stage. Their dancing was an unfettered celebration of life, with every woman having a place in the pageantry.

Tears came to my eyes and I was surprised by how deeply their performance moved me. Their choreography struck me as a fitting metaphor for the dance of God's kingdom. People of all shapes and sizes, nations and tribes are invited to enter the greater wholeness of the Maker's genesis-vision.

When he spoke, Jesus proclaimed, "The kingdom of God is at hand." The first people who heard these words most likely interpreted them nationalistically—a new political order was about to be established by God for the sake of Israel. They soon learned that Jesus was announcing the reality of something more universal and more personal—the potential for each of us to live in rhythm again with the genesis-vision of our Creator. Jesus was announcing the power and potential for us to dance together in harmony with the divine aria of love.

In the chapters included in Part Three I explore what Jesus meant when he said, "The kingdom of God." Through these chapters I am suggesting that:

- It has always been God's desire to bring us into greater wholeness.
- Everything matters, and Jesus leads us toward an integrative path where we can learn to love the Creator and all of creation.
- We need spiritual transformation in our lives to achieve greater wholeness.
- Jesus fulfilled the "deeper magic" of the universe that gives us the power to love.
- We have the ability to be agents of healing in our world.

You are free to dance when you feel accepted, supported, and loved. And learning to love is the essence of making a life in the Way of Jesus.

CONVERSATION

Dance?   Do you think dancing is an apt metaphor for the invitation to live in the Way of love? Why or why not? What makes our culture reticent about dancing? Why is it so often relegated to an adult nightlife activity?

Everybody dance!   Is there space for anyone to enter the dance of God's kingdom? Who would you like to see welcomed into the dance who seems underrepresented?

EXPERIMENTS

Get your groove on.   Dancing can be a powerful integrative activity that dynamically connects the body, will, and emotions. Historically, dancing has been a part of most world cultures—and traditionally children and older people are included in this celebration of life through body movement. Alone or with friends or family turn the music up and the lights down and find your groove. Do you feel self-conscious? What was this experience like, and how could it be a metaphor for a life with God?

Dancing as a spiritual practice.   One of the most poignant pictures of King David of Israel is the description of him dancing "before the LORD with all his might" (II Samuel 6:14). *Put on some music and move your body as an expression of worship, gratefulness, and reverence.*

CHAPTER NINE

THE TINY SEED AND THE BIG TREE

From up in the rafters, my friend Michelle carefully manipulates the large puppet of a bearded young man. The loud screeching of a chainsaw reverberates through the sound system and suddenly—*snap*—a tree crashes across the stage, crushing the marionette. The puppeteers are performing a story about recent events in Humboldt County, California. On December 10, 1997, Julia "Butterfly" Hill climbed up into the branches of "Luna," a 180-foot-tall tree to protest a lumber company's plans to cut an ancient but unprotected grove of redwoods within the Headwater forest. While Julia sat up in the tree bringing global awareness to the issue, tensions escalated between environmental activists and the management and employees of the Pacific Lumber Company. The local economy was dependent on the lumber industry, and families would suffer if logging operations ceased. One day a logger cut down an adjacent tree that crushed and killed activist David "Gypsy" Chains. The incident was deemed an "accident" (despite lingering suspicions) and galvanized efforts by activists to protect the grove of 1,000-year-old trees.

David "Gypsy's" death is a dramatic midpoint in Michelle's puppet show that concludes with Luna being legally protected and Julia Butterfly climbing down from the tree where she had lived for more than two years. After Michelle and the other puppeteers take their bows, a sympathetic audience listens to a representative from a local environmental group make an impassioned plea for continued diligence. "Great performance!" I say to Michelle, as the audience trickles out of the small theater space.

When I told my friend Gary about the puppet show I had seen, he said, "That sounds like a bunch of nonsense—sitting up there in a tree. I feel sorry for your artist and activist friends who are so deluded and idealistic. There are more important things to be concerned about than old trees—like, for instance, your eternal destiny."

We live in a fragmented world where we all yearn for wholeness—yet we can't seem to agree about when or what will make us complete. Jesus came announcing, "The kingdom of God is at hand," and then told many allegorical and mysterious stories about the reign of God—leaving us to speculate about what, exactly, he meant by what he said. Perhaps as a further symptom of our lack of wholeness, we bring our limited faith and finite understanding to our conceptions of God's reign. One person's ideal of kingdom come is another person's worst nightmare. Some of us want a king *without* a kingdom—a God who is far away but ready to swoop in at the last moment to save us out of this place. And some of us want a kingdom *without* a king—an Earth home where justice, order, and beauty reign without divine sovereignty or moral responsibility. In any case, it takes eyes of faith to believe the message Jesus proclaimed: "The kingdom of God is within you" (Luke 17:21).

THE SEEDS OF GENESIS-VISION

A mighty redwood like Luna begins with a tiny seed slightly larger than a pinhead. But from the smallest of seeds grow the tallest trees. Many *Sequoia Sempervirens,* or redwoods, survive for thousands of years and reach heights of more than 350 feet—as tall as a thirty-five-story building. Jesus once said that the kingdom of God is like the seed of a mustard tree, "which a man took and planted in his field. Though it is the smallest of all your seeds, yet when it grows, it is the largest of garden plants and becomes a tree, so that the birds of the air come and perch in its branches'' (Matthew 13:21–32). Within every seed is the potential to grow up into what it was made to be—to fulfill the genesis-vision of its DNA. The genesis-vision of the Creator's dream for our lives has been planted in each of us. And we were created to be generative—to flourish and grow to fulfill our good destiny in the kingdom of love. In another story, Jesus said that our lives are the soil in which the seeds of God's kingdom can grow. Those seeds fall on soil that is hard and dry, or shallow and weedy, or fertile and healthy, ''where it produce[s] a crop—a hundred, sixty or thirty times what was sown'' (Matthew 13:8). If, indeed, the genesis-vision of God's kingdom has been planted in each of us, then it is the task of a lifetime to discover how to cooperate with the generative activity of God yearning to sprout up inside of us.

Unfortunately, devout and religious people are often no more fruitful in their lives than people who are irreligious. I was once part of a think tank where we sought to address this conundrum, considering the question, If we were made to be generative, what hinders this process? A seed needs both soil and sunshine to grow up into what it was made to be. Our growth is often frustrated by the choices we make—opting for *either* sunshine or soil, we take fragmented paths that make us less than fruitful. Our tendency is to live in polarization, taking paths that are blue or yellow instead of healthy green.

FOLLOWING A BLUE PATH

''I just got my belly button pierced and it really hurts,'' Michelle tells me, pouring me a second cup of coffee. Business was slow at the café when Michelle sat down at my table. A model-thin fashionista with dyed black hair, Michelle currently plays the role of a glamorous party girl—working at the café in the mornings, protesting with puppeteer activists in the afternoons, and going out to clubs every night. Although she has a degree in natural resource management from a prestigious east coast university, Michelle is waiting tables for a couple of years so she can be free to travel and, in her words, ''suck the marrow out of life.'' Eventually she plans to settle down, devoting herself to helping women and children in Africa through her knowledge of sustainable agricultural practices and safe water treatment. Through frequent trips among Colorado, Europe, New York, and San Francisco, using credit cards and money from her family, Michelle maintains an extensive network of friends that she calls her "framily"—friends who are like family. When she describes her swirl of companions it sounds like a cross between the United Nations and the Rainbow Coalition: Israeli students, lesbian academics, Bosnian refugees, German expatriates, Afro-Cuban musicians, Asian hipsters, Islamic artists, gay Puerto Rican bartenders—and lots of overeducated east coast kids like herself. It is as if Michelle is trying to bring about world peace one friendship at a time.

How do I fit into this scheme? I'm the straight-Caucasian-family man—"her pastor friend," she tells people—an intriguing anomaly to her atheistic sensibilities. "I believe in love instead of God," she quips. Michelle relates to me like I'm either her rabbi or her older brother. "I have a feeling our conversations will end up in a book you write someday," she says knowingly.

For Michelle, life surges like blue blood pulsing through healthy veins. She typifies what we could describe as someone on a "blue path"—acutely aware of her body, the Earth, and humanity. A person on a blue path is more attuned to the physical and social realities of the present than moral or theological concerns about the future. Someone on a blue path is passionate about social justice in ways that fit their personal sensibilities. Michelle, for instance, searches for meaning in the immanence of social harmony, ethics, and ecological sustainability. A person on a blue path yearns for the reign of God by imagining and working toward a time when there will be world peace, global unity, and sustainability in the natural world—a time when together we fulfill the command to love our neighbors as ourselves.

FOLLOWING A YELLOW PATH

Gary pulls up in front of my house in his 4 × 4 pickup truck with an American flag sticker and Jesus fish decals attached to the back bumper. Barrel-chested and wearing a Christian logo T-shirt, blue jeans, and white tennis shoes, Gary greets me with a friendly smile. "How's it going, brother?" he asks warmly, slapping me on the back. Gary works as a construction superintendent for a large building developer, but has taken the afternoon off to talk with me about bringing a group of students to the city for what he calls "an urban plunge." In his spare time Gary is a youth volunteer at a large suburban church. As we walk toward the café where Michelle works I ask what's new. He tells me that his family has just moved into a larger house further from town, but closer to the delta where he enjoys boating and fishing. A new evening service has started at Gary's church that he is really excited about, "because I can watch the game and still make it to church on Sunday nights," Gary explains. "And the worship band is really great!" Gary is in a men's "accountability group" and is also the local contact person for a national men's movement. "Have you seen anyone get saved lately?" he asks as we near the entrance to the café. When we arrive Michelle is working the counter, and I order a regular coffee and Gary orders a large mocha latte, a muffin, and orange juice. "I love my snacks," he says, "but I'm afraid it's starting to show in my waistline."

When we get settled at a table, Gary solemnly asks, "So, Mark, how's your walk been lately?" What Gary means is, "Have you been praying, reading the Bible, and staying away from pornography?" I mention a few things about my work and family life. "Well, you can be praying for me, because I've been tempted a lot this week. I'll tell you what," Gary says, "I don't know how you can handle being around all these attractive younger women. But, praise God for grace and forgiveness!"

With a tender conscience and reverent heart, Gary stares up into the sunny yellow radiance of God's mercy and eternal judgment. If Michelle aligns her spiritual life horizontally along a blue path, Gary orients himself vertically along the opposite axis, following what we could describe as a yellow path. He is acutely aware of unseen forces and the moral dimension to existence. A person on a yellow path is often more focused on the future than on the present. Someone on a yellow path is passionate about seeking purity and forgiveness in the areas where they are morally aware. Gary searches for meaning by worshiping a holy and transcendent God, and by preparing himself and others to meet their Maker. A person on a yellow path yearns for the reign of God by imagining and working toward a time when all people kneel before their Creator—fulfilling the command to love God.

THE LOSS OF GENESIS-VISION

"Excuse me," Gary says, pointing to his cell phone. "It's work. I have to take this call."

When Gary steps outside, Michelle comes over to our table. She looks disturbed, so I ask, "What's wrong?"

"Are you sure your virgin ears are ready to hear what I have to say?" I nod. "Okay. I've been sleeping with somebody who works here for the past month, but his fiancé is moving to town this weekend—so we are going to have to break it off. We have a real intense connection and the sex has been great—so I'm really going to miss him. I'm hoping to stay connected by making friends with his fiancé."

"It sounds complicated. What if she finds out that the two of you have been involved?"

Michelle begins to wipe her eyes as she answers. "Well, I'm a little concerned that this is becoming a pattern with me. I did the same thing with an older married man when I was in college. It was very messy and they eventually divorced. I hate to think it was my fault, but I know they weren't happy together either."

"Have you considered the possibility that there is a moral dimension to your sexuality," I ask delicately, "that might affect the outcomes in your relationships?"

"What do you mean?"

"Well, there may be some divine guidance on how to have healthy boundaries. Are you familiar with the Torah commandments about trust, fidelity, and monogamy?"

"Remember, Mark, *all* of my grandparents died in the Holocaust. God abandoned us—so my family was not very religious. We celebrated the Jewish holidays, but I don't think my parents believe in God any more than I do. I know it seems like I'm wrecking my life by the choices I make, but I prefer to think that we have many lives within one lifetime. Each relationship I've had is like one life that is good while it lasts. I can keep starting over. Does that make any sense?"

"I see your reasoning," I say, "but if this is true, you will still be the same character in each new life—and the repeated choices you make are determining the kind of person you are becoming."

Gary is back, and I briefly introduce him to Michelle. As Gary and I discuss his plans to bring a group of teenagers to the city, I try to make it clear that we try to help students practice walking in the ways of Jesus. "I notice you keep saying 'the Way of Jesus'—what's that all about?" Gary interjects somewhat suspiciously. "I've never heard anyone else use that term before."

I spend a few minutes trying to explain the way I understand the message of Jesus—that the present availability of God's kingdom means we can learn to love God by caring about everything that God has made.

Gary looks puzzled and says, "That's not what I understand the gospel to be about! I was told that I was a sinner going to hell, and that if I believed in Jesus and confessed my sin, God was legally obligated to forgive me and let me into heaven. You can try to love people, but we are so broken and wicked that you will always keep messing up. There is no way that we can live much better than we do. That's why the gospel is *all* about God's grace and forgiveness."

THE SHEMA AND THE NEARNESS OF GOD'S KINGDOM

Jesus often used images of wholeness and completion to describe the fulfillment of God's kingdom. He once told a story about a woman who lost a gold medallion from a precious necklace. She searches the house until she finds it and "calls her friends and neighbors together and says, 'Rejoice with me; I have found my lost coin.'" Jesus concludes the parable saying, "In the same way, I tell you, there is rejoicing in the presence of the angels of God over one sinner who repents" (Luke 15:8–9). The deeper truth revealed by this story, and others like it, is that, like the woman's gold medallion, though we have often become lost, fragmented, or disconnected from the source of our life in God, we can be found and made whole again.

God has always been inviting us back into the greater wholeness of genesis-vision. When Jesus proclaimed, "The kingdom of God is at hand," he implicitly addresses our desperation for restoration and healing in our relationship with the Creator, the self, the Earth, and one another. His announcement was an invitation to return to the genesis-vision of our Maker. Here I'm using genesis-vision to mean the DNA of God's will and dream for our lives. Jesus sought to awaken our imagination for what life could be like if we learn to surrender to the rule and reign of God again. Although the vocabulary of "kingdom" is less developed in more ancient texts, we see a pattern of God calling people to greater wholeness. One of the earliest examples of genesis-vision, the DNA of God's kingdom, is summarized through the Hebrew Shema, based on the ancient commands delivered through Moses:

> Listen, Pay attention! The LORD our God, the LORD is One.
>
> Love the LORD your God with all your heart, and with all your soul and with all your mind and with all your strength. These commandments that I give you today are to be upon your hearts. Impress them on your children. Talk about them when you sit at home and when you walk along the road. When you lie down and when you get up. Bind them as symbols on your hands and fore-heads. Tie them on the door frames of your houses and on your gates. (Deuteronomy 6:4–9)

We were made to orient our entire beings to the good dreams of our Maker. The command to love God was a centering vision of life reinforced in ancient times by rituals, daily habits, clothing, decorations, and continuing conversations. This greatest com-mand is the basis for the "Shema Prayer," which observant Jews continue to sing in the mornings and evenings of each day. *Shema,* in Hebrew, emphatically means "Listen! or pay attention!" The Shema Prayer is often the first words sung over a child at birth and the last words on the lips of a person taking their final breaths. The instruction to love God with one's whole being summarizes the meaning and destiny of our lives.

Loving "your neighbor as yourself" was an implicit corollary to the command to love God. Jesus confirmed the significance of the Shema when he answered an expert in the law who asked, "What is the greatest command?" (Matthew 22:36). He added that "the second is like it: 'Love your neighbor as yourself.' All the Law and the Prophets hang on these two commands" (Matthew 22:39–40). You seek greater wholeness by learning to love God with your whole being, and you love God by caring about all that God has made. The reality of the kingdom of God is fulfilled among us to the extent that we learn to love both Creator and creation. In his life and teachings Jesus modeled what this means. He said, "I have not come to abolish the law or the prophets, but to fulfill them" (Matthew 5:17). Through his words and example, Jesus taught how to embrace and cultivate genesis-vision. And through his ethical teachings he described how to pursue the kingdom of God in various dimensions of human experience (relationships, conflict resolution, money, sexuality, ambitions, attitudes, and so on).

YEARNING FOR GREATER WHOLENESS

A few weeks later Gary called to explain that he wouldn't be coming along on the trip he organized for his group of students. "Why the change in plans?" I asked. He sheepishly told me that, effective immediately, he was no longer working with students at his church. Gary had a secret he had kept hidden from everyone. Recently a woman contacted the church and revealed an inappropriate sexual relationship that Gary had had with her many years before—when she was a teenager and he was the youth leader. "I finally had to tell my wife about what I'd done, but also decided that I should confess my ongoing porn addiction. Now my wife feels like I've been living a lie, and can't be trusted anymore. This week has been a living hell, and I feel like my life is destroyed. I have a lot to rebuild."

I listened and offered my support to Gary in his process of healing and restoration. I now understood more fully why God's grace and forgiveness were so important to him. Every week Gary had been going through a cycle of guilt, shame, and confession that, on Sundays, was released through singing and hearing teaching about God's love and forgiveness. It was hard for Gary to embrace the social dimensions of the gospel when guilt and judgment loomed so large in his consciousness. Through these difficult circumstances, Gary is discovering his need for greater wholeness—to have an experience with God that is more connected to the details of his humanity, relationships, and social ethics.

Michelle had been away traveling for about a year when she called one day to invite herself over for dinner. When she arrived I was surprised to see the change in her appearance. She wore simpler clothes, and her hair was back to its natural color. She was also more calm and centered than I had ever remembered. While living in Africa the previous ten months she had made some changes to simplify her life—becoming a vegetarian and committing herself to a monogamous relationship. As always, she had plenty of stories.

"I had a bizarre spiritual experience last month," Michelle said. "I went to a Womyn's Spirituality weekend with my friend and thirteen other women on some land in Southern Oregon. On Friday night we sat in a circle as two shamans conducted a ceremony to welcome the spirits of the four directions into our gathering. I was skeptical but curious about observing their practices as sort of a sociological study. I thought most of the rituals were pretty hokey, but some of the women were really amazing."

"What made the experience so bizarre?" I asked.

"Well, on Sunday morning they had this ceremony to release the spirits they had invoked for our gathering. I suddenly started shaking and felt like something was taking over my body. I screamed and began vomiting repeatedly. I don't know how I could have vomited so much. It lasted about two hours and then I felt fine. What do you think it was?"

"Had you eaten anything strange—or taken any controlled substances?" I asked.

"No, I hadn't even had breakfast. It was only 9:30 in the morning!"

"Wow, it definitely sounds like you connected with some unseen spiritual being," I offered.

"That's exactly what it felt like. It was extremely scary. The women reasoned that sometimes the spirits linger and manifest themselves before leaving. I don't quite know what to do with this experience. It doesn't fit into any of my rational categories. I've tried to explain it in terms of science and psychology, but I can't. I wasn't even an active participant in the ritual. Do you think it might have been God?" Michelle asked.

"It seems like you were possessed by something that entered your body against your will—almost like a soul violation. That doesn't sound like God to me. My understanding is that there are both good and evil forces in the spirit world. I don't think a God of goodness would present to you in such a violent or invasive way. I wonder if what you experienced was something from the dark side."

"It did feel dark and spooky—so I wonder why the spirits chose me?"

This experience seemed to lead Michelle to contemplate moral and spiritual dimensions of life that she had previously avoided. She is becoming more sensitive to the differences between light and dark spiritual forces. Was there a particular reason why the spirits were so interested in her? I brought up the possibility that Michelle's difficulty with believing there is a God may have more to do with her moral choices than she first realized. I wonder if this incident was meant to bring Michelle a step closer to greater wholeness by helping her begin to yearn for a connection with the transcendent nature of a good God.

BLUE + YELLOW = A GREEN PATH

Perhaps you can identify with both Michelle's and Gary's struggles to move from their fragmentation to the greater wholeness of the kingdom of God. Of course the distinctions I've made between blue and yellow paths are somewhat artificial and meant to illustrate the difficulty we have holding love for Creator and creation together as one reality. It is our lack of wholeness that makes us want a king without a kingdom or a kingdom without a king.

If we tend toward these polarities, is one preferable over the other? And would Jesus best be described as a yellow path person seeking transcendence or a blue person seeking immanence, or both? It is clear that Jesus followed neither a yellow nor a blue path, but a synergistic combination of the two: a green path. The color green is a symbol of health, vitality, and life. Remember that Jesus once said, "I have come that they may have life, and have it to the full" (John 10:10).

In late November I heard the sad news that Luna, the tree where Julia Butterfly staged her famous two-year "tree sitting," had been slashed by vandals who cut through two-thirds of her trunk using chain saws. Environmental activists were outraged and devastated by this act that now threatened the life of the ancient tree. Experts debated whether the tree would be saved or lost and if Luna could ever be become whole again.

Shortly after vandals had slashed Luna's trunk, a complex system of metal braces were bolted across the base of the giant redwood to hold the tree together as it heals. To sustain life, a tree must stay both rooted in the soil and open to the energy of sunlight and carbon dioxide. If a tree is cut or pulled out of the soil, where it draws water and nutrients, it will eventually die. Similarly, if a tree is shielded from the radiance of the sun it will eventually wither away. The life of a tree is an apt metaphor for the green path toward making a life in the way of Jesus. To see the Creator's genesis-vision fulfilled in our lives we need to be both rooted in the soil of our humanity, people, and place and open to the transcendent energy of God.

The dirt of life in the here and now provides the nutrients to cultivate a life with God. We also need exposure to the energy of the Spirit of God surrounding us. Jesus demonstrated a life that was grounded in humanity and struggle and open to the energy and breath of God. We find him in the marketplace caring for the needs of people and on the mountainside connecting with the eternal Father. His life was an example of dynamic unity and synergy between the pursuit to love God *and* everything that God has made. And this is the life we are being invited into.

Julia Butterfly Hill is the daughter of a traveling evangelist. Growing up, Julia performed puppet shows for the children who came to her father's revival meetings. And the tree-sitting environmental activist is still something of an evangelist, on the road speaking at green rallies, festivals, and conferences. In an interview about her spiritual roots and aspirations, Julia humorously quipped, "In the Beginning, God's original intention was to hang out in a beautiful garden with two naked vegetarians. What a great vision!" (*Common Ground*, San Francisco ed., April 2006). Julia is trying to reconcile the apocalyptic God-vision of her youth with the kingdom of God that is already here to embrace and protect. We each search for how to find ourselves in the greater wholeness of genesis-vision—learning to care about everything that God cares about. And this is an important step along the path toward making a life in the Way of Jesus.

CONVERSATION

Fragmentation.   How do you see a polarization between yellow and blue paths being played out in our society? (For instance, in politics, social policy, or entertainment.) Where do you see green—examples of where loving God and caring deeply about the needs of our time are deeply integrated?

Yellow or blue?   Which character did you relate the most to— Gary or Michelle? Are you naturally more drawn to a vertical (yellow) or horizontal (blue) orientation to life? What is the first thing that pops into your head as you consider what it might mean for you to become more green and integrated? In what areas of life would you like to be more whole and complete?

Everything matters.   In the Maker's economy, everything is important and everything matters—our spirituality, our relationships, and our personal and social ethics. How do you think we can learn to live awake to God in a world where all of our choices matter?

EXPERIMENTS

Seeds and plants.   Buy a small house plant. Nurture it and watch it grow to remind you of the seed of genesis-vision that longs to grow up inside of you. If this sounds too complicated, buy a jar of mustard seeds and put them in a prominent place as a reminder.

The Shema.   Practice orienting your mind and heart around the Creator's vision of unity and wholeness. Say a version of the Shema Prayer in the morning and evening each day for the next week. Better yet, say the prayer together with the people that you live with.

The following version would be considered the first section of the traditional Jewish Shema with the added phrase, "Love your neighbor as yourself."

> Listen! Pay attention! Hear, O Israel: The LORD our God, the LORD is one. Love the LORD your God with all your heart and with all your soul and with all your strength. And love your neighbor

as yourself. These commandments that I give you today are to be upon your hearts. Impress them on your children. Talk about them when you sit at home and when you walk along the road, when you lie down and when you get up. Tie them as symbols on your hands and bind them on your foreheads. Write them on the door frames of your houses and on your gates.

Praying kingdom come. Jesus invites us to pray, "God, Your kingdom come, your will be done, on earth as it is in heaven" (Matthew 6:10). Make the prayer, "Your kingdom come, your will be done," your mantra this week as you travel about. While writing this chapter I looked out the window to see my neighbor Deanna talking with a group of men. She has been selling her body for drugs for as long as I can remember. Whenever I see Deanna I quietly pray, "God may your kingdom come to her—she is a little sister princess child, and I long to see everything you imagined for her life before the creation of the world to be restored here and now." There are places where land is scared by destruction—pollution, toxic wastes, debris, feces, urine-soaked alleyways, dirty needles on beaches, or broken glass. When I walk in these places, cleaning up what I can, I pray, "Your kingdom come. Bring healing to Earth scarred by selfishness or neglect. Make these places clean and fresh, that children may walk here without fear."

CHAPTER TEN

BREAD AND WINE AND THE DEEPER MAGIC

Early one morning my neighbor Kate called to tell me what had happened. In the middle of the night, a woman was killed in the apartment adjoining Kate's. "She was shot four times in the chest over a drug deal gone bad," Kate said. "I'm all shook up! It happened in the room directly adjacent to my bed—three feet from my pillow! I woke up when I heard the shots. One of those bullets could have gone right through the wall!" I invited Kate and her partner over for dinner that night to talk more about the incident. We made pizza and they brought over a bottle of wine to share. Outside on the porch, between puffs on a cigarette, Kate said, "I'm struggling to understand why this happened. Don't we naturally want to do good in the world? I've tried to have faith in humanity, but events over the past few months are beginning to shake my confidence."

Despite the enduring yearning we have to live out God's genesis-vision, there are other forces at work in our world and within ourselves that inhibit us from living out this great dream. Jesus' statement that "the kingdom of God is near" implies conflict with other kingdoms—a great contest between the good reign of God and the empires of greed, lust, and selfishness. We are, in many ways, at war with ourselves.

As Kate and I were talking, a man on a bicycle stopped in front of us on the sidewalk. Quickly he handed a ten-dollar bill to another man who, in return, gave him a small bag of crack. With last night's drug-related murder fresh in my mind, I had more courage than usual to confront them. "I don't want you doing that," I yelled from the top of the stairs.

"I'm sorry," the man on the bike said. "We'll go somewhere else."

"I don't want you doing that anywhere," I said. "That stuff will eventually kill you."

"Hey, I said I'm sorry, what else do you want me to do?" he asked.

"I want you to get a new kind of life," I said sternly. Then I told him what had happened the night before and explained how drugs make the neighborhood unsafe for children and older people. Calming down a bit, I introduced myself. He shook my hand and told me his name. "Frank, do you have kids?" I asked. He told me he has eight children and they live just down the street. "Your children need a father who is present and caring," I pleaded, "but it's hard to be that kind of father when you're smoking crack and cruising around. I believe there is a different kind of life available to you—and I would be glad to help you discover it. If you want my help, you know where I live."

As I was saying this, I was fully aware that I was no better than Frank. I was holding a glass of wine in my hand—a good gift of creation that I could misuse if I chose to. In one way or another we all have our own demons—self-destructive tendencies that threaten wholeness and harmony.

What gives a person the power to choose genesis-vision over destructive self-will? Many people who have faced their darkest demons have learned that to pursue wholeness they needed a power beyond themselves. We need to be transformed in order to fulfill the mandate to love the Creator and creation. The work of Jesus' life was to renew our imagination for the kingdom of God and show us how we can live generatively. But Jesus also promised that new energy for life would come through his sacrifice. He believed that his crucifixion and resurrection would bring the power to live in a new way. The event of Jesus' death was the inexplicable catalyst for the early church. Paul of Tarsus once said, "We preach Christ crucified: a stumbling block to Jews and foolishness to Gentiles, but to those whom God has called, both Jews and Greeks, Christ *the power* of God and the wisdom of God" (I Corinthians 1:23–24). In the experience of the early disciples, the power of Jesus' resurrection brought the spiritual metamorphosis required to inhabit the kingdom of love. Jesus confirmed our need for transformation when he said, "No one can see the kingdom of God unless he is born again" (John 3:3). We were born once in our physical bodies and we thirst for spiritual rebirth.

BREAD, WINE, AND CHOCOLATE

It's springtime, and that means birthday season. By the number of parties that fill our weekends (sometimes two on Saturday and three on Sunday!), you would think that we parents all schemed to synchronize our children's births between late February and early May. Birthday parties among our friends are often family affairs, with games and activities for the kids, and tasty food and beverages for the moms and dads. At this "faerie" birthday, a luscious table is set in the middle of a meadow. Barefoot children with dirty faces run in and out of the afternoon shadows, snatching food with giggles. And the adults graze—at a table spread with goat cheese and tomato pesto, hummus and crackers, shrimp cocktail, salads, grilled sausages, crusty bread, and wine. "You should try the zinfandel," Martin said pouring me a glass. "But you may also like the pinot that Serina picked." At the other end of the table Bob is holding court talking excitedly about alternative energy sources, bicycles, and hybrid fuel efficiency. "As a society we have to start thinking more about where our energy comes from," Bob says emphatically. The sun is still warm in the cooling mist of late afternoon as we enjoy good food, good wine, and the company of good friends. "I think I could live on crusty bread and red wine," Maria says, "and maybe a little olive oil—I could be happy for the rest of my life with those three things."

"What about chocolate?" someone asks. "Okay," Maria adds, "four things!"

Maria's comment makes me think of the modest lunches Lisa and I have shared on our trips to Napa Valley's wine country. It's so simple and satisfying to have a glass of wine with some bread and cheese on the luscious grounds of a winery on a hot summer day. These lunches remind me of an old phrase about all the Maker provides for us: "wine that gladdens the heart[s] of [people], oil to make [their] face[s] shine, and bread that sustains [their] heart[s]" (Psalm 104:15). Growing up, I was unaccustomed to people drinking wine, so I always thought it strange when it was used during communion. Yet in the time and place where Jesus lived, most people were familiar with bread and wine as reminders of daily provision. This is probably why Jesus chose them to symbolize the power that would be available through his sacrifice. And he bewildered the crowds by telling them, "I am the bread of life" (John 6:48), and "My flesh is real food and my blood is real drink" (John 6:55). What Jesus was getting at was that just as we need physical food to fuel our bodies, we need spiritual energy to pursue a generative life of love. The early followers of Jesus seemed to experience this flow of spiritual power tangibly—almost as a physical sensation. And for that reason the Apostle Paul wrote, "Do not get drunk on wine, which leads to debauchery. Instead, be filled with the Spirit" (Ephesians 5:18). In any case Jesus made it clear that we don't "live by bread alone" (Luke 4:4).

JESUS, THE SHEMA, AND THE DEEPER MAGIC

"Could I talk to you about something?" Deborah asks, while I grab another hunk of bread and refill my glass. She is looking very serious. "I've been reading this article in the *New Yorker* about the new Mel Gibson film. Have you heard of it?"

"You mean *Lethal Weapon 5*?" I say, joking.

"No! You're kidding, aren't you?"

"You mean the film about the crucifixion of Jesus. I've heard there are concerns that it might be anti-Semitic." (Deborah and her husband, Bob, are both Jewish.)

"That's what I wanted to ask you about." Deborah adds, "I've always been intrigued by Jesus, but have hesitated to explore much further because so often Jesus is portrayed as an antagonist to Jews. And also, if political leaders use the name of Jesus to justify war and imperialism, then how could I be interested in that same Jesus? Does that make any sense?"

"Many agendas have been attributed to Jesus that I'm not sure he would condone or support," I say.

"So, from your perspective, what exactly was his message?"

"Well, I'm sure you are familiar with the Shema Prayer?" Nodding her head, she says, "Of course. You know how important these things are to Bob. We sing the Shema every night as we put the kids to bed."

"Our family also says a version of the Shema. So, I understand that the vision for this prayer is a state of unity, wholeness, and integration—a harmony between Creator and creation. It's a reminder that we were made to love God and love one another in a state of *shalom*-peace."

Thoughtfully, Deborah responds, "I really resonate with that. When I hear you say that it makes me think that, deep down, you and I really long for the same things."

I continued, "So, as I understand it, the message of Jesus was that shalom is now possible. Through his teaching and example Jesus showed the way toward the shalom of God—how we can fulfill the vision to love God and one another. But simply knowing that we were made to love hasn't brought shalom near. We seem to lack the power to love. Many people believe that the crucifixion and resurrection of Jesus fulfilled a cosmic mystery. C. S. Lewis I believe called it 'the deeper magic of the universe' that gives us the power we need to seek God's shalom. People came to believe that through the sacrifice of Jesus, an energy was released, some would call the Spirit, that allows us to love God and people from the deepest place of our being. When Jesus traveled, proclaiming, 'The kingdom of God is near,' he was announcing that a new kind of life is now possible, or, as a friend likes to say, 'There is a new way to be human.'"

Pausing for a moment, I add, "I'm sorry for such a lengthy answer to your question—but I'm sure you knew you were asking me about something that is really my passion."

"That's okay. I'm very curious about all this," Deborah replies. "So this article in the *New Yorker* seemed to suggest that antagonism developed when Christians began blaming the Jews for Jesus' death. Is that a common sentiment?"

"Well, first of all, Jesus and his disciples were all Jewish."

"Are you serious? I'd never heard that," she says with a look of surprise.

"In fact, what would later become Christianity began as a Jewish sect. Jesus wouldn't have been historically significant as a rabbi, had it not been that many miracles were attributed to him and hundreds of people claimed to have seen him after he rose from the dead. The sect of Jesus really gained momentum when the simple people who followed him suddenly had the courage to subvert the Roman Empire. They began to live in a radical new way—sharing their houses, food, and clothes with one another, welcoming strangers and caring for orphans and widows. The historian Aristedes once commented, 'This is a new people, and there is something divine in the midst of them.'"

"So you are saying that most of this took place within the Jewish community?" Deborah asks.

"Yes, but soon Greeks and other ethnic groups also began to experience the power of Jesus. A big debate in the first century was whether anyone who was *not* Jewish could follow the Way of Jesus. Many of the books and letters of the New Testament share the story of the struggle to assimilate non-Jewish people into the Way. There were heated debates, for instance, about whether gentile followers of Jesus should be required to follow the circumcision regulations and kosher laws of the Talmud."

"I had no idea that Judaism and Christianity were so closely related," Deborah comments. "It's not the impression you get these days."

"Eventually the Way of Jesus took on an identity beyond its Jewish roots and, over time, many of the connections were forgotten. Antagonism developed with religious Jews over Jesus because some Christians felt that Jewish people who didn't embrace Jesus were rejecting the prophesied Messiah. Ironically, in the first century, what distinguished the Way of Jesus was inclusivity—the message that anyone, from any race or tribe, could have access to this new power to love."

"This is all very fascinating to me," Deborah says. "I wish we could keep talking, but it looks like it's time to cut the birthday cake."

THE MECHANICS AND THE MESSAGE OF POWER

Every time Lisa and I visit Napa Valley, we try to go on at least one winery tour. The elegance of a wine tasting room often stands in stark contrast to the machines, hoses, and steel vats where the grapes are processed and the wine is actually made. Being something of an oenophile, I'm always curious about the specific details of the current vintage: where the grapes were sourced; brix content at harvest; length of skin contact; number of punch-downs during primary fermentation; and how long the wine has been aged in either French or American oak barrels. By the time I've asked so many questions, Lisa has usually wandered off to the gift shop. You can enjoy wine without knowing how it's made—but knowing all the work and attention that goes into it makes me appreciate it even more. For other people, knowing so many details about the process seems ridiculous. They know that wine tastes good. In the end, it's probably more important to learn how to enjoy tasting wine than knowing the mechanics of how it was made.

I think there is a similar connection between the kingdom of God and the power-giving sacrifice of Jesus. For many people it has been enough to know that the power to love is now available. Early followers of Jesus, for instance, had a very simple soteriology (doctrine of salvation). They knew the kingdom was promised and there was power available through Jesus. Jesus and his disciples emphasized two basic and related ideas: first, the present reality and availability of the kingdom of God; and second, the sacrifice and victory of Jesus as the power of God. We see this in how Jesus and his disciples talked about his message. After his resurrection Jesus appeared and continued to speak "about the kingdom of God" (Acts 1:3). The disciple Phillip proclaimed "*the good news of* the kingdom of God and *the name of* Jesus *Christ*" (Acts 8:12). And similarly, the Apostle Paul preached "*the kingdom of God* and taught about the Lord *Jesus* Christ" (Acts 28:31). How are these two concepts related? The sacrifice of Jesus is *how* we gain access to God's power. Making a life in the kingdom of love is *what* we need the power for.

Just as I may be fanatical about how wine is made, some people verge on obsession with understanding how the transforming power of God works. We could become so preoccupied with trying to understand and agree on doctrines of salvation that we forget the main point. I sense that an overemphasis on the mechanics of salvation in our time has overshadowed the point of Jesus' sacrifice: that there is power to live generatively, fulfilling the genesis-vision of God. This imbalance may explain why so many people are familiar with the historical elements of Jesus' life, but relatively unfamiliar with his essential message: "The kingdom of God is at hand." We sometimes forget that the goal of understanding is better living—and that the kingdom of God is ultimately something to experience, taste, and enjoy. How much information do we need to know before we can embrace the transforming power of God? Paul of Tarsus said, "For the kingdom of God is not a matter of talk but of power" (I Corinthians 4:20).

HOW WE SAY "YES" OR "NO" TO THE WAY OF THE KINGDOM

The next place Lisa and I visited was a small family winery started by a father and now operated by his son. The son is young for a winemaker, but already has many years of experience. He poured us tastings of each of their six varietal bottlings. I could tell by tasting that this man has high standards, a distinctive style, and a consistent vision for winemaking. The cabernet sauvignon, made from Howell Mountain fruit from the north valley, was exceptional. We bought a bottle to keep until Christmas. It was closing time, but this friendly winemaker invited us downstairs to the cellar where he had a few jobs to do before leaving for the day. We watched as he and his assistant "topped off" the fermentation tanks with argon gas to inhibit oxidization—a conscientious vintner's practice. When I asked the young winemaker about his work, he explained the details and complexities of his enterprise: managing fields and workers, ordering supplies and machinery, payroll and accounting, the marketing and staffing of the tasting room—in addition to the actual craft of winemaking. I've visited other larger commercial wineries where the heirs to the family business simply showed up for board meetings, charity auctions, and photo ops.

This experience reminded me of a story Jesus told about a vintner and his two sons. The father asked both sons to go to work in his vineyard. The first one said, "'I will not'... but later changed his mind and went." The second son said, "'I will, Sir,' but did not go." Then Jesus asked his audience, full of religious people, "Which of the two did what their father wanted?"

"'The first,' they answered."

Then Jesus gave this indicting explanation: "I tell you the truth, the tax collectors and the prostitutes are entering the kingdom of God ahead of you" (Matthew 21:28–31).

It isn't always the usual suspects who have the will to engage the power of the kingdom. My friend Willow is learning to apply this insight to how she sees her mom. When we were talking one day she said, "My mother is the kindest and most compassionate person I have ever known. She really shows Jesus in how she lives and treats people, but isn't religious. When I became a Christian I was told that my mother was going to hell, because she wasn't 'saved.' People encouraged me to distance myself from her and to view her as a bad person. But I was always confused because she lives in a more loving way than most Christians I know." Tears started streaming down Willow's face as she began to cry, "After all these years of seeing my mom as lost, it feels good to think that despite what I once thought, the energy of the kingdom of God may actually be at work in her life." You can say "yes" with your mouth and "no" with your life, or "no" with your mouth but "yes" with your life. This is one of the great mysteries about the kingdom of God.

EYES TO SEE THE KINGDOM OF GOD

At the next winery we were seated beside a reserved and stately looking couple from another part of the country who were on their first trip to Napa Valley. They were engaging and friendly until they found out where we were from. The woman frowned and said, "We drove an extra sixty-five miles just to avoid *that* city on our way up here. How can you stand to live there? It's such a disgusting place."

Her comment reminded me of a recent conversation I had with a religious leader who had moved to San Francisco from a part of the country similar to the couple's. As we talked, it didn't take long before both of us realized that we were looking at God's kingdom from very different perspectives.

"This city is an evil place," he said, waiting for me to nod in approval. Between bites of fish taco I offered a response: "I'm not sure I agree with that assumption. Jesus proclaimed, 'The kingdom of God is among you,' so we can be confident that the Creator is actively working to restore people from every tribe and nation—even in this city."

Setting down his burrito, he responded, "Well, I guess I've never thought about it like that before. But still you'd have to admit that there are very few Christians in this city."

"I used to say something similar, but gradually I began to realize that I was looking through my own cultural blinders. I tried to measure God's kingdom by counting the number of gatherings where there were people who looked like me. I eventually discovered that there are many vibrant communities of faith among Asian, African American, and Latino communities as well as many other ethnic and immigrant groups. In places where it isn't popular to be religious, people of faith really say 'yes' to the kingdom by the fruit of their lives—expressing love in hidden places."

My companion was not yet convinced. "Yes, but we are not supposed to be hidden. Don't you think there comes a time when we have to stand up for what is right and let our voices be heard?"

I got back to one of my favorite themes. "We are letting our voices be heard by how we live our lives. I meet many people who have a hard time believing there is any power to the kingdom of God because of their experiences with people who identify as Christians. If we need to speak louder, it should be through how deeply we love others, inspired by the example of Jesus and empowered by the Spirit."

"Still, don't you think there comes a point when people need to know where we stand on moral issues? If, for example, someone did ask you what you think about all the immorality in this city, what would you say?"

"Have you ever noticed that Jesus rarely answered the questions people asked him? In fact he often responded with another question. Jesus invites each of us into a better way of life under his direction. Most people don't need to be convinced that there is something broken about them. They might not describe their lack of wholeness using the word *sin*, but they sense their woundedness nonetheless. In the Gospels we don't see Jesus spending a lot of time trying to convince people that they are wrong, except for religious leaders. Instead he awakened people's imaginations to a better way of life.''

Taking the last bite of his burrito, he continued to probe. ''Of course you will agree with me that according to the Bible, homosexuality is clearly wrong?''

It is always more convenient to condemn or make light of an issue we are distant from, don't understand, or don't personally wrestle with—and we usually find it easier to judge another person's choices more than our own. Consider how often Jesus resisted the demand for his pronouncements on the ethical debates of his day. Why do we so quickly assume that it is our business to judge another person's behavior? Don't we have enough to do working out our own salvation? If we have a responsibility, it is to help people fall in love with the message and power of Jesus. I am confident that if anyone decides to begin making a life in the Way of Jesus, the Spirit will reveal to them what changes are necessary to move further along the path of life. Jesus is a patient and caring teacher and promised that we can trust him to take us into a better way.

VINES, BRANCHES, AND FRUIT

From the winery we stepped out into the fields of the vineyard to feel the warm breezes of a summer afternoon. The aroma of jasmine, planted along the roads, wafts through the air. The dirt at our feet is arguably the best wine-growing soil in the world—worth more per acre than most people's homes. The surrounding mountain ranges, early morning fog, and daily extremes of heat and cold make this a perfect climate for growing grapes. Some of these trestled plants are more than a hundred years old, and produce excellent ''old vine'' zinfandels, a grape varietal that thrives on rocky soil where it can labor to extract complex and intense fruit flavors.

I take a cluster of unripened grapes in my hand and notice how much smaller these grapes are than the table grapes we eat at home. Jesus used vines and fruit as an allegory for how we access power to live in the genesis-vision of God. "I am the vine," he said. "You are the branches. If a [person] remains in me, and I in [them] [they] will bear much fruit" (John 15:5). He also mentioned that the branches that do not produce fruit are eventually thrown away. "How can they tell which plants in the vineyard are fruitful and which ones to uproot?" I wondered. On that question Jesus said, "Let both grow together until the harvest" (Matthew 13:30).

So much emphasis in our religious culture has been put on determining who is "saved" and who isn't. The reasons why people are concerned about this question aren't always malevolent. Some people just want to see as many people as possible experience new life in the kingdom of God. Jesus made it clear that we can't know whether or not someone else is accessing the power of the kingdom. Yet we show signs of transformation by the fruit of love in our lives: "This is to my Father's glory, that you bear much fruit, showing yourselves to be my disciples" (John 15:8). Perhaps it has never been our responsibility to decide who has or hasn't been reborn to see the kingdom. What matters more is that we seek to be fruitful and engage the power of transformation ourselves.

How do we "remain" connected to the power that allows us to enter the greater wholeness of God? Jesus said that we "remain" connected to this power through surrender and obedience: "If you obey my commands, you will remain in my love, just as I have obeyed my Father's commands and remain in his love" (John 15:10). You abide in the power of Jesus by acknowledging the authority of God over your life and by submitting to God's will. You did something like this as a child when you depended on your parents to give you food and comfort, understanding that they also made the rules. What are God's rules for us as children? Jesus said, "My command is this: Love each other as I have loved you. Greater love has no one than this, that he lay down his life for his friends" (John 15:12–13). Jesus was showing us the way to love and making a way to love by laying down his life for others.

I come to the end of this chapter thinking that we tend to make a very simple message very complicated. Maybe for us it seems complex because we are such enigmatic and conflicted social creatures.

We were made by love. We were made to live into the greater wholeness of love. We need a power beyond ourselves to truly love our maker and one another. We can choose to obey the power of love. And through the "deeper magic," this is now possible.

CONVERSATION

A threat to greater wholeness.   Do you agree with the statement, "In many ways we are at war with ourselves?" Where do you see the power of love transcending the empires of selfishness and greed?

Tasting the wine.   How much do you think a person needs to understand or acknowledge about the work of Jesus before he or she can access the power of the deeper magic? Do you think that a fruitful life of love is empowered more by surrender to the will of God or an understanding of "orthodox" theology? Or both? Explain.

Which son did what his father asked?   Considering the parable of the vintner and the son who said "no" but still went to work, what do you think it means to live "yes" to the kingdom of God? Is entering the kingdom of God as simple as surrendering to the authority and power of love?

Signs of fruitfulness.   We know whether we are connected to the source of love by the fruit of love displayed in our lives. Where do you see signs of love bearing fruit in your love for people?

EXPERIMENTS

Assuming the best.   What if only God knows who is saved or unsaved? How would your approach to people change if you assumed that every person you see wants to pursue the kingdom as much as you do? For one day, try treating everyone you come in contact with as a fellow seeker and see how it affects your attitudes and conversations.

The bread and wine. The Eucharist or "Lord's Supper" is a common rite for people who seek the Way of Jesus. It is the only ritual that Jesus taught his disciples to practice. The earliest disciples of Jesus seemed to treat it with little formality (or institutional governance) as a meditation at the meals they shared together in their homes—a reminder that we rely on power outside ourselves to seek the kingdom of love. Even people who are skeptical about religion take their choice to participate in this rite quite seriously—since it is an essential sign of dependence on the name and power of Jesus. Before a meal with family or friends, use bread and wine (or grape juice) as symbols to give thanks for the sacrifice of Jesus that unleashes the deeper magic.

Read the Gospel of John. John is the most philosophical and mystical of the four Gospel writers who were included in the canon of the New Testament. Writing for a later Greek audience, John talked about the kingdom of God using words like *light, life, love, and spirit.* Chapters 14–17 of John's Gospel in particular offer a poetic exploration of the energy and power of love related to the sacrifice of Jesus.

CHAPTER ELEVEN

COMPASSION: THE PATH OF A HEALER

The Road Ahead
Lonely Highways, Dusty Fields
flatland midwest humidity
My rust-colored AMC Matador barrels down the road toward
    justice/mercy/love
You Leave Home to Jericho you roam
through fallow fields and winter trees stripped bare
skeleton branches reaching for the air
and they are waiting. . . .
Waiting for the sons and daughters to be revealed.
Waiting for the hands that will soothe and heal.
And down the road
I see the Nazarene, embraced as Messiah and Rabbi King
I see our desperation for substance become living abundance:
Loosening the chains of injustice
Breaking the yoke of oppression
sheltering the stranger

feeding the hungry
clothing the naked
comforting the sick
welcoming the weak
and WE will no longer turn away
from our own flesh and blood
WE will be called "repairers of broken walls,"
And "restorers of streets with dwellings."
The road ahead for us
is a road toward justice/mercy/love

by Mark Scandrette

Walking through our neighborhood with a group of friends one day, I met a man who seemed eager to talk. When I drew closer I noticed that his curly gray hair was crawling with lice and larger spidery bugs. Though I struggled to understand his slurred Spanish, we made some kind of connection, and he reached out to me with a full embrace, laying his head on my shoulder. I hesitated for a moment and then wrapped my arms around him for a long hearty bear hug. It took me a moment to recognize Jesus in disguise.

With healing hands, Jesus embraced people rejected or forgotten by society. As a sign of the kingdom of love, Jesus touched those shunned because of infectious diseases and put his hands on the eyes of the blind and on the ears of the deaf to heal them. He welcomed and held little children in his arms, even while his disciples looked on disapprovingly. He also made himself vulnerable to people in the streets, allowing them to touch him—like one woman who had been bleeding for many years who reached for his clothes and was miraculously cured, or another woman who worked as a prostitute who touched his feet, weeping and washing them with her tears. He invited the poor and oppressed into a community of hope.

Through the example of his life, Jesus invites us to follow the path of a healer. How can we love a God we cannot see? By loving the people we can see. We follow the master by entering the struggle of those who are hungry, thirsty, lonely, naked, or in prison. The ancient prophet Isaiah once wrote:

> Is not this the kind of fasting I have chosen:
> to loose the chains of injustice
> and untie the cords of the yoke,
> to set the oppressed free
> and break every yoke?
> Is it not to share your food with the hungry
> and to provide the poor wanderer with shelter—
> when you see the naked, to clothe him,
> and not to turn away from your own flesh and blood?
> Then your light will break forth like the dawn,
> and your healing will quickly appear; . . .
>
> (Isaiah 58:6–8)

The promise of this prophecy is that through seeking to follow the path of a healer, we may ultimately be healed ourselves, as we step further into the power of the kingdom of love.

THE PRACTICE OF COMPASSION

When he saw the crowds, he had compassion on them, because they were harassed and helpless, like sheep without a shepherd.
MATTHEW 9:36

The first way we touch the people we encounter is through our eyes. To begin to flow in the compassion of Jesus means learning to see people the way God sees them, deeply aware of their struggles and suffering and wanting to do something to help. Admittedly we don't naturally see people in the generous way God sees them. We instinctively make certain judgments or harbor prejudices.

In my mind I can still see the face of the dead young man found lying facedown in the yard next door early one Sunday morning. At first the investigators thought he died falling off the roof of our house. A police officer followed me up a rickety ladder onto an adjoining roof to survey the scene. A crowd of neighbors gathered in front of the building, and we invited them in to look through our living room window. Six feet below lay the body of a nineteen-year-old man wearing black Converse All-Stars, sagging khaki pants, and a dark hooded sweatshirt. His head was freshly shaven. "Gangster," I thought disdainfully.

In the months before I had often been awakened by loud music and breaking glass coming from the street, where a group of young men sat on their cars drinking late into the night. Exasperated, I went outside to plead with them to be quiet so my family and I could sleep. Now we watched the medical examiner take photos of the body, documenting mucous spots on the cement with white chalk. When they turned the body over I saw his bloated face and was overwhelmed by the sadness of this tragedy. My neighbor, an older Mexican lady, turned to me and asked, "Why do so many young men in our neighborhood get involved in gang activity?" Though I had probably seen this young man walking down the street a hundred times, it was only now that he was dead that I looked into his face with compassion rather than disdain. I am still learning to see and respond to people with the loving heart of the Creator.

A prayer I have used and taught is, "God help me to think your thoughts and feel your feelings for the people and places that I see." It is a mantra that helps me identify with the heart of God for all people. How we think and talk about one another matters because attitudes determine action. We can choose to speak derisively, telling cruel jokes or stereotyping, or use words that encourage honor, dignity, respect, and hope.

In our family we work together on renewing our attitudes toward people—and it seems to be working. I once overheard a debate among my kids about the issue of homelessness in our city. Our youngest son Isaiah suggested that maybe the mayor could send the homeless to New York. His sister Hailey, aghast, informed Isaiah that "the homeless are people and you can't just move them around like objects." My middle son Noah said, "I'm getting comfortable knowing homeless people—except I don't think we should call them homeless, it doesn't seem respectful, because they have homes—their home is just outside."

As seekers of the kingdom of love, what should our attitude and posture be? Jesus saw himself as one who proclaimed hope—empowered by the Spirit to announce God's favor on all people. When he began his public life he stood up in the synagogue and read the following mandate from the ancient book of Isaiah:

The Spirit of ADONAI ELOHIM is upon me,
because ADONAI has anointed me
to announce good news to the poor.
He has sent me to heal the brokenhearted;
to proclaim freedom for the captives,
To let out into light those bound in the dark;
to proclaim the year of the favor of ADONAI.

(Isaiah 61:1–2, Complete Jewish Bible)

I remember reading these lines as I sat on my front steps watching all the activity on the street and wondering what my attitude should be toward all the people that I see. Just then a car drove by with the stereo thumping, blasting bass that made the windows on my house shake. The two men inside the car wore puffy dark jackets and hooted at the women on the sidewalk. Then it occurred to me: "It is the year of God's favor on men who wear puffy jackets and drive tricked-out cars with stereos blaring." Then two young women walked by holding hands, dressed in masculine clothing. "It is the year of God's favor for these women," I thought. And then I looked down at myself and realized, "It is even the year of God's favor on bratty midwestern kids like me. Now is the time when the Creator longs for all people to experience wholeness and peace."

THE PRACTICE OF SERENDIPITY

Some of the most magical healing moments in the life of Jesus come from times when he was on his way to somewhere else. They often occurred as interruptions to his meals, meetings, or itinerary. In one incident a group of men tore through the roof of the house where he was staying to seek help and healing for their disabled friend. Most of these events could not be anticipated or planned. Jesus followed the path of a healer by embracing serendipity—fortuitous, providential happenings. Jesus was aware that the power of God flowed through his being, drawing people to him unexpectedly.

When our car broke down for the fifth time in three months, I spent an entire day tracking down replacement parts, having the car towed to a repair shop, and negotiating about parts under warranty. "I'm supposed to be spending my time on important matters," I thought, "not dealing with this stupid car." (I have since transitioned to travel almost exclusively by foot, bicycle, or train.) The "car problem" completely wrecked my attitude for the day—and still nothing was resolved. I woke up early the next morning anticipating another frustrating day—except that I chose to trust that the reign of God was somehow at play in my unpleasant circumstance. I approached the day with expectancy.

That afternoon, when Noah and I were walking home from yet another repair shop where we'd had the car towed, we came upon a garage sale. I recognized a woman sitting on the sidewalk—we had met once before. As we talked she began to cry. "My two-month-old baby died last night," she said. Her husband approached and I listened to the story, and asked if I could pray with them. Noah and I and the couple huddled together in a circle, and we all cried and prayed over the loss of the baby. They said, "I think God or an angel sent you to us. We've been wandering aimlessly around town since last night, not knowing what to do." Over the next few days I mobilized a support network, accompanied them to the county coroner's office to view the baby's body, and helped make funeral arrangements.

Serendipity turned a day of disgruntlement about my car to a chance meeting through which I could help a sorrowful family. The example of Jesus teaches us to be a channel of God's love. If you are open to the Spirit, people who need care will be drawn to you in mysterious ways.

THE PRACTICE OF GOOD RELIGION

Religion is often a poisonous word in current vernacular, but perhaps we would change our minds if we recognized that "religion that God our Father accepts as pure and faultless is this: to look after orphans and widows in their distress and to keep oneself from being polluted by the world" (James 1:27). My wife Lisa grew up in a family that welcomed ninety foster children into their home in twenty years. The two of us spent the first five years of our life together making friends with children and families in low-income housing projects—and it is staggering to consider that there are children at risk just like this in virtually every town and city. We are invited to practice "good" religion by caring for the needs of children and older people who are being neglected or forgotten.

And our families are the first place we can start to practice good religion. Even as he was being executed on the cross, Jesus' thoughts turned to the care of his mother, who was likely a widow. Later leaders in the early church wrote letters reminding disciples "that they should learn to put their religion into practice by caring for their own family and so repaying their parents and grandparents, for this is pleasing to God" (I Timothy 5:4). Most of us don't have to look any further than our own families or kinship networks to identify an elderly person who is in need of care or companionship, a child who has lost a parent, or another relative living in suffering, mental illness, or addiction.

THE PRACTICE OF ADVOCACY

Jesus modeled the ancient command and practice of advocacy: "Learn to do right; seek justice, encourage the oppressed, defend the orphan, plead for the widow (Isaiah 1:17). Recognizing that human suffering is related to systems of power and inequity, he advocated on behalf of the weak. He confronted the dominance of civil and religious authorities and their oppressive control over the common people. And he taught his followers to live subversively under foreign occupation—paying taxes and carrying the packs of Roman soldiers, but honoring another kingdom and king. And Jesus warned adults that they would be held responsible if their choices led children into sin. The struggle for justice ultimately led to his persecution and death. Through his example, Jesus invites us to be healers through the practice of advocacy.

Immigrant, refugees, and other poor people struggle to make ends meet and often don't have the language, skills, or confidence to advocate for themselves. The wealthy and educated advocate freely on their own behalves, even hiring lawyers and politicians to preserve their status and safety. I was surprised, for instance, to learn that the affluent neighborhoods in my city have disproportionately more services and police presence than poorer neighborhoods with far greater needs. Our faith community realized that we could lend our voices to speak out on behalf of our neighbors so that their voices will be heard. Some of us attend public meetings, or monitor the streets and call city officials, and we have organized a campaign to encourage neighborhood pride and community involvement.

In our time of increasing mobility and international trade, the call to justice is both local and global. A friend who works with Latin gang members in our city discovered that the young men dealing heroin on our street corners are from a town in Honduras where a U.S. company opened a factory that tainted their water supply and destroyed the local economy. What appeared to be a neighborhood problem was related to international trade, corporate power, and greed. My friend works to help these young men discover a better way of life, but also meets with government officials to address corporate responsibility.

Public policies and our personal actions will determine the kind of world our children and grandchildren inherit. Future generations are now being shaped by our Earth-keeping practices, our economic choices, and our management of debt and trade. As healers we are invited to consider what kind of legacy we are leaving for those who are not yet born.

THE PRACTICE OF ABUNDANCE

When I think of all the suffering in the world, I am easily overwhelmed. We hear statistics about famine, disease, or genocide and are often vexed or paralyzed by the magnitude and complexities of these issues. You may find yourself asking, "Where do I start?" or "What real difference can I make in the global scheme of such needs?"

I'm not sure that Jesus approached these concerns from a perspective of scarcity, like we tend to. My sense is that instead of assessing how bad the problem is, he asked, "What resources do I have to offer?" Jesus gave whatever energy he had toward addressing the needs of others. He leveraged his life to be a healer through the practice of abundance.

In the well-known parable of the sheep and the goats, Jesus suggested that "the righteous" are instinctually motivated to give to others out of their abundance. They asked, "'Lord, when did we see you hungry and feed you, or thirsty and give you something to drink? When did we see you a stranger and invite you in, or needing clothes and clothe you? When did we see you sick or in prison and go to visit you?"' And the king replied, "'Whatever you did for one of the least of these brothers of mine, you did for me'" (Matthew 25:37–40). We practice abundance by asking, "What can I offer to those who are hungry, thirsty, lonely, naked, sick, or in prison?" and "Where are the people and places of greatest need?" And then we offer ourselves generously through time, relationship, skills, money, and our material resources. More than just writing a check, we present our very selves to flow with the abundance of the Creator's energy.

So many of the problems in our world seem to elude our comprehension and our ability to resolve them. The psychological effects of famine, war, or domestic abuse linger long after the hunger is gone or the fighting has ceased. Some situations seem beyond mending—I think of chronic generational poverty and mental disorders as two perplexing examples. Where power and human will are involved there is great resistance to change. Anyone who follows the path of a healer will eventually come to face the limits of human intervention. Dealing with these challenges and ambiguities should not make us throw up our hands in despair or retreat into passive complacency. In Mark, we see the story of the disciples of Jesus coming to him frustrated because they could not cure someone who was demon possessed (in the language of our time this might mean mentally distressed). Jesus replied, "This kind can come out only by prayer and fasting" (Mark 9:29). When we reach the limits of our abilities we can call on a power greater than our own. At times I've laid my hands on a neighbor who is passed out drunk, praying for divine help when treatment programs and other interventions have failed.

Jesus accessed the power of the kingdom to heal people who were sick, disabled, or mentally ill. And he promised his disciples, "Anyone who has faith in me will do what I have been doing. He will do even greater things than these" (John 14:12). Peter the disciple saw a lame man begging near the temple and said, "Silver or gold I do not have, but what I have I give you. In the name of Jesus Christ of Nazareth, walk" (Acts 3:6). The man got up and walked. Is the apparent scarcity of miracles in the First World evidence that we lack faith or compassion? Perhaps Peter didn't have any money because he had already given it all away. If we believe that all problems are essentially related to the spiritual, then we are invited to spend ourselves on behalf of the poor and then beg God for miracles for what we cannot do ourselves.

THE PRACTICE OF PRESENCE

Just as Jesus lived among the poor, the lonely, and the outcast, we are urged to live with equal compassion and humility: "Your attitude should be the same as that of Christ Jesus: Who, being in very nature God, did not consider equality with God something to be grasped, but made himself nothing, taking the very nature of a servant, being made in human likeness" (Philippians 2:5–7). We follow the path of a healer through the practice of being present to each other.

One of the challenges in learning to be healers is that we are often geographically or culturally removed from the places of greatest need. Our contemporary patterns of housing and travel tend to isolate wealth or even just middle-class comfort from poverty. It is easy to ignore the hunger or injustice we can't see. To be present, we have to try intentionally to put ourselves in the path of need, crossing boundaries by changing where we go and who we identify as our neighbors. This could be as simple as walking down a new street or changing where you shop or eat. Or it may require visiting another neighborhood, city, or country, or even relocating to live in a place with more needs or diversity.

If this requirement sounds intimidating, frightening, or inconvenient, that's because following the Way can be all of that and more. Imitating the healing ways of the master requires us to move beyond the boundaries of personal comfort, reorienting and making space to practice being present to one another. One of my most vivid experiences of boundary crossing occurred as we moved to San Francisco's Mission District. Becoming part of our neighborhood was a humbling transition that stretched us to practice being present to others in new ways.

We moved to San Francisco during the technology boom of the late '90s. We had a very difficult time finding an apartment for our family of five. We stayed with friends and slept in the basement of a church building for six months. Eventually we found a small home to purchase, but to occupy it we had to negotiate with tenants who were under rent control. When I first knocked on the door of the lower flat of the old Victorian, holding our youngest child in my arms with the other two children clutching the pockets of my pants, a teenaged girl appeared, barefoot in shorts and a tank top. "Hello, is Miguel home?" I asked.

"I don't know, he might be at work," she said with her arms crossed, twisting bubble gum from her mouth around her fingers.

"Do you know if he got my letter?" I inquired tentatively. She replied, "We read Miguel the letter, but he doesn't want to move out. It's hard to find another place right now."

I pleaded, "Please try to talk to Miguel. We will pay your relocation costs." She smiled at the baby. "I will try, but you know he's kind of crazy sometimes."

A month and a half later I approached the door again with a checkbook. Keys were handed over and polite handshakes were exchanged with Miguel, Salvador, Roberto, and Felicity (the teenaged girl I had spoken to earlier). I stood in the empty apartment calculating the work it would take to make it clean and livable. The children, so glad to be "home" after six months of sleeping on floors in public buildings, took off their shoes and ran up and down the narrow hallway. Moments later Lisa stopped them, when she noticed their white socks were now dark with stains, and said, "You'll have to wear shoes until we have new floors."

We began bagging up the trash that had been left behind. In the makeshift windowless room that Felicity shared with her thirty-year-old boyfriend Roberto, we found a few soiled stuffed animals, candy wrappers, and a note from a clinic explaining postoperative instructions for a first-trimester abortion. A forgotten student ID revealed that Felicity was only fourteen.

The back bedroom, where the children would sleep, was Miguel's room, where he had often sat on a single bed drinking beer and watching Spanish TV. Bonita, the woman upstairs, told us that Miguel got a little crazy when he drank. "One time a young prostitute ran up the steps to my back door screaming—Miguel was chasing after her with a knife, trying to stab her to death. We had to call the police. But other than that, Miguel was a very nice neighbor," she said.

The bathroom was covered in black mildew. The small back-yard, a plot of cement, was filled waist deep with garbage: old auto parts, broken bicycles, bags of beer cans, and rotting food in Styrofoam Chinese takeout cartons. A dead fish floated in a bucket of water. It would take months to discard the trash, tear out the carpets, knock down the shanty room, repair the mildew damage, repaint and carpet to make the apartment and yard safe for children. Our kids quickly got to know Pablo, the little boy who lived upstairs.

"Your people will rebuild the ancient ruins," I mused while bagging up the garbage. ". . . And will raise up the age-old founda-tions," I repeated as I knocked down the shanty room walls with a sledge hammer. "You will be called Repairer of Broken walls, Restorer of Streets with Dwellings" (Isaiah 58:12).

We learned many painful lessons about being present to others when we were confronted by violence, theft, loneliness, hostility, and many sleepless nights. We found out that whole refugee families were living in single bedrooms and that the streets were not safe for children or older people because of drug trafficking. The problems of a neighborhood were now our problems as well. "Surely he took up our infirmities and carried our sorrows," wrote the prophet Isaiah (53:4). Jesus modeled the practice of presence by identifying with the struggles and sufferings of the people of his day. We become healers by also joining in the sufferings of others.

One day an undercover narcotics officer stopped at our door. Flashing his badge, he asked, "Do you realize what was going on in this house before you moved in? The former tenants used this place to traffic guns, drugs, and prostitutes and to harbor fugitives. Your move here really helped clean up this neighborhood." At a Christmas party, our neighbor Grandma Lupe told everyone, "This block used to be really bad, with lots of shootings. Mark and Lisa have brought peace to this corner. Mark even makes the sleeping drunk men leave our front door so we can go outside." Though it would be convenient to conclude from this that we have somehow been a gift to our neighborhood, it would be more accurate to say that our neighborhood has been a gift to us—by teaching us how to expand our capacity for love.

UNTIL OUR LOVE IS MADE COMPLETE

It is clear that Jesus didn't heal every person, and that his mighty acts were signs of a kingdom that is still being revealed. As long as spiritual darkness is at work somewhere in the world, there will be physical, emotional, and spiritual poverty produced by scarcity and greed. So what difference do our efforts make and how do we measure success? Perhaps it would be best to ask, "Am I part of the problem or part of the solution?" and "Are we doing all that we can?" Jesus said that if we abide in his Way, we will bear the fruit of love in our lives. Until the completion of all things, we seek the path of a healer, holding to this promise:

> If you spend yourselves on behalf of the hungry
> and satisfy the needs of the oppressed,
> then your light will rise in the darkness,
> and your night will become like the noonday.
> The LORD will guide you always;
> he will satisfy your needs in a sun-scorched land
> and will strengthen your frame.
> You will be like a well-watered garden,
> like a spring whose waters never fail.
>   (Isaiah 58:9–11)

CONVERSATION

Attitudes.   Are there categories of people you struggle to see with the generosity and understanding of Christ?

Advocacy.   How do you think the call to advocacy is appropriately played out in civic and political arenas? What are the costs of speaking out on behalf of an unpopular or marginalized group?

Relocation.   Is the idea of relocating to live among people in greater need exciting or scary to you? What criteria might a person use to decide where they should live and who their associations should be with?

Making comparisons.   When you hear about what other people are doing to care for the needs of others, do you feel encouraged, guilty, grateful, or conflicted? Why do you think we tend to compare or justify our level of social involvement? How can this be resolved?

Fears.   Many people hesitate to get involved in caring for others because they are afraid or feel they lack experience with certain populations of people. Can you relate to this? What has helped you overcome your fears in the past?

EXPERIMENTS

Empty space.   For two weeks, keep track of how you spend your time. What do you notice? Many of us don't have the space in our lives to stop and attend to the people that God may send to us. You can begin by evaluating your schedule and making adjustments so that you have more margin and open space to practice serendipity.

Travel patterns.   Try changing the normal pattern of where you drive, eat, or shop, looking to connect with a segment of the population that you wouldn't normally associate with.

Being perplexed.   We often avoid getting involved in situations of need because they are often beguilingly complex and not easily resolved. Is the goal always to solve problems? Or might it sometimes be more appropriate to accompany someone through the difficulties of a seemingly unsolvable issue? Choose one local need or issue that you research and take action on to the point that you are entering the chaos and having to call out to God to solve the unsolvable.

Give to the needy.   Most of us spend what we earn on ourselves—and our level of personal spending usually increases when we receive a raise, a bonus, or other unexpected funds. Consider where you are spending your money and how it could be used to bring hope and relief to hurting people. Do a check on your finances. What percentage of income do you normally set aside to support charitable causes? How could you get more creative and involved in where that money goes?

CHAPTER TWELVE

BERYL: A SEMIPRECIOUS JEWEL

It is often in the midst of our wounds and frailty that we find the greatest opportunity to discover the power of love. I've included the story told in this chapter because I think it illustrates the potential we have to give and receive love in a world that is aching for the fulfillment of God's reign. I hope it serves as a reminder that it's never too late to learn how to love and be loved.

I first saw Beryl at the meeting of a small Baptist Church in East Oakland. With long greasy gray hair, she was hunched over a pew, wearing an old polyester dress. When I reached out to shake her hand I could smell the odor of soiled clothes and unwashed skin. "Beryl is the oldest member of our congregation," I was told. "She has seventy years of perfect attendance pins." Next to Beryl stood Roger, her "companion," an elderly man with short hair and thick glasses, who wore an ill-fitting plaid polyester suit with white socks.

Just after Christmas Beryl fell and couldn't come to church anymore. One day I went to visit her at her home in a nice neighborhood. I first noticed the piles of debris and swarms of flies buzzing around the front porch. When I knocked, Roger came to the door. The hallway and rooms were piled waist deep with boxes of old books, broken tools, and bags of rotting food.

He led me down a narrow path back to a dark room where Beryl lay. She greeted me with a smile, as I reminded her of where we had met. I asked her how she was feeling. "Oh I'm fine," she said, "I just haven't been well enough to leave this room for the past two months. I'm good for nothing." Roger shuffled around and cleared the way for me to sit in a chair next to her bed. As we talked I looked around the room. Prescription bottles and dirty dishes covered every flat surface. Piles of filthy clothes and bags of garbage filled the spaces not taken up by the bed, where Beryl lay propped up eating fried chicken, surrounded by stacks of newspapers and old mail. The sheets were worn and soiled, and when I looked down, I noticed dried feces on the floor. The stench in the room made it difficult to breathe.

"Beryl, have you been to the doctor since you fell?" I inquired.

"I don't think the doctor could do anything for me. I'm too old," Beryl said with resignation.

"Do you feel any pain?"

"No. I'm just tired and depressed."

"Are you able to get up to bathe or use the bathroom?"

"Roger helps me with those things—do you know what my name means?" Beryl asked abruptly. "I'm a semiprecious stone—one of the nine jewels from the streets of gold in the book of Revelation." Looking into Beryl's grey-blue eyes, past the wrinkles and greasy hair, I think I can see the little girl she once was.

I asked her more questions about her life story, like where she grew up and what she had done through her many days. She had worked as a municipal court clerk for thirty-six years. She never married. This was the house where she had lived with her parents and where she continued to live after they died in the 1950s. The church was really her only family, and people in the church community had cared for her throughout her life by making sure that she went to the doctor or by fixings things in her house. Within her limitations as a person Beryl had found a place to serve others. For ten years she was the church bookkeeper and also helped in the Sunday School. She had Roger show me the old red dress with seventy perfect attendance pins strung together down the front. Beryl had written thousands of poems, mostly based on the weekly sermons she heard. I read a couple of the poems that Roger handed me from a pile by the bed. On the wall behind my head was a Raggedy Ann doll like the ones Beryl had made for the children of missionaries. "My Raggedy Ann dolls are in twenty-three countries," she said, proudly.

The whole time we talked, a dog barked and scratched at the door. Roger occasionally yelled at the animal, and when he finally got up to put the dog outside I asked, "How long has Roger lived here?"

"For five years."

"How is it that he came to live with you?"

Beryl explained that Roger went to her church. He had lost his apartment and was living out of a truck in the church parking lot. She invited him to come and live with her to help with cooking and cleaning.

"So Roger does the cleaning?" I asked suspiciously.

"Yes. And he runs errands for me and drives me to the doctor and to church." I gathered that throughout her life Beryl had offered hospitality to many people in need. There was the family Beryl met while inviting children from the projects to Sunday School who stayed with her for fifteen years. Beryl had many stories about the people who she had helped out, though some of them, it seemed, had taken advantage of her.

Since all the other rooms in the house were filled with stuff, I wondered where Roger stayed at night. Beryl told me that Roger slept in the bed beside her. "Is it a romantic relationship?" I inquired.

"No. Roger asked me to marry him, but I'm too old. He's seventy-five and I'll be ninety-three next week. He's a good companion. I don't know where I'd be without him."

"Do you feel safe sharing a bed with him?"

"His parts don't work anymore. He just lays there."

When Roger returned he spoke gruffly to her, "Now eat your food, Beryl, it's getting cold."

I asked if I could pray with them, and took Beryl's hand. Later Roger showed me out. At the front steps I turned and said, "I think Beryl needs our help. She needs to go to the doctor." With some irritation Roger replied, "Well, if she don't want to go, we can't make her."

"I also think it would help Beryl if we could make the house cleaner," I offered.

"I do my best," Roger said defensively. I could see that despite his limitations, Roger truly cared about Beryl and really did his best to love her.

In the afternoon on Beryl's ninety-third birthday, I arrived at the house with a bakery cake and candles, and Roger and I sang her Happy Birthday. Roger found a couple of dirty plates and I cut the cake with a butter knife, and we ate it together with our fingers, while the television blared in the background. "You shouldn't have brought me a cake," Beryl said. "I'm nobody special. I'm worthless."

"Beryl," I answered. "It makes me sad to hear you say that. I wanted to celebrate your birthday with you because you are valuable to God and to all the people who love you. Do you know the poem from the Bible that says, 'I praise you because I am fearfully and wonderfully made'? Beryl, *you* are fearfully and wonderfully made." Between bites of cake Beryl responded, "Well, I don't feel like it. I feel worthless." With great concern I asked, "How is it that you came to feel this way? Did something happen in your life that made you feel worthless?"

Beryl then told me a story in a rather matter-of-fact way: "When I was ten we lived out in the country. I was friends with the children down the road and we used to play together in their chicken coop. One day their dad had me pull down my pants and sit on his penis. He would make me do that every time I went over there."

"I'm so sorry for what happened to you. I imagine it made you feel ashamed and confused. Did you tell your parents?"

"I've never told anybody." Beryl replied. "But I still think about it all the time." Beryl looked as sad as a little girl and had tears in her eyes. I asked her how she thought that experience affected her throughout her life.

"Well, I never married because of it, and it really made me feel like I was good for nothing. I've never been good at caring much about myself."

"I can see how that experience may have made it more difficult to have healthy boundaries with people," I interjected. But Beryl still had more to say. "I guess I've let other people take advantage of me. There was a delivery man who use to rape me every week when he came to pick up my laundry."

"How long ago was this?" I asked.

"Just a few years ago. I was already an old woman."

"Did you tell anyone from the church?"

"No, I figured it was what I deserved."

I groped for something to say that matched the depth of Beryl's pain. "Hearing about that makes me feel really sad. I want you to know that you are loved and valued. I want you to embrace the fact that you really are a precious jewel in the sight of God."

Embarrassed, Beryl smiled. "I don't feel like a jewel."

I answered, "Well, according to the scriptures, you are a princess in the kingdom of God. One of the reasons that Jesus went to the cross was to bring healing to the whole person—to remind us that we are truly loved. It is never too late to regain your sense of dignity and self-respect."

When I went home that day I told Kaitlyn about Beryl. Kaitlyn came to live with us during her recovery from six years of traumatic childhood sexual abuse. Perpetually expressive and always smiling, laughing, or crying, Kaitlyn wears her heart on her sleeve. Even as a teenager she showed tremendous compassion toward people in their suffering—in her hometown and around the world. But finding a way through the anger and confusion of abuse was a long journey. "There is someone I would like you to meet who was once a young woman like you," I told her. "I think you could help Beryl—and through caring for her you might discover greater wholeness within yourself."

The following Sunday Kaitlyn came with our family to visit Beryl. We brought posters we had made that affirmed Beryl as a person of worth and beauty. I read the affirmations to her as we hung the posters with tape around her room. "Beryl, all the statements on these posters are true about you. You are a princess in the kingdom of God. We want you to remember how valuable and precious you are. But as I look around at your house, I'm thinking the conditions here don't seem very princess-like. Do you think so?" Beryl replied, "Well, I guess not. Roger tries his best to take care of me, but he's also getting old." Kaitlyn sat down next to Beryl and took her hand while I continued, "Sometimes we need the help of others to affirm our royalty. With your permission, we could get some help to bathe you, clean your clothes and sheets, help you to the doctor, and make your house more like a place fit for a princess. Kaitlyn is trained to help people with their health needs and could come visit you regularly. Would you mind if we helped you live more like the princess that you are?''

''I would like that,'' Beryl said, grinning.

''Having a clean and neat place to be might also help you to feel better. I can organize a group to come haul away the things that are making your house sick. Big changes will need to be made. We will have to decide what to keep and what to throw away. I know I'm young enough to be your grandson, but to help make these changes, I may need to act like a papa. Are you okay with me acting as your papa for a little while?''

''Yes,'' Beryl said with a smile. ''I always thought I could take care of myself, but now I think I need some help.''

Kaitlyn assisted Beryl to the bathroom, gently bathed her, and put clean sheets on the bed. In the other room I talked with Roger about the implications of these changes. ''Roger, it's good that you have cared for Beryl. Right now she needs more help than you can give her alone. Let's care for Beryl together by making the house clean and neat.''

The next week fifteen volunteers arrived, and we spent three days sorting, shoveling, and hauling debris. We discovered several rooms piled to the ceiling with old clothes, newspapers, and broken tools. The kitchen and dining room were piled with hundreds of grocery bags filled with spoiled food, mixed with dung from decaying rats. Roger has a tendency to hoard, forgetting what he already has, and constantly going out to find more: machetes, old books, broken vacuums and television sets, suitcases, clothes, and new power tools. It was difficult to sort the good and usable from the debris. As we loaded the trailer, Roger followed behind, salvaging paper clips and rusty pieces of pipe. He put as many ''valuables'' as he could in the four junked cars he kept parked on the street. In the morning we would return to find that he had hauled many things back into the house. While trying to help Roger manage his stuff, I had to face some things about myself. I could see similarities between Roger's behavior and my own—the urge to pick things up off the street, to hold on to things that

I don't need, to live with a sense of scarcity and greed—but also the good desire to see things that were once abandoned get fixed and made useful again. Roger could see the value in broken things, and maybe that was what drew Beryl and Roger together.

By the end of the week, the house was in order, Beryl had been to the doctor, and Kaitlyn was coming to help every other day. We began to sort through Beryl's finances and established some healthier relational boundaries with Roger. Kaitlyn gently cared for Beryl, making sure that she was clean, comfortable, and eating healthy food. Over the months they become good friends, laughing and crying together over many long talks. By reaching out to Beryl, a grown-up hurt little girl, Kaitlyn was learning to face the wounded child within herself. Slowly, through better nutrition and exercise, with Kaitlyn's help Beryl gained the strength to return to church—and her church family celebrated her recovery with open arms.

Sometime later, while my plane taxied the runway in Kansas City, I received a call: "Mark, I think Beryl is dying!" Kaitlyn screamed. "Call 911," I said. On a layover in Chicago I got another call saying that Beryl was dead. She had died peacefully in Kaitlyn's arms. I began to make funeral arrangements and fielded questions from paramedics about what to do with her body. At Beryl's funeral, old and new friends alike shared about what Beryl had meant to them. She was someone who needed love but also had a lot of love to give. Kaitlyn continues to wear a watch Beryl gave her—as a reminder of their connection during the last days of Beryl's life and the healing they found together. We were all enriched by helping Beryl spend her last days in dignity, as the precious jewel that she is.

CONVERSATION

Secret wounds. The wounds of Beryl's childhood seemed to affect her throughout the rest of her life. Do you think Beryl could have experienced greater wholeness and integration if her secret wounds had been addressed earlier? How can we make more space in our communities of faith to help one another discover support and healing from such wounds?

A wounded healer.   Despite the hurt and loneliness Beryl experienced in life, she found ways to bring love to others. Beryl's story illustrates the seeming contradiction between being wounded and being a healer. How can we acknowledge and deal with our wounds while also affirming and encouraging one another to care for the needs of others?

Messes and bad smells.   How do you tend to react to clutter or strong body odor? These are often signals that a person needs more love and support. What barriers or fears might you need to overcome in order to welcome more messy people into your life?

EXPERIMENTS

Worthless or priceless?   Sometimes we need to have our sense of worth affirmed by others. A warm smile or a kind word can do a lot to help someone remember that they are valuable and important. Go out of your way to encourage someone by affirming when you see the generative activity of God in their life. Go out of your way to greet people you see in stores or walk by on the street.

Helped by helping.   Think of a way you feel wounded or broken. Find a concrete way to help someone you know who is struggling with the same or similar issues.

Care for the elderly.   People in advanced stages of aging are often isolated and overlooked in our society. Visit an older person you know, or look into volunteering at a local assisted living facility, or provide respite for someone you know who is the primary caregiver for an aging relative.

PART FOUR

IMAGINING AND INHABITING THE WAY OF LOVE

FREEDOM TO RUN
AND PLAY

Repent and believe the good news.
MARK 1:15D

Generally I'm not an airplane conversationalist. But recently on a connecting flight from Salt Lake City, I sat down next to a sales executive who was eager to talk. As the plane taxied for takeoff he introduced himself. A newcomer to the Bay Area, he quizzed me about the real estate market and good neighborhoods. Gradually, our discussion turned to more personal matters, and he leaned closer and whispered, "One thing I've learned in the short time I've been here is that there are a lot of attractive women in the Bay Area—exotic and beautiful girls from all races in different shapes and sizes! Eye candy everywhere—do you know what I mean?" Stammering, I replied, "Well, the Bay Area is definitely diverse." Hoping to change the subject I asked, "Do you have a family?"

"I have a wife and two daughters living in Dallas." He showed me a picture of the two girls, ages six and nine.

"They're beautiful children," I commented. "Will they eventually move out here with you?"

With a sigh, he paused and then replied, "Well, that's what I'm not sure about. It looks like I might be heading toward the big D. My wife and I are probably getting a divorce."

I was surprised that he would reveal such personal information, and I offered sympathy, adding, "I imagine the divorce will be difficult for your daughters as well. Are they aware of what is happening between you and your wife?"

"We haven't told them yet," he said, taking a gulp of water. "This the first Christmas since we've separated. I'm actually on my way back from taking them to see their grandparents in the Midwest."

"Do you mind if I ask what happened between you and your wife?" I ventured. "You don't have to tell me if it seems too personal."

Fumbling with a package of roasted peanuts, he slowly responded. "Well, I messed up and got involved with another woman—but I really feel like she drove me to it. Since our daughters were born she hasn't really done anything to improve herself. I've been on her to finish school and get a job. When she found out about the other woman she got angry and started acting out, neglecting her responsibilities in our family. But the real problem between us is that she doesn't share my spiritual beliefs. My spiritual beliefs are very important to me."

Fascinated, I asked, "What are your spiritual beliefs?"

He seemed to sense an opportunity to testify, and spoke with renewed confidence, "You see, I'm a Christian. God is the center of my life. I've always gone to church. In fact when I moved out here the first thing I did was go looking for a good church. I've met someone and we've been going to church together every Sunday for the past two months. My faith is so important to me—I want to share it with the woman in my life. But my wife—that's a different story—she and I didn't have that spiritual center—and she wouldn't attend church with me. I guess I made a mistake by getting involved with her in the first place."

"I can see how that would be difficult," I offered. "How long were the two of you married?" After counting with his fingers he answered, "Almost six years."

Thinking of the ages of the girls, I asked, "Did you have both of your daughters while you were together?"

"Yeah well, I'm a little embarrassed to say it, but I got her pregnant when she was nineteen. We lived together after our oldest was born and eventually got married when we found out that our second daughter was on the way."

When the flight attendant walked by he asked for two extra bottles of water. "I am so thirsty," he said. "I'm just coming off a three-day bender. You know how it is. I feel so hung over and dehydrated." He quickly opened a bottle of water, and kept talking. "I left the girls with my parents and spent the weekend in a hotel with my old college buddies—going out to clubs, partying, and meeting the ladies." Between sips of water he makes a point: "This is a perfect example of why it isn't working out with my wife. She's always complaining about how she doesn't get to do what she wants. I don't understand that. If I want to go out and have a good time, I make it happen. I'm not waiting to make something of my life. Do you know what I'm saying?"

"This is just a guess, but maybe she felt obligated to stay home to care for your daughters," I ventured.

"Well, I suppose," he replied.

"I know that going through separation and divorce can be a painful and lonely experience. I'm wondering if you have a support system—family and friends—to help you through this. You said that your spiritual beliefs are very important to you. Do you have a spiritual mentor, pastor, or a group of friends you respect who are helping you process your decisions?"

"Um, well, not exactly," he answered slowly.

I tried to explain. "I mention this because I know that having a safe place to go for wisdom, accountability, and support could be really helpful for you right now."

Suddenly he changed the subject. "I don't think I asked you this earlier—what is it that you do for a living?"

"I am the director of a nonprofit organization in San Francisco," I replied. "I also speak and write about Christian spirituality and have worked as a pastor in several churches."

Abruptly he turned away, plugging headphones into his ears, and we spent the rest of the flight in uncomfortable silence. I suspect that when he found out we shared similar beliefs, he regretted being so transparent. Our conversation unwittingly revealed the inconsistency between what he said he believes and how he actually lives.

LIVING INTO BELIEF

We all struggle to live into what we say we believe. Perhaps this is why so many of us doubt the relevancy and potency of religious faith—we can think of so many poseurs, fakers, and impersonators. Many of us shy away from claiming to believe anything because we fear becoming hypocrites or impostors. With a cynical shrug we wonder, "Is it all just words and mumbo jumbo—or can what you say you believe really make a difference in how you live your life?"

Religious belief, particularly in cultures influenced by ancient Hellenistic and Greek philosophies, tends to be defined by intellectual assent to a set of theological propositions. We often speak of beliefs in terms of our rational agreement with certain facts or truth statements (such as the authority of scripture, human sinfulness, the deity of Christ, or a theory of atonement). Often the mind agrees with these statements of belief without the cooperation of the will or body. Is this why so many of us can maintain strong "beliefs" that appear to have little or no bearing on how we actually live our lives? Our culture allows us to claim belief without validating faith by actions. Our use of the phrase "I believe" could more accurately be substituted with "I agree" or "That makes sense to me" rather than "I act on this information with fidelity and trust."

The statement, "Repent and believe the good news," in the language and context in which Jesus spoke, was a call to action intended to provoke a visceral and bodily response. When John the Baptist announced the message of the kingdom, people asked, "What should we do?" and John answered, "The [person] with two [coats] should share with him who has none, and the one who has food should do the same" (Luke 3:10–11). When John noticed religious people coming to be baptized, given their tendency to reduce spiritual realities to rituals and endless theological debates, he cried, "You brood of vipers. . . . Produce fruit in keeping with repentance" (Matthew 3:8). In other words, show your belief in the present reality of God's kingdom by learning to walk in the way of love.

Like a lot of people, my friend Jill was taught that having faith in God's grace implies that we don't need to do anything to change ourselves. She waited passively for transformation to come to her life, fearful that making any effort would put her in danger of trying to earn her salvation. And yet she was deeply frustrated by the lack of progress in her issues and character. A renewed emphasis on *Sola Fide* (faith alone) during the Protestant Reformation popularly evolved into the assumption that belief in God's grace is opposed to deeds or effort. In reaction to contemporary assumptions, shaped by the churches' abuse of indulgences and the pervasive notion that salvation can be earned through "works" alone, the reformers proposed that salvation is accessed by grace alone through faith in the sacrifice of Jesus. Gradually, and I believe unintentionally, their emphasis on grace overwhelmed the necessary component of an active response, to the extent that in many traditions any effort or "good deed" is construed as an erroneous attempt to earn merit with God.

Making faith and deeds mutually exclusive has not been helpful. Belief that is functional and transformational recognizes that grace—God's effort on our behalf—is not opposed to action or effort. James the brother of Jesus wrote, "Faith by itself, if it is not accompanied by action, is dead.... Someone will say, 'You have faith; I have deeds. Show me your faith without deeds, and I will show you my faith by what I do'" (James 2:17–18). Similarly, Paul of Tarsus once wrote, "Continue to *work out your salvation* with fear and trembling, for it is God who works in you to will and to act according to his good purpose" (Philippians 2:12–13). We express faith in God by learning to cooperate with the energy and agenda of God's reign. Perhaps a story will help illustrate this.

FREEDOM TO RUN AND PLAY

When my kids were small we moved to a neighborhood that was not a safe place for children to play. The sidewalks were covered with trash, broken glass, dirty needles, and human waste, and our local playground was run down and crowded with people taking drugs. I decided that once a week I would take my kids out to the beach where they could feel free to run and play. On our first excursion I held their tiny hands as we crossed the street, buckled them into their car seats, and drove out to a gorgeous beach along the Pacific Coast. When we arrived my children stood in the sand clinging to my legs and clutching my hands. "Why are they just standing here?" I wondered. "Why aren't they running and playing in this beautiful place?" Suddenly I realized why they were afraid. In the city I had taught them to stay close and hold my hand. They were not accustomed to the safety and wide open freedom of the coast. I gently detached myself from their grasps and ran down the beach doing summersaults. "Come on, kids, run and play!" I shouted. Their looks of panic quickly turned to smiles as they followed along, rollicking on the sand and splashing in the waves. It was a great day. I even brought snacks and sand toys.

When I think about this story and start to unpack it, I see some parallels to the theological ideas of earning and effort. Who held the children's hands on the way to the car? Who drove the car? Who paid for the fuel? Who showed them how to run and play? Who brought snacks and sand toys? Did my children have to earn this trip to the beach? No, I did everything necessary for them to rollick, splash, and play. But as their father, I expected them to take full advantage of the opportunity I provided for them. For those who can believe, Jesus has done everything necessary to bring us into the new way of genesis-vision. His sacrifice, death, and resurrection unleashed the power and freedom to live in the way of love. The grace of God propels us into new actions, thoughts, choices, and habits. We are invited and expected to run and play in the freedom and beauty of the kingdom of God.

How do we change? And what steps are necessary to experience freedom and transformation? In the chapters included in Part Four, I explore how we can learn to cooperate with the power of the Spirit that is available to us by being tuned in to hear the voice of God, cultivating a new imagination for life, and inhabiting belief through action. In these chapters I am suggesting that transformation happens through:

• Time, space, and intentionality
• New vision and understanding

- Rigorous self-examination
- New experiences and experiments
- Intentional group encounters
- New decisions, behaviors, and patterns
- Guidance and mentoring
- Pain and suffering
- Surrender to the work of the Spirit

Discovering how to run and play in the ways of the kingdom is the essence of making a life in the Way of Jesus.

CONVERSATION

Dealing with incongruity.   Stories about public faith figures who live incongruent lives are perpetually circulating in the media. How have you learned to process or explain these inconsistencies? Do you think such hypocrisy is avoidable or inevitable?

Learning to run and play.   How would you explain the connection between God's mercy and our efforts to be obedient? Where have you seen transformation in your own life or in the lives of the people you know?

Examining our own incongruities.   Where do you struggle to live into what you say you believe? Is it easy or difficult for you to own your own shadow tendencies? Do you think it is healthier for us to keep our personal struggles private or public?

Realism without legalism.   Do you think there is a way for us to help one another seek the standard of love without gossiping or being judgmental? How could this be done? (See Matthew 18:15–19.)

EXPERIMENTS

Spread good gossip.   Bad news often spreads faster than good news. Make an effort to spread a rumor about the good deeds, beauty, and transformation you see in the lives of people you know.

Allow others to speak into your life.   We are often blind to or embarrassed by areas of inconsistency in our lives. (Sometimes it is the elephant in the room that we choose to ignore.) Without being overly self-deprecating, try asking those around you to speak into your character formation. (For example: Do you think I am acting selfishly? What should I do about it? Or, Where do you see a need for growth in my life?) Most people will be caring, supportive, and honest. Remind yourself that it is okay to have areas of growth in your life, since we are all in the process of being transformed.

Make connections between your beliefs and practices.   In a journal, write down five to ten statements that summarize your core spiritual beliefs. Under each statement write, "And because of this belief I practice (fill in the blank)."

CHAPTER THIRTEEN

CONTEMPLATION: THE PATH OF A MYSTIC

Music, like love, makes the world go 'round. You can hardly go anywhere without hearing a song. At dawn I am often awakened by the ballad of a wandering musician crooning soulfully in Spanish while he plucks on a pawnshop guitar. The pulse of hip-hop fills urban streets and rural highways with a thunder of syncopated words and bass beats. In west coast cities, Mariachi bands wearing cowboy hats and carrying accordions play for tips in restaurants and along the boulevard. In Chinatown an old man sits strumming Elvis songs on a two-string Erhu for the tourists passing by. You can hear country songs and cool jazz echoing through subway tunnels or under bridges in most large cities. Sometimes a song can change the world. Ecstatic praise emanates from a thousand tiny Pentecostal storefront churches every night at dusk. "Redemption song" blares from college dorm rooms, at civic rallies, and inside psychedelic head shops. In the Haight-Ashbury I walk by a mural of the late Bob Marley with words he borrowed from Jesus and King Solomon scrawled in graffiti: "Don't gain the world and lose your soul, wisdom is better than silver or gold." Closer to home I hear my sons practicing their cello and violin in the living room and listen to my daughter's sweet phrasing of Celtic ballads. And as I write in my bedroom, I hear Dan, a musician who lives in the flat below, composing and recording his own film scores and melodies. The music we hear on the stereo, on the street, or in our heads create the soundtracks for our lives. With a tearful gulp of sentimental memory I recall the song my mother sang to me every night before bed when I was a child. In her clear and warm Patsy Cline voice I can still hear her singing:

> I come to the garden alone
> while the dew is still on the roses
> And the voice I hear, falling on my ear,
> The Son of God discloses.
> And He walks with me, and He talks with me,
> And He tells me I am His own,
> and the joy we share as we tarry there,
> None other has ever known.
>
> C. Austin Miles, 1912

Music comforts, inspires, animates, and empowers. A song can bring voice to the cry of revolution. A song can awaken imagination or resonate with our deepest emotions and convictions. Poets and prophets speak of God's power and presence like a song. "The LORD is my strength and *my song*; [God] has become my salvation" sang the ancient seer of Israel (Isaiah 12:2). The kingdom of God is a song that thunders throughout the universe and beats quietly within our hearts. The prophet Isaiah announced that as the nation learned to cry out to their Maker, they would begin to hear the voice of God all around them: "Whether you turn to the right or to the left, your ears will hear a voice behind you, saying, 'This is the way; walk in it'" (Isaiah 30:21). The voice of God is eager to teach us how to walk in the way of genesis-vision.

GETTING "TUNED IN" TO THE SONG OF GOD

If the voice of God is a song, how can we make the kingdom and power of love the soundtrack for our lives? Back in the days of the transistor radio, I remember twisting the dial to get "tuned in" to invisible frequencies. Some people still fiddle with the rabbit ears of an antenna to adjust the reception on their TVs. My friend Nate has a knack for tapping into wireless Internet signals using his laptop. On a recent trip through L.A. we found ourselves lost on the corner of Wilshire and Grant. He found a signal that enabled him to pull up a computer map that showed us which way to walk. You tune into the invisible song of God's kingdom by adjusting the dial of your will and adopting the posture of a receiver. This is the path of a mystic—learning to hear the song of the soul, to perceive beyond the visible, to listen to the inaudible aria of divine presence.

A mystic is simply a person who believes in the existence of realities that are beyond intellectual apprehension but are accessible by subjective experience. The chronicles of ancient Israel offer historical precedents for mystical phenomena, including divine appearances, audible voices, revelations, dreams, visions, and prophecies. Figures such as Enoch and Noah were described as people who "walked with God" (Genesis 5:4; 6:9). Various liturgical poems and songs celebrated conscious awareness of the divine: "Blessed are those who have learned to acclaim you, who walk in the light of your presence, O LORD (Psalm 89:15).

Jesus was a mystic in the sense that he lived in conscious awareness of the transcendent reality of God. Everything we admire about the life of Jesus—his compassion, wise teaching, mighty acts, and sacrifice—were funded by the private disciplines of his inner life—how he learned to be tuned into the presence and power of God's song. He demonstrated that the transforming power of God's kingdom is accessed through receptivity, mindful surrender, study, simplicity, silence, and solitude. Through the example of his life, we are invited to follow the path of a mystic.

AMBIVALENCE ABOUT MYSTICISM

You've probably seen someone dancing, singing, or talking to themselves and wondered if they were crazy—only later to discover that they were listening to music or talking on their cell phone. We live in a time of great attraction and suspicion about the mystical or unseen dimensions of reality. The prevailing influence of scientific rationality has led to great skepticism about supernatural experiences, and simultaneously created an intense hunger for divine encounters and guidance. We tend to approach the unseen world with great caution and ambivalence, as something powerful yet dangerous. Weary of the overuse of phrases such as "God told me" or "I had a vision," we prefer to stick with the unambiguous facts. We're well acquainted with caricatures of the overly "spiritual" person, obsessed with their personal psychology, esoteric knowledge, or narcissistic navel gazing. So we are cautious about delving too deeply into the "inner life" or "inner voice." And yet, the profound challenges we face in society, the demands on our time, resources, and relationships, and the prevalence of stress, anxiety, and depression suggest the need for practices that give us access to wisdom, guidance, and power beyond ourselves. You balance the rationality of the mind and the activity of the body by cultivating the mystic within.

RECEPTIVITY AND MINDFUL SURRENDER

My friend Burke couldn't sleep because of the woman he had had dinner with the evening before. "I just lay in bed all night thinking about our conversation," he told me, "her small gestures, and how beautiful she looked sitting across the table from me in the candlelight." I remembered being similarly smitten when I first met Lisa, my wife. For years I was more conscious of her, living in another city, than the people I saw every day. Those we cannot see may be our most constant companions. We've all had experiences when we are acutely aware of someone who is not physically present to us. A mother thinks about her child away at school. A son thinks of his mother lying in a hospital bed. A refugee remembers the family she may never see again. And we pray to a God that we cannot see with our eyes.

Paul of Tarsus taught his disciples to "pray continually" (I Thessalonians 5:17). My friend Tom likes to tell a story about a day when he spent four hours "practicing" the presence of God. "It was the most amazing four hours of my life!" he later said. "I eventually stopped because I became so ecstatic with peace and joy that I feared I was going insane." We were made to live conscious of a God we cannot see, finding a connection to the eternal within and beyond ourselves.

It is in our nature to be *tuned in* and surrendered to something or someone—an image or ideal, a government or corporation, or a charismatic personality. We can even make ourselves objects of idolatry. As a mystic, Jesus lived with receptivity and mindful surrender to God. In the accounts of his life, he referred to the Maker as the central focus of his will and actions. By adolescence he identified God as his true father—as when he said to his parents, "Why were you searching for me? Didn't you know I had to be in my Father's house?" (Luke 2:49). Later, at his baptism, a mysterious voice spoke from the sky, "You are my Son, whom I love; with you I am well pleased" (Mark 1:11). Jesus tuned his will toward hearing and obeying the voice of God. He once answered his critics by saying, "I do nothing on my own but speak just what the Father has taught me" (John 5:19). On the eve of his crucifixion, Jesus epitomized his complete trust and attention to God when he prayed, "Father, if you are willing, take this cup from me; yet not my will, but yours be done" (Luke 22:42).

People seeking mindful surrender to God often adopt habits that serve as cues or reminders to pray, according to the rhythms of the day. The early disciples seemed to follow a pattern of "divine hours," praying at certain times: morning, noon, afternoon, and evening. A friend of mine suffering from a chronic illness kneels by his bed each morning to echo the words of Jesus: "Father, not my will but yours be done." Prayer is a vital way we learn to be receptive to the song of the kingdom of love.

A RELIABLE GUIDE FOR "TUNING IN"

For Jesus, the sacred texts of the ancient Jewish tradition served as a basis of knowledge and inspiration for his sojourn. At the age of twelve he was found in the temple "sitting among the teachers, listening to them and asking them questions" (Luke 2:46). Jesus was raised in a culture and tradition that was conscious of God's progressive revelation through events in human history. We know that he was familiar with the Jewish sacred writings because he utilized them in his teaching: "Beginning with Moses and all the Prophets, [Jesus] explained to them what was said in all the Scriptures" (Luke 24:27).

What separates a mystic from someone who is merely eccentric or out of touch with reality? The answer is that they ask how God has already spoken into history. Jesus located his personal revelation of God within the reliable pattern of the Jewish scriptures. He recognized a continuity between his life and message and the witness of ancient writers. In one instance he answered his critics by using a quote from a psalm, asking, "Have you never read in the scriptures?" (Matthew 21:42). In another incident he retorted, "You are in error because you do not know the scriptures or the power of God" (Matthew 22:29). A mystic processes their experience in light of previous revelations and is committed to knowing the history of those who came before them who have sought to live *tuned in* to the song of God.

We are helped by knowing the ancient sacred writings. This may sound like a trite suggestion to those familiar with reading the Bible like a textbook full of facts. What if we are invited to read the Bible as a written record of those who have sought to "walk with God"—that we may be inspired and guided in our own efforts to live in mindful surrender to the work of the Spirit? We can read the scriptures as a living story that we enter into through the actions of our own lives.

Many people find it challenging to read the Bible with any intensity or regularity. I'm struck by how easily I can read a magazine or novel for an hour, but reading the Bible for fifteen minutes can seem like forever. Yet if we are serious about being *tuned in* to the song of God's kingdom, then we need to discipline ourselves to pay attention to the scriptures with the same dedication that we would bring to any other pursuit. Like playing scales is to the musician or conditioning the voice is to the opera singer, studying scripture is an essential practice for a mystic. Many people find it helpful to read the scriptures out loud as families or households—discussing how it relates to their own journeys of faith.

In ancient times the scriptures were predominantly used as an oral instrument for daily meditation. Joshua, the leader of the Israelite exodus, was told, "Do not let this Book of the Law depart from your mouth; meditate on it day and night, so that you may be careful to do everything written in it. Then you will be prosperous and successful" (Joshua 1:8). Perhaps even more than reading, we are helped by using the scriptures as a tool for contemplation. From the time when I was a small child I watched my father memorize and meditate on scripture, and he taught me to slowly repeat phrases written on small cards until they became part of me. I learned to ruminate on texts that spoke to my particular struggles and longings. In the famous song about word as light, David exclaimed, "I meditate on your precepts and consider your ways" (Psalm 119:15). Meditation on scripture, especially the psalms, is a tool for training the mind to be tuned in to the song of God.

SILENCE AND SOLITUDE

A few years ago I discovered that I was conceived in Pamplona, Spain, where my parents were visiting friends a month before the Festival of San Fermin and the running of the bulls in that year. This, I believe, explains my general sense of raging restlessness, my fascination with the *terroir* of Spanish wines, and why I always tear up when I hear Flamenco guitar being played. I was born in a U.S. military hospital in what was then West Germany. In subsequent transfers my family moved to Chicago, South Dakota, Minneapolis, rural Alabama, New York City, San Francisco, and San Antonio.

Never having felt "native" to any region or country, I have nonetheless attached personal significance to scattered places. My list includes the mountains and beaches of Santa Cruz in Northern California, which I discovered on my first silent retreat. I wondered what I would learn about myself and how might I hear the voice of the Creator by practicing silence and solitude for twenty-four hours. At midnight I rented a car at the San Francisco airport and drove over Highway 17, the winding mountain road to Santa Cruz. Parked at the beach, I slept restlessly until sunrise. The next day I was completely alone, pacing white sand beaches and wandering among the redwoods.

I remember the noise that filled the first hours of my retreat—symptoms of withdrawal from normal anxieties, compulsions, and distractions. I needed a period of detox in order to be present to myself and aware of the voice of God's rest. Turning to poetry, I reflected on the internal chaos I had to overcome to live with more clarity and peace:

Friday Spiral Down
Two Weeks No Rest
Caffeine Belly Rush
Sluggish Mind Racing
Toward distracted fantasies of illicit relief
Infected Left Eye-Itch
Late Again—Crabby Bone Tired
Success, Achievement, Accolade
This discordant pace violates
the gravity of my internal symmetry
Hesitatingly,
I shorten My Stride to Coincide
with the Cadence of Genesis-Vision
Footfall after Footfall tensions ease
as I assume the rhythm of Sabbath Rest

It's not surprising that Jesus "often withdrew to lonely places and prayed" (Luke 5:16). He needed time and space to hear the clear whisper of God's voice beyond the clatter of schedules and crowds. He didn't retreat in order to escape. In silence and solitude he found strength to be more fully present to those he was called to love.

Throughout his life, Jesus modeled the practice of silence and solitude. At the beginning of his public life he spent forty days wandering in the wilderness wrestling with temptations. Later, after he began proclaiming his message in Galilee, Mark's Gospel tells us that "very early in the morning, while it was still dark, Jesus got up, left the house and went off to a solitary place, where he prayed"(Mark 1:35). Before making important decisions, he stayed awake all night to pray. Later Jesus began inviting his closest friends to join his solitary wanderings in the mountains. In the final moments before his arrest and crucifixion, Jesus knelt in the garden of Gethsemane. After his resurrection, Jesus told his disciples to go into Jerusalem to wait for the Spirit. They waited and prayed for ten days in an upper room, and then the Spirit came with earthquakes and tongues of flame.

Through extended times away from the normal demands of your schedule, you can make space for God to speak and open yourself to the voice and power of the Spirit. If there was ever a time when we needed solitude and silence, it is now. We are a people prone to distractions and a hurried pace: airplanes, mobile phones, car stereos, television, movies, and the world at our fingertips through our computers. The path of a mystic invites us to make space for God to speak by intentionally pursuing periods of silence, solitude, and rest. What do we accomplish by waiting? Often in the silence the static and distortions that clutter the mind rise up in full force. Just as Jesus chased down demons in the silence of the wilderness, the space of solitude allows us to see what we really wrestle against inside ourselves.

Is it practical to escape the demands of our schedules to pursue silence and solitude? When our kids were small Lisa and I swapped child care duties so that each of us could spend four hours alone each week. Eventually we scheduled a full day every month for each of us to get away on retreat. Many people are rediscovering the practice of Sabbath as a weekly time for rest and contemplation. Silence and solitude can also be practiced together in families and groups. Early on Friday mornings we hike up a hill to pray with others from our community. And once a year we all go on a three-day silent group retreat. I find that it works best for me to be outside, walking in the mountains or near water. Some people feel most settled sitting in a cabin or at a bench in the park. I imagine Jesus found "lonely places" he could return to that became familiar and safe.

But what if in the silence God doesn't speak? Sometimes the practice of solitary prayer can feel dark and lonely. There may be times when the warmth, presence, or guidance you expected prove elusive—and you spend the whole time fighting distractions or chasing away despair. Our comfort is that through persistence we will find the stillness to hear God's voice, remembering the words of the prophet Isaiah: "In repentance and rest is your salvation, in quietness and trust is your strength" (Isaiah 30:15).

More than anyone I know, my friend Derek has learned to hear the voice of God. The scriptures can only take you so far, giving general guidance but not revealing what you should do next Monday. In a hotel room in Paris early one morning, Derek thought he heard a voice saying, "Go to New York." With $100 in his pocket he went to the airport to see if he could afford a flight. Amazingly, there was a ticket available, and he boarded a jet to New York on the morning of September 11, 2001. As the Twin Towers of the World Trade Center burned and fell, Derek's plane landed at J.F.K., just before the airports were closed. Derek then realized that the voice had led him to New York to comfort people traumatized by the attacks. He spent the next three weeks wandering the streets, caring for dazed and displaced people.

SIMPLICITY

Historically, mystics and prophets have lived as voluntary ascetics so they could be more receptive to the voice of God. They often restricted their wardrobes, diets, housing, and travel to be less encumbered. Simplicity is a process of setting voluntary limits in order to devote more energy to your ultimate goals. The goal of simplicity is the training of the body, mind, and soul to cooperate more fully with the power of the Spirit. Jesus lived a life of simplicity and invited his disciples into the same path. When he called his earliest followers, they left their fishing boats and tax collection booths in order to devote themselves more completely to the agenda of the kingdom. Would-be followers of Jesus were cautioned to count the cost of becoming disciples of the master. In an incident recorded in the Gospel of Luke, one religious teacher came up to Jesus exclaiming, "I want to follow you," and Jesus replied, "Foxes have holes and birds of the air have nests, but the Son of Man has no place to lay his head" (Luke 9:58). Jesus unapologetically invited people to abandon their pursuit of pleasure or wealth in order to seek the reign of love. He told his disciples, "Sell your possessions and give to the poor. Provide purses for yourselves that will not wear out, a treasure in heaven that will not be exhausted, where no thief comes near and no moth destroys. For where your treasure is, there your heart will be also" (Luke 12:33–34).

Making a life in the Way of Jesus requires us to rethink our dominant cultural values about money, security, and status. We hear the teachings of Jesus in a cultural context in which economic materialism is the default expectation—and the typical person works long hours to pay for debts amassed trying to live up to an overindulgent lifestyle. Jesus invites us to abandon our preoccupations with achieving wealth or leisure in exchange for the better way of radical contentment. Paul of Tarsus explained this aspect of simplicity: "For we brought nothing into the world, and we can take nothing out of it. But if we have food and clothing, we will be content with that." He goes on to say, "People who want to get rich fall into temptation and a trap and into many foolish and harmful desires that plunge [them] into ruin and destruction. For the love of money is a root of all kinds of evil" (I Timothy 6:7–10). Our economic choices directly affect our ability to flow with the power of the kingdom of love.

Many of my friends have tested their sense of contentment by giving away valued possessions, making vows not to buy anything new for a year, or limiting their personal spending to give more away. Some have even quit lucrative positions to pursue an inspired dream or a more simple life of service. During a reevaluation process like this, people often realize that sometimes what they own actually owns them, taking valuable time and energy to maintain.

My good friend Darren Prince, who is part of an urban order among the poor, is fond of saying, "The spiritual life is more about subtraction than addition. Most of us don't need anything more added to our lives to be fulfilled. It is more likely that what we really need is to subtract from our schedules and possessions to have more space for God and people." The quest for simplicity and contentment, rather than being legislated by rules, can be guided by a question: "How can I manage my life to be the most free to hear the voice of love?" You will find the best rhythm of simplicity through careful experimentation.

Jesus directed his disciples to train themselves to be controlled by the will rather than the cravings of their bodies. When he discovered his disciples sleeping, he said, "Watch and pray so that you will not fall into temptation. The spirit is willing, but the body is weak" (Matthew 26:41). Our bodies are not naturally accustomed to being oriented toward the Spirit, but they can be disciplined through exercise, a more limited diet, occasional fasting or abstinence from other normal pleasures and comforts. Paul told his apprentice, Timothy, "Train yourself to be godly" (I Timothy 4:17). As a society we are becoming increasingly aware of the dynamic interaction among the mind, soul, and body.

Stress, for instance, can bring on a variety of physical symptoms, including heart and intestinal problems. Eating too much can make you feel sedated or lazy. Caffeine makes many of us agitated. Lack of sleep often produces irritability and even temporary insanity. Many people are discovering that paying closer attention to their diet, sleep, and exercise helps them be more centered and present to God's voice. Through practices of physical, material, and economic simplicity you focus your life energy and open yourself more fully to the regenerating work of the Spirit.

CONTEMPLATIVE ENGAGEMENT

I suspect that my use of the word *mystic* may, for some, conjure images of a nomadic eccentric or hermit, consumed with personal religious experiences or disaffected with society. Being a mystic is not an escape from life in community. The contribution of prophets and mystics is the clarity they receive through prayer, solitude, and simplicity to serve others. Some have referred to this as the call to be an "engaged contemplative," and this is precisely the kind of mystic that Jesus was—tuned in to the voice of God and simultaneously connected to his community and society. Jesus even participated, on some level, with the conventional religious life of his culture. He offered himself to be immersed by John in the Jordan. He spoke in synagogue meetings, taught in the temple courts, debated with religious authorities, and followed religious customs and ceremonies.

What Jesus recognized, which other people often missed, was that the religious buildings, ceremonies, and hierarchies were "a shadow of the things that were to come" (Colossians 2:17). He challenged the rules imposed by religious leaders and subverted their teachings and authority. He often met secretly with high-profile religious leaders who wanted to follow his way. His ability to speak prophetically to the people within religious institutions came from the fact that he remained engaged in dialogue.

Once Christianity was legalized within the Roman Empire in the fourth century, the distinctiveness of being a "follower of the Way" was obscured by the popularity of the new religion. Many people retreated to the desert in order to cultivate a way of life that they felt would be a provocative alternative to the cult of the empire. Gradually people began to visit the "desert fathers and mothers" to learn from their peculiar way of life, and this served to renew the church from the margins of society. Similarly, we are invited to be engaged contemplatives who seek to hear the voice of God while staying connected to the people and communities from which we come.

SINGING ALONG WITH A NEW SONG

When I was small I learned to mouth the words of the songs my mother sang to me. I still carry that music with me, the voice of my mother's love. Those songs shaped me, became part of me, and I learned to sing them myself—loud and strong, with my own intonations, pitch, and harmonies. The kingdom of God's love—the genesis-vision—is the song that reverberates throughout the universe, with power to animate all who hear it. The music is contagious. As we learn to tune in and listen to the voice of our Maker we are invited to mouth the words, to sing loud and strong, to add our own phrasing and harmonies, to join the chorus of those who have gone before us—becoming part of the eternal aria of the Creator's love.

> [Yahweh] put a new song in my mouth,
> a hymn of praise to our God.
> Many will see and fear
> and put their trust in the LORD.
>
> (Psalm 42:3)

CONVERSATION

On being a mystic.   Are you comfortable using the word *mystic* to describe the spirituality of Jesus? What other words would you use to describe his existential awareness of the voice and power of the Spirit?

Contemplative engagement.   Sometimes the deepest impact on society comes from those on the margins who practice *vital irrelevancy*—living distinctively while staying engaged with the needs of people. What might this look like for someone in your life situation?

Prayer practices.   What daily practices help you stay aware of God and surrendered? Have there been techniques you have used successfully in the past that could be renewed?

Dark night of the soul.   Have you ever had the sense that God was speaking to you? The risk of listening for God's voice is that God might not say anything. How have you handled this in the past?

EXPERIMENTS

Keep a journal.   Daily journal keeping can be a helpful form of meditation. If you don't keep a journal already, begin a daily morning journal in which you reflect on the internal and external events of your life. Once a month, read through your journal entries, reflecting on the patterns of successes and struggles the journal reveals.

Pray the psalms.   A discipline that might help you with both prayer and study is reading the Hebrew psalms. For thirty days, read five psalms each day, aloud if possible. An easy way to keep track is to read by the date. If it is the fifth day of the month, you would read Psalms 5, 35, 65, 95, and 115—adding thirty to the day. On the thirty-first, read Psalm 119.

Practice the presence of God.   Like my friend Tom, try to spend four hours "practicing" the presence of God.

Take a silent retreat.   Try taking a twenty-four- or forty-eight-hour silent retreat. Avoid bringing books or other distractions, and spend the time in contemplation, solitude, and prayer. Many people find that they spend a good amount of time sleeping on their first silent retreat—what does this say about the schedules we keep?

Add by subtracting.   Brainstorm a list of five actions or decisions that would help you simplify your life and leave more room for God to speak. If the spiritual life is more about subtraction than addition, what would be helpful to subtract? Experiment with limiting clutter, commitments, and activities.

CHAPTER FOURTEEN

DANCING INTO
THE CIRCLE

"It's time to do the Hokey Pokey" crackles the voice over the microphone at this small farm-town roller-skating rink. We form a circle, and a worker, dressed up in a bunny suit, skates out to lead us in the song: "You put your right hand in, you put your right hand out, you put your right hand in and you shake it all about." We go through all the parts of the body this way—left arm, right leg, left leg, head in, head out, and "we shake it all about." The motions are challenging as we balance and teeter on our roller skates, especially on the chorus where we all spin in the middle of the circle waving our hands and clapping, "You do the Hokey Pokey and you turn yourself around—that's what it's all about!" At the song's finale we sing, "You put your whole self in, you put your whole self out, you put your whole self in and you shake it all about, you do the Hokey Pokey and you turn yourself around, that's what it's all about!"

Entering the kingdom of God is a lot like doing the Hokey Pokey on roller skates. We slip—slide, rock, and reel around and around learning to bring our whole selves into the circle of the Creator's reign. If the voice of God is like a song, we were made to hear the music, dancing and swaying to its rhythms and funky beats. The way you enter the kingdom dance is by learning to bring all the parts of yourself into the hokey-pokey circle of genesis-vision.

TRUE WORSHIP

The term *worship,* as it is often used, evokes images of exuberant singing with outstretched arms, or the dignified ceremony of a Mass or liturgy. In its most elemental form, true worship is the surrender of the body to the will of its Maker. In his letter to the Romans, Paul of Tarsus urged, "Offer your bodies as living sacrifices, holy and pleasing to God. *This is your spiritual act of worship*" (Romans 12:1). More than ardent singing or reverent posturing, the most devout thing you can do is to surrender your body to the way of love. You can only offer to God what belongs to you—your mind, body, time, resources, and influence. This is your personal kingdom—the things that are directly under your jurisdiction and control. You choose how to spend your time, what you will think about, how you move your body, where you will spend your money, what you do with your property, and how you relate to others. When I tell my kids to tidy their rooms, I often remind them that their space in the house is part of their personal kingdom that they have been entrusted with. If we want to see change in the world, we will have to begin by changing ourselves—or rather by surrendering our bodies and wills to the dance of genesis-vision. We enter the hokey-pokey circle of God's reign by systematically leveraging every part of ourselves to serve the cause of love.

Jesus is a model of what it means to surrender to the way of love. When I was in college, a mentor invited me to consider how well my actions and priorities matched the goal of imitating the example of Christ. I began asking, "Does the way I live contribute to the greater wholeness of God's kingdom?" I was guided in this process by the words, "Let us throw off everything that hinders and the sin that so easily entangles, and let us run with perseverance the race marked out for us. Let us fix our eyes on Jesus, the author and perfecter of our faith..." (Hebrews 12:1). I realized that there were certain things I needed to say "no" to in order to seek the path of love. Making a life in the Way of Jesus requires leaving behind the distractions and sins that keep us from more fully entering into the dance of God's reign.

Sarah, a friendly and compassionate professional, asked me to meet with her and help her think through some changes she wished to make in her life. She hoped that by seeking coaching and spiritual direction she could begin to address the obstacles that were blocking the person she wanted to become. Longing for a greater sense of community and purpose, yet feeling isolated and lonely, Sarah often attempted to fill the void with extra work assignments, shopping, or watching TV. During our conversation, she slowly revealed her addictions to eating and spending and their results: unhealthy weight and very serious credit problems. In a few weeks she would be leaving for an extended vacation during which she hoped to kick-start some new habits and direction. Her holiday plans included renting an expensive and luxurious house she could not afford, where she intended to spend many hours alone watching television. After listening to her hopes and plans, I suggested that her desire for change could be reflected in how she organized her upcoming trip (for example, by choosing economical accommodations, daily exercise, healthy meals, and limited media consumption). As we talked, I could see Sarah's face revealing her growing discomfort. Finally she said, "This all makes sense to me, but . . . I guess I'm not quite ready to make the changes that are necessary."

I appreciated Sarah's honesty. Perhaps you can identify with her predicament: knowing that specific changes are needed, but fearful or unwilling to take new action. Most of us have the intelligence or common sense to recognize what we need to make over. We could change if we really wanted to. The problem is that sometimes we simply don't wish to. This struggle is a sign of our shadow side and the reality that we often choose paths that are harmful or destructive, preventing us from collaborating with the Creator's agenda of love.

REIMAGINE!

When Jesus announced, "The kingdom of God is near," he invited a response, saying, "Repent." The word *repent* has ominous undertones in the cultural vernacular of Americana. For me it conjures memories of barn roofs near highways in the rural South, often painted in blazing red with the word "REPENT!" in angry capital letters. The word literally means "rethink your thinking" or "reimagine" your life in view of new alternatives. The instruction to "repent" or "reimagine" is meant to shock and arrest, to incite us to rethink our goals and priorities, to call into question our previous ways and awaken us to new possibilities. We reimagine our lives by allowing the Creator to examine our thoughts, attitudes, motives, and behavior. We see an ancient example of this in a song attributed to David, King of Israel:

> Search me, O God, and know my heart;
> test me and know my anxious thoughts.
> See if there is any offensive way in me,
> and lead me in the way everlasting.
>
> (Psalm 139:23–24)

It takes courage and vulnerability to ask, "How am I out of rhythm with the way of love?" We are told to repent or reimagine our lives because there is a better way, as the Apostle Paul suggested: "God's kindness leads you toward repentance" (Romans 2:4). Allowing the Maker to gently examine your character is an entrance into the kingdom dance.

WHAT TO START AND WHAT TO STOP

When Frank and I met, he wanted to hear my "testimony"—the story of how I began making a life in the Way of Jesus. Frank's own story was a dramatic tale of betrayal, child neglect, drug addiction, and drunken brawls. After several bottles of wine one Friday night, Frank suddenly had an epiphany and gave his life to Jesus. He immediately stopped drinking or using drugs and started going to church. I'm sure my boring and unsalacious "testimony" of childhood conversion disappointed Frank. My spiritual awakening was gradual and didn't involve cheap motels, multiple arrests, or time in jail. I wanted to hear something about Frank's journey to greater wholeness in the time since that epic moment eight years before. What Frank and I have in common is that we are now both in the school of conversion—the process of continual repentance—learning to move with more elegance to the rhythms of the master. To transition from basic two-step to sexy tango, we need to continually evaluate what to say "yes" to and what to say "no" to.

In the New Testament, there is a consistent diagnosis and prescription for what it means to "reimagine" our lives. The example and ethical teachings of Jesus are a reliable guide to this. The Sermon on the Mount (Matthew 5–7) is a summary of Jesus' teachings on how to more fully surrender the parts of your personal kingdom to the kingdom of God, and these concepts are echoed in the pastoral letters of the Apostle Paul (notably Colossians 3 and Ephesians 4–6). Many people have found it helpful to commit these passages to memory. Together these texts provide a systematic curriculum for what to stop doing and what to start doing to progress through the kingdom dance school. Paul of Tarsus, with his penchant for lists, suggests what we need to stop doing to learn our new dance moves:

> Put to death, therefore, whatever belongs to your earthly nature: sexual immorality, impurity, lust, evil desires and greed, which is idolatry. Because of these, the wrath of God is coming. You used to walk in these ways, in the life you once lived. But now you must rid yourselves of all such things as these: anger, rage, malice, slander, and filthy language from your lips. Do not lie to each other, since you have taken off your old self with its practices and have put on the new self, which is being renewed in knowledge in the image of its Creator. (Colossians 3:5–10)

Later Paul listed new steps to start practicing for the dance of love:

> Clothe yourselves with compassion, kindness, humility, gentleness and patience. Bear with each other and forgive whatever grievances you may have against one another. Forgive as the Lord forgave you. And over all these virtues put on love, which binds them all together in perfect unity. (Colossians 3:12–14)

When I first began considering my spiritual formation as an intentional endeavor, my mentor suggested I write down my plan and goals. At the top of a piece of paper I wrote out my ultimate goal: to seek the kingdom of God. I made two columns: (1) What will help me move toward this goal? and (2) What hinders me from this goal? I began evaluating how I was spending my life energy. "What obstacles are keeping me from seeking the Way? What is distracting me? What new things can I do to live more consistently with this vision of life?" Perhaps the most important thing I did was look at my schedule. Did how I spent my time reflect my ambition to live by the example of Jesus? Gradually I developed a list of things that I needed to stop doing and a list of things I needed to start doing to cooperate with the agenda of God's reign. For example, I decided to stop watching TV, and I started volunteering at a mental hospital. Once or twice a year I continue to go through this process of discernment.

SHADOW PATTERNS

Nearly everyone has some pattern of destructive habits that serve to sabotage relationships or frustrate personal goals. Sometimes we tenaciously hold on to these shadows. Our chronic shadow habits are often signs of deeper or more foundational soul sickness: fear, anger, jealousy, and so on. While "sin" is often viewed as an incident or episode of indiscretion, in actuality it is part of the total system of our thoughts, values, planning, and cultural assumptions. When examined more holistically, we may come to recognize that any incident of "sin" is symptomatic of an entire pattern of life set up in opposition to the way of love.

For example, a character named "Crabby Dad" makes occasional visits to our home. He is an anxious and demanding father figure who speaks harshly, gives orders, and lacks empathy. Needless to say, no one is happy when Crabby Dad makes an appearance. Fortunately his visits have become less frequent as I have begun to deal with anger and impatience as a pattern rather than an isolated incident. My anger and impatience are products of a total system of beliefs and practices: connected to overwork, fatigue, lack of rest or care for the body, an unhealthy drive to be validated through achievement, a sense of perfectionism, and a desire to control other people. I am wrong not only in my anger. I am also wrong in the total pattern of my reasoning, values, and life management. It has been helpful for me to ask, "Why do I become anxious?" and "When do I become angry?" and to make intentional changes in the entire pattern of my choices.

A LEGACY OF SHADOWS

The wounds of sin and our shadow selves are both individual and collective. Jesus once cautioned, "The things that cause people to sin are bound to come, but woe to that person *through whom* they come" (Luke 17:1). Our choices have a direct effect on other people, and our influence can set up chains of struggle and temptation for others. You may be conscious of the ways your parents or elders influenced the nature of your own shadows. And those of us with children may be well aware of the ways we have passed on our own issues and temptations. If we look out on our world and see problems, they are our problems because we have collectively chosen to stand aside in idle rebellion against the contagious dance of love. Together, in some measure, we are responsible for the conditions on our planet—slave trafficking, colonialism, sexism, sectarian violence, and war are examples that come quickly to mind. The disciple Peter described the death of Jesus as a means of delivering us from "the empty way of life handed down to [us] from [our] forefathers" (I Peter 1:18). We begin to reimagine our lives by acknowledging that we have inherited and perpetuated empty ways of life that must be dismantled and replaced by new patterns of living.

We reimagine our lives by recognizing that the empires of this world stand in opposition to the kingdom of God. Government policies, economic systems, and prevailing social and cultural values constitute aspects of the kingdoms of this world that are critiqued by the melodious song of the kingdom of God. Part of repentance is examining how we have consciously or unconsciously participated in sustaining systems of power, greed, and oppression. In a global sense, the insidious nature of sin not only places a person "in danger of the fires of hell," but can also make life on Earth a living hell. What this suggests is that repentance involves both personal piety and a commitment to becoming advocates for peace and justice. The prophet Micah summarized the goal of repentance when he wrote:

[God] has showed you, O [people], what is good.
And what does the LORD require of you?
To act justly and to love mercy
and to walk humbly with your God.

(Micah 6:8)

DECONSTRUCTION AND GRIEVING

When I first met Ryan and Holly, they were at the height of their success. Ryan was the leader of a well-known touring band, playing music in front of thousands of adoring fans at important venues and churches. Gradually the intrigue of fame wore thin, and they began to wonder if they were part of perpetuating a way of seeing faith that promoted hype and success over substance. Ryan walked away from his band and, along with Holly, began a three-year journey of rethinking assumptions about what it means to be followers of the Way. I watched Ryan, in particular, move from his confident stage persona to a diminished and tentative figure who was becoming increasingly dejected and depressed. Gradually they both began to realize that their anger at religious, political, and economic systems was more profoundly anger with themselves—because they had been willing participants who had benefited from those structures. Their process of grieving and deconstruction is now bearing fruit in the ways they are constructively learning to walk in greater wholeness.

Grieving and deconstruction are natural rhythms in the dance of the kingdom. We awaken to the way of the kingdom by dying to our previous patterns and assumptions. Consider how frequently surprise, suffering, and pain come as elements of growth and transformation. The disciples of Jesus were often blind-sided by new revelations, and for many of them this pattern of surprise and disruption continued throughout the rest of their lives. Paul of Tarsus had a blinding deconstruction at a midpoint in his life, and the Apostle Peter struggled to overcome his prejudices long after the resurrection of Christ. If spiritual progress is often slow and gradual, we should expect that we will continue to be challenged, humbled, and corrected. James the brother of Jesus encouraged followers of the Way to "grieve, mourn and wail. Turn your laughter to mourning and your joy to gloom"

(James 4:9). Deconstruction is necessary to rebirth, and sometimes it is the best we can offer to our Creator: "The sacrifices
of God are a broken Spirit, a broken and contrite heart, O
God, you will not despise" (Psalm 51:17). Paul of Tarsus once
commented that "Godly sorrow brings repentance that leads to
salvation and leaves no regrets" (I Corinthians 7:10). We can
only enter fully into the kind of life we are being offered if
we adequately grieve and deconstruct the shadows of our past.
We should welcome disruption, grief, and surprise as signs of
transformation.

CULTIVATING A NEW IMAGINATION

One night at 2 a.m. I awoke to the knock of police at my door.
Shining a flashlight in my eyes, the officer apologized and asked
if I had heard gunshots. Across the street someone had been
murdered, execution style, with a pistol to the back of the head.
Looking past the officer, I saw the street taped off where investigators were searching for bullet casings. I stood on the steps for
a long time, watching them trace bullet trajectories and thinking
of what had just occurred. I lay awake most of the night wondering what it means to be a good neighbor in a place where
people are routinely shot and killed. I realized that I had been
letting the propriety and respectability of my social class shape my
imagination more than a vision for living as a healer in the world.
As I dozed in and out of sleep and prayer, John the Baptist kept
coming to my mind, a dreadlocked wild man dressed in camel's
hair, calling people to repentance. That night I strengthened my
resolve to defy convention and live with more abandon, creativity,
and imagination. I asked God for new pictures of myself to guide
me toward new adventures. I saw myself walking the streets of
my neighborhood with more courage and less propriety as an
ambassador of peace.

Imagination is the capacity to see future possibilities in pictures. Part of repentance is learning to reimagine your imminent
destiny. If I asked, "What will you be doing tomorrow night
between nine and ten-thirty?" you can probably conjure moving
pictures of the likely scenarios: You, going to the freezer to get a
bowl of ice cream. You, reading a book or sitting in front of the

television. We were made with the innate capacity to be guided by our images of the future. We are invited to reimagine new scripts for the movies of ourselves we see in our heads.

Generally you move toward a perception of your identity. Our tendency is to consciously or unconsciously adopt controlling metaphors that condition our choices and responses. You may define yourself by an ethnic or cultural identity, by your vocation (business person, artist, medical worker, minister, academic, technologist, contractor, laborer), by your location (rural, suburban, or urban), by your social class (wealthy, poor, upwardly mobile), or by a role you adopted in your family of origin (the obedient child, the rebel, the clumsy one, the smart-aleck). These roles help simplify our choices, but also place limits on our ability to imagine and live into new possibilities. The voice of Jesus from the Revelation declares, "Behold, I am making all things new" (Revelation 21:5). The song of God invites us to discover a renewed identity in the kingdom of love.

RETHINKING VOCATION

The Apostle Peter describes the seekers of Jesus as "a chosen people, a royal priesthood" (I Peter 2:9). And John echoed the language of priesthood in his vision of revelation: "To him who loves us and has freed us from our sins by his blood, and has made us to be *a kingdom and priests* to serve his God and Father—to him be glory and power for ever and ever!" (Revelation 1:6). We know from watching the lives of living monarchs that being a princess or prince involves certain privileges and responsibilities. The best examples of royalty use their time, resources, and positions to serve the public interest and not their own pleasures or whimsies.

How do we understand what it means to be a priest or priestess in the kingdom of God? Priests in the ancient Hebrew tradition read the law, offered sacrifices, and administered just decisions. But they also gave instructions about sanitation, building codes, and public health. There was no distinction between what was sacred and what was secular. For the ancient Hebrew priests, all of life was sacred and worth attending to. As seekers of God's kingdom, we are called to care more and not less about the world that we live in.

We are being invited to reimagine our perspectives on vocation. Your true vocation is not how you draw a paycheck but your unique contribution to humanity. Each of us has a vocation in one of the domains of life, and every vocation has potential for great dignity. It may be in business, public service, teaching or caring for children, medicine, science or engineering, or a life in the arts. I once met a woman who worked as a school social worker in an inner-city neighborhood. She approached me after my lecture with tears in her eyes and said, "Thank you for affirming the dignity of my work. The people in my church community are always asking me to get more involved in their programs, and I'm misunderstood when I say that I am already fulfilled in my calling as a social worker. I know that I am doing God's work when I care for these children and families."

My friend Damon is paid well for his work at a large technology company. Damon's employer tells him what a great job he is doing and encourages him to take on more and more responsibility. And yet Damon is troubled by the fact that, after long hours, he is mentally and physically exhausted. "Why," he asks, "am I spending the best hours of my life serving the company's agenda instead of discovering how to bring greater wholeness to the world?" Damon wants to spend more time cultivating a spiritual center and caring for the needs of the poor. He contemplates what it will cost to make his decisions based on a kingdom agenda—possible loss of promotions and status, less income, and fewer investments for retirement. "It feels like if I leave my job I will be jumping off a cliff." Jesus promised that if we seek first the kingdom, all the things we need will be provided (Matthew 6:33). What for Damon feels like jumping off a great cliff might actually be a small gentle step into the arms of God's abundance.

Reimagining your vocation does not necessarily imply quitting your job or making a drastic change. Sometimes it is simply a matter of shifting your expectations or work ethic. When John the Baptist announced the kingdom of God, soldiers and tax collectors asked, "What should we do?" Perhaps they were assuming that they were supposed to quit their jobs and do something else. John told them to do their work in a new way, operating according to different ethics than those commonly employed in their trades (Luke 3:12–14). My friend Ken left his work in business to become a minister, hoping to do the work he thought was more significant to God's kingdom. Reflecting on that decision, he said, "At the time I thought that the only way I could be used by God at my job was by witnessing to my coworkers. I didn't have a very holistic understanding of God's purposes. Only later did I realize how many opportunities I missed to participate in the healing of creation. I worked for a clothing company and often traveled to developing countries where our products were manufactured. I was in a position to influence the conditions of workers in sweat-shops and factories and advocate for environmentally sustainable practices." Now, ten years later, Ken has returned to business and has started a company that serves his employees and community.

BIG AND SMALL DECISIONS

Our lives are composed of the collective choices we make. Some of those choices are monumental: What career will I choose? Who will I marry? Where will I live? Our destinies are formed by both macro-level *and* micro-level decisions—including our small moment-by-moment choices. We frequently become consumed and paralyzed by the task of making major life decisions, not realizing that our lives are primarily formed by the many minute choices we make every day.

Phil and Kim are considering a dramatic life change—quitting their jobs and retraining to move to China to help with develop-ment work. They have struggled with whether they are making a good decision or not. In the process they have begun to ask, "How can we begin to live into the life we have imagined from the place where we now are?" Together they brainstormed a list of simple ideas they could start with (taking a class to learn Mandarin, developing friendships and serving in a local Asian community, watching films and reading books that give voice to the Asian experience). They realized that there are small steps they can take now that will help them discern their direction, clarify their bigger decisions, and propel them toward their destiny.

In the process of repentance, sometimes the number of changes you feel you need to make can seem overwhelming. The place to start is with your next step. What are you being invited to stop? What do you need to limit? And what new thing do you need to start to move forward to enter the hokey-pokey circle of the kingdom dance?

THE SONG AND DANCE

After dinner at the wedding the tables are cleared out to make room for the dance. The bride and groom take their first steps out onto the dance floor, and slowly people muster the courage to stand and move their bodies to the beat of the music. A middle-aged man hears the music to his favorite high school radio tune. Sucking in his stomach, he tucks his shirt into tight dress pants and waddles out onto the dance floor to remember what he once knew. He moves heavily, awkwardly, and I am afraid that he might hurt himself or someone else as he strains to move his body to the rhythm of the music. He is learning to dance again.

Entering the kingdom of God is a lot like learning to dance again. Somewhere in the deepest part of ourselves we have heard the music of our Maker and long to get our groove on, moving according to the ancient rhythm of genesis-vision. We repent and reimagine how we live in our bodies, knowing that a revolutionary force, the Spirit of God, is at work in us, wooing us toward health, wholeness, love, and peace. Inspired by this vision, I once wrote a poem about what life could be like for us together as we learn to reimagine:

> In my mind's eye
> I am flying high across the sky
> Swooping in and out and dropping low,
> Touching the ground of city streets
> Like a spirit of God hovering over primordial waters
> Of lump clay earth.
> I am waking up
> I am daring to dream again
> I hear the voice
> I hear the voice
> I hear the voice over the waters saying to you and to me:
> "I am here.
> The hidden whisper of love.
> That beautiful and terrible story you hunger to hear.

Be still!
Be still sacred scared child.
Awake!
Awake from your stubborn numb slumber
Open those sleepy eyes to my morning daylight
It will not burn away any good it finds in that hungry cracked
    heart.
ReIMAGINE!
Life with me
Taste and see the splendor of
my blooming spring garden rest weary home
Weep while you can.
While you still feel
While the pain is still real
While my love still heals."
ReIMAGINE!
Nonfiction in full color
Humanity and divinity live in concert together.
The "I" and the "we" making sweet synergy.
It's the song we all long to hear
Let the aria resound, may the earth shake with the reverber-
    ation of your ancient apocalyptic prodigious creativity.
ReIMAGINE! All our voices in harmony with yours, Lord.
Samba, Romba, Rhimba
Afro-Cuban beats
Italian Opera
Salsa Latina
Tai-Chi Mariachi
Three Chord Punk Rock bleats and the symphony
The Trance, Trip-Hop, Hip-Hop, Doo-wop, Swing
Big Band Bleeding Heart Acoustic Folk Middle Eastern Dirge
Zeideco, Howling Blues and the Salvation songs of plantation
    slave spirituals singing:
"We shall overcome." "We shall overcome."
ReIMAGINE!
A spiral, whirling miracle, of you and me and us swept up in
    the Creator's remaking.
ReIMAGINE!

CONVERSATION

Patterns.   Can you think of an example of how the issues you struggle with are related to your total pattern of life management (similar to the example of Crabby Dad)?

Small choices.   How have you seen small choices and incremental changes affect the direction of your life?

Your true vocation.   How would you relate the work you do to your true vocation in the scheme of God's kingdom?

EXPERIMENTS

Examining your personal kingdom.   On a piece of paper, write the words *time, body, mind, resources, relationships.* In each category, think through the ways you have chosen to manage your personal kingdom. How are you using your life energy in ways that move you toward or away from the kingdom of love?

New experiences.   New experiences help jolt us out of complacency and create an opening for proactive change. Make a conscious choice to do something different from your normal pattern each day for one week. *Change your schedule.* If you normally stay up late, go to bed early one night. *Change your surroundings.* Put yourself in an unfamiliar situation. *Change your sensations.* Try a new activity. Modify your eating habits. Notice how a new schedule, surroundings, and sensations can expand your horizons.

When you are older.   Since I was quite young I've found it helpful to imagine myself at later points in life. When I met my wife, I tried to imagine our life together as we became older. Every now and then I try to think of what I will look like and who I will be when I am fifty, seventy, or eighty. This exercise helps me orient and monitor my daily activities toward the best imagination of who I hope to be someday. What pictures do you see of yourself as you age? What do you hope to be like when you are eighty?

CHAPTER FIFTEEN

ENTER THE JESUS DOJO

We could smell the sawdust and see the power tools—but for the first six weeks of eighth grade woodshop class we were glued to our desks studying an instruction book and taking pop quizzes. My hands were itching to touch the pine boards and press the trigger on a power drill. By week six we were literally salivating for the chance to make something with our hands. At the end of the semester I was thoroughly disappointed that all I had to show for my work was a small wooden candy bowl that I reluctantly gave to my mother.

Two years later I transferred from the big city to a small rural high school in central Alabama, where the only elective class was Agricultural Science—or "Ag" for short. On the first day of Ag class, the teacher, Mr. Mac King, handed me an Oxy/Acetylene torch and taught me how to cut steel. The next week I learned how to arc weld when he slapped a welding mask on my head and sent me into the shed to draw a few beads with high-voltage current. Every week there was a new project—for instance, building kitchen cabinets. We replaced the playground equipment at the elementary school, installed new bleachers in the school gym, and fixed creaking floorboards and broken windows in classrooms. Mr. Mac King also got us involved in his own personal projects. We rotated the tires and changed the oil in his pickup truck, repaired the leaking bottom of his fishing boat, and manufactured new shutters and steel stairs for his home. I even crafted a beautiful cedar chest that he gave to his daughter as a graduation gift. His approach may have been unorthodox, and possibly illegal, but I learned more about the trades from him than I would have in twenty years' worth of textbooks, lectures, and pop quizzes.

Sometimes our dignified and sophisticated approaches to education yield poorer results than more primitive and applied methods. When Jesus said, "Repent and believe the good news," it was an invitation to become students of the master. And like being in Mr. Mac King's Ag class, those who responded to his call were immediately swept up into his work and mission, inhabiting their belief by learning to do what he showed them. The way Jesus taught his disciples, as a first-century rabbi, was more like being in woodshop or a karate dojo than a lecture hall. Jesus taught his disciples on hillsides, along the road and in the marketplace, giving them assignments and sending them out as advocates to towns and villages—even before they understood what they were doing.

If we want to believe Jesus' message and become the kind of followers his early disciples were, we may have to shift our expectations about what spiritual education looks like—leaving the metaphor of the lecture hall to enter the "Jesus dojo." A *dojo* is a Japanese word meaning "the place where you learn the way." Jesus once declared, "I am *the way* and the truth and the life" (John 14:6), implying that he is both a savior *and* a teacher for life—he provided the way to God *and* he teaches us how to live in the Way of God.

Many of our structures and venues for religious education are set up to be passive and cognitive rather than active and participatory. Most people, for instance, think of a church as a place to sit and listen—not a context in which they will be coached and stretched to practice new skills. How do the schedule and programs of a church reveal what is thought to be most important? How is success measured? (Too frequently by attendance, buildings, and budgets.) Even home groups are often just smaller venues for knowledge and study. We might ask, Did Jesus give his life on the cross so that we could sit around reading and discussing books about him, or so we could join the revolution?

EAST MEETS WEST

While hiking together recently, I asked my friend Wolfgang about his spiritual journey. Raised in postwar Germany, Wolfgang had some painful experiences with the church that alienated him from Christian belief. His quest for integration prompted him to travel the globe in search of insights and techniques that would lead to greater wholeness. He studied with many gurus and teachers, eventually developing his own practice of inner simplicity, yoga, and daily meditation. At one point in our hike Wolfgang urged me to say something about my own pilgrimage. As I began he interrupted, saying, "Mark, my impression is that you are more Buddhist than Christian."

"What do you mean?" I asked.

"Well, your spirituality seems so much about awareness and practice—embracing all of life as sacred. Those aren't things I associate with Christianity."

We stopped to look at a waterfall, and after some contemplation I responded, "I see my beliefs as deeply rooted in the life and teachings of Jesus, the Judeo-Christian scriptures, and trustworthy streams of Christian tradition. Perhaps it doesn't sound like the Christian belief you are familiar with because in Western society, experience and practice are so rarely emphasized."

Nodding, Wolfgang added, "We seem so obsessed with the rational and theoretical, and maybe especially being German, I find myself wanting a path that helps me move from my mind into my body, to be aware of life in the here and now. I want to experience this waterfall, for instance, not just analyze and dissect it with thoughts and words."

"I understand the desire for just being," I said. "Yet, for me the epic narrative of creation and redemption is still significant." I offered, "But I do find myself trying to strike a balance between the mind of reason and the richness of practice and experience. We need not be opposed to rationality."

"That reminds me of an encounter I had during one of my trips to India," Wolfgang said. "Someone was hit by a car and everyone started screaming and crying. No one helped or called for an ambulance as the person lay dying. The people had a beautiful way of being present to their feelings and experiences, but were paralyzed by their lack of reasoning. It was there that I realized that the consciousness of the East needs the rational mind of the West."

REASON AND EXPERIENCE

Our conversation illustrates the tension we often feel between reason and experience. The Western obsession with theory and rationality can be spiritually toxic. I believe this explains a growing fascination with Eastern mysticism and more practice-based spiritualities. Like so many people, I was taught that Christian belief is based on facts and, explicitly, *not* on experience. Instructions and warnings like "Don't trust your feelings" and "Experiences and emotions can lead you astray" betray the Western quest for certainty and objectivity—a desire to make faith reasonable and appealing to the scientific mind. The difficulty with a purely rationalistic view is that life is full of many uncertainties, ambiguities, and subjective experiences. If the expression of orthodox faith can only be rational and verifiable, then belief must be relegated to an exercise of the mind and statements about words.

Paul of Tarsus noted that "the kingdom of God is not a matter of talk but of power" (I Corinthians 4:20). I think of how personally addicted I am to words and ideas that are often fragmented from my sensations, feelings, and relationships. We struggle to live in our bodies what we believe in our minds. How is it that so many of us have energy to debate about words but lack the passion to seek love and reconciliation? Or why do we tend to look for God in the pages of a book more than in the face of a friend? In the West we have more ideas about God than encounters with God, treating the message of the kingdom more as an elegant theory than a present reality. Is the name and power of Jesus something to be understood or a presence and power to encounter? From our fragmentation we struggle for a unity between thought and experience.

FAITH AND OBEDIENCE

How do people groomed in a Western mindset recover from the separation of body, mind, and spirit? Let me quickly suggest that the solution is not to swing the pendulum from West to East. We've already discussed how two things can be true simultaneously—in this case the rationality of a biblical narrative *and* our subjective experience of the present reality of the kingdom of God. Jesus suggested that his message is best understood through obedience. Once when he was asked to defend himself in rational terms, Jesus responded, "If anyone chooses to do God's will, he will find out whether my teaching comes from God or whether I speak on my own" (John 7:17). We verify the truth claims of Jesus by learning to obey what he taught.

During my life I've watched many friends abandon faith, though most never took the risk of obedience. Their "belief" was more like an unconsummated intellectual game, and the stakes were low. "I'm done believing," they would say—and I wanted to ask, "When did you ever start? When did you seek solidarity with the poor? How did you try to love your neighbor as yourself? When did you work to discipline your appetites? Have you struggled to exchange love of money for the pursuit of greater wholeness?" We think that our beliefs or unbelief flow from logical evidence, when it may be that our beliefs are more influenced by the choices we make in our moral and ethical lives. Perhaps we can only believe to the extent that we are willing to obey.

Although many would say that San Franciscans are irreligious, you can see thousands of people huddled outside of synagogues and churches sipping coffee and smoking cigarettes after early morning Alcoholics Anonymous meetings. In those meetings people are learning to trust a God whose name they might not even know, accessing power to make changes—seeking reconciliation, healing, and restoration. My friend Elizabeth, who just celebrated her two-year sobriety birthday, explains that she has learned to have what she calls "functional faith." Like a simple pair of walking shoes, functional faith, rather than being elegant or fancy, is utilitarian and basic—but it can help you get around in the real world. The Jesus dojo is about learning to connect faith with the messy details of everyday life.

LIFE IN THE JESUS DOJO

• *You enter the Jesus Dojo through new experiences.* Perhaps you have been in a setting in which someone spoke or a group discussed the theme of compassion and justice in the teachings of Jesus. Several years ago I realized that merely talking about it wasn't helping me live any differently. I heard the rattle of grocery carts outside our door every morning as homeless people dug through our trash to collect recycling. Sometimes we saw these same people holding signs out by the freeway. With a group of friends, our family decided to become friends with our homeless neighbors. Instead of having our normal church meeting we went underneath the freeway overpass where nearly a hundred people, many struggling with addictions or mental illness, were living in tents. We cooked together, told stories, and played games. Eventually these neighborhood parties became a regular occurrence. Having this new experience helped us reflect on and internalize what Jesus taught in more profound ways.

I often hear people comment about the life-changing experiences they have had while on a mission's trip or disaster relief project. "We worked hard together all day, slept on concrete floors, and ate rice and beans all week," they say, "and it was really great!" If these experiences are so helpful to formation, we may want to consider how to make them more a part of our normal patterns of life and community. Most of us live within a short distance of places where there are similar needs and opportunities.

• *You enter the Jesus dojo by moving from ideas to action.* It is pretty clear that Jesus had some strong things to say about money, wealth, and empire. Reading or discussing a teaching like "Sell your possessions and give to the poor," we are often quick to suggest that Jesus could not have meant for us to take him seriously. "Of course," we reason, "he only said this to remind us not to become overly attached to our possessions." But what if he intended these statements to provoke transformation? The early church certainly took his words literally: "Selling their possessions and goods they gave to anyone as [they] had need" (Acts 2:45). The soles of our walking shoes connect with the grit of asphalt as we struggle together to apply the hard sayings of Jesus.

Last year I worked with a group of friends to develop a two-month project to explore the radical teachings of Jesus on money and stuff. We called the project HAVE2GIVE1, inspired by the statement, "The person who has two [coats] should share with him who has none" (Luke 3:11). We publicly invited people to join us in a campaign to divest of half of what we owned, giving the proceeds to the poorest people in the world through disaster relief. Our groups met once a week to work through the details about how to sell our clothes, music, bicycles, and automobiles. We collected others items for garage sales and recycling. We also took a systematic look at everything Jesus taught about generosity, trust, contentment, and simplicity. One evening we brought our personal budgets and told each other how much we earn and spend. The things we learned together during that time spurred us on to create some group resolutions about how we wanted to change our habits in regard to money and possessions. I was surprised by the number of people who were ready to sign up for such an audacious project—which made me suspect that many people would take bolder steps to pursue genesis-vision if they were merely invited to do so.

- *You enter the Jesus dojo by creating a social culture where formation is expected.* Through social conditioning many of us have learned to approach church or group life as consumers or spectators. It may take a lot of work, but we should try to change our contracts with one another so that action and obedience are anticipated group norms. In our faith community we are learning to gently explain that it is our regular practice to discern an action we will take together. The projects or assignments we commit to create momentum for the next time we are gathered. Some examples: This week, write a letter or have lunch with someone you need to reconcile with; Before our next meeting, take one tangible step to love someone you perceive as your enemy; During the next week, do one thing each day to secretly honor a person you live or work with.

• *You enter the Jesus dojo through greater intentionality.* Many people will tell you they aspire to follow the ways of Jesus. A hip-hop diva may declare her allegiance to Jesus while receiving an award—just as a president might amid the crucible of an impending war. What separates mere sentiment from true substance is intentionality.

Near my thirtieth birthday I came to the painful realization that I was not becoming the person I hoped to be. Part of my dilemma came from the realization that, if the gospel of Jesus is holistic and integrative, then everything matters. Where do I start? How do I begin to live by the example of Jesus? I invited a trusted mentor to speak into my life. He gave me gentle but firm advice: "Mark," he told me, "the abilities that got you to thirty aren't going to get you to forty. If you are serious about seeking the ways of the kingdom, then you need to be deliberate, specific, and systematic in your approach—and you are going to have to work at developing your character, skills, and capacities."

I began reading the Gospels in search of images that I could use to summarize how Jesus lived. My first list included four images: companion, artist, healer, and mystic. Using these images as guides I began to ask, "How can I be a companion, artist, healer, and mystic?" For several years these categories have shaped my planning and experiments (and they are reflected in the four themes of this book). I try to have two or three tangible goals or activities attached to each image that are also reflected in my schedule. As you read the Gospels, I encourage you to come up with your own short list of descriptors to guide your experiments.

Our family is part of a community of faith in San Francisco called SEVEN—because we want to live into the Way of Jesus seven days a week. As a group we are committed to a deliberate approach to making a life together in the Way of Jesus. We reviewed the Gospels and identified seven themes based on how Jesus lived *and* what he taught: service, simplicity, creativity, obedience, prayer, community, and love. We spend seven weeks every year focusing on each theme and have designed a one-year, project-based, group formation process we call "the Jesus dojo" that meets weekly. We have also developed common rhythms and vows based on these seven themes that we invite one another to take each year. Our specific practices and rhythms are continually evolving because we see each year as a new phase of our experiment. A summary of our vows (omitting specific rhythms and practices) is included next, but I encourage you to review the Gospels yourself and make a list of themes that fit the language and sensibilities of your community and context.

1. *Service.* We are made to collaborate with our maker in caring for all of creation. We recognize the sacredness of work and use the capacities of our minds and bodies to serve others with our talents and skills according to the needs of the place where we find ourselves.
2. *Simplicity.* We acknowledge the abundant provision of our Maker and seek to live in trust, radical contentment, and generosity within an empire of scarcity and greed.
3. *Creativity.* We seek to be awakened in our imaginations and actions, inspired by the epic story of God's kingdom and creation, and connected to our cultural context. We want to live artfully, taking risks, experimenting, and using the language and mediums of our culture to explore the story of God's kingdom together.
4. *Obedience.* We recognize Jesus as our teacher and authority, and wrestle with how to surrender to the way of love in every detail of our lives. We submit ourselves to one another in love and strive to keep our vows to God and our commitments to one another.
5. *Prayer.* We seek the fruitfulness and guidance of the Spirit that comes from being centered and surrendered to the will and presence of our Creator. We practice rhythms of prayer, study, silence, and solitude that help us remain open to the voice and power of the Spirit.
6. *Community.* We seek to practice forgiveness and reconciliation, honor, encouragement, humility, and hospitality in all of our relationships. We are committed to taking the journey of faith in solidarity with our sisters and brothers around the world.
7. *Love.* We acknowledge that love is the greatest force in the universe, and in every dimension of our lives we seek to cooperate with the reign of God's love.

• *You enter the Jesus dojo by making promises.* If the invitation into the kingdom dance leads us toward repentance and transformation, how exactly do we change? In short, by whatever means are necessary. We have the intelligence, resources and capacity to learn to live in new ways, if we choose to do so. Change happens by turning desire into concrete resolutions. If you want to see change, you will have to do something different. Jesus suggested an initial step in this process is announcing your intentions. He said, "Simply let your 'Yes' be 'Yes,' and your 'No,' 'No'" (Matthew 5: 37). An ancient secret for change is found through making and keeping vows. King David of Israel once declared:

> For you have heard my vows, O God;
> you have given me the heritage of those who fear your
>   name....
> Then will I ever sing praise to your name
> and fulfill my vows day after day.
>   (Psalm 61:5,8)

A vow is a solemn promise made before God and people, to take or refrain from a specific action. Some would relate this to the concept of spiritual disciplines. A vow translates sentiment into tangible action. Paul of Tarsus, for example, once made a vow and did not cut his hair until his short-term promise was completed. I like to think of vows as experiments in truth, opportunities to see if making a specific change over a certain period of time will produce desired results.

Recently a group of friends and I decided that we wanted to become more centered and better at listening to God's voice. We promised each other that for thirty days we would sit still for fifteen minutes in the morning and evening each day. We all noticed the effects this change had on our sense of focus and peace.

Most of us know that it is difficult to keep resolutions or change on our own. That's why so many of us join gyms or weight loss clubs or attend recovery meetings. When a group of people make promises together they can support and encourage one another through the process of transformation. Common vows can be seen as improvisational experiments in obedience. By making temporary vows with one another, we can learn which practices are the most helpful to making a life in the Way of Jesus.

• *You enter the Jesus dojo by taking an experimental approach to life.* Tired of sitting and writing all day, I close the computer and walk out the door in search of a presence that is more real than words. The Israelites tasted manna in the desert and roasted quail by their campfires. John the Baptist ate grasshoppers and wild honey. And tonight I am scavenging the streets for my dinner. I want to remember what it is like to wander with primitive trust in the great mystery. And the streets yield what I need for my journey—along with ample food to take home to my family: hot caffeine-free herbal tea when I'm cold; a cup of water when I am thirsty; a piece of banana bread and two French pastries when I am hungry; pasta with meat sauce, still warm atop the garbage can, along with organic salad and two dozen chocolate chip cookies wrapped in tin; and, in a bag by the bus stop, five loaves of hearty European artisan bread and two dozen exquisite ginger cookies.

I recall Jesus and his disciples walking through the grain fields on the Sabbath, picking the heads of wheat while earning the scorn of more dignified religious leaders who would not stoop to scavenge for their food or break their own rules. No, tonight I will be free—I will walk fifteen miles and roam city streets in the silence of prayer, looking up at the stars under a bridge in darkness, feeling the wind on my face and tasting the salty air. I will remember that the Earth was made to provide for our needs through the Creator's abundance—not the work of our hands or the cash in our pockets. I want to experience the goodness that money cannot buy, resisting internal and external forces that pressure me toward greater security, control, and conformity. I will remember that life is ultimately about risk and adventure and that we die a certain death when we resign ourselves to propriety and convention. I will affirm, perhaps only in symbolic gesture, the spirit of the wandering Messiah-prophet, spreading the propaganda of hope, like soul graffiti, on the canvas of Earth and eternity.

"As for you, the anointing you received from him remains in you, and you do not need anyone to teach you. But as his anointing teaches you about all things and as that anointing is real, not counterfeit—just as it has taught you, remain in him'' (I John 2:27).

CONVERSATION

Reason and faith and experience.   Do you agree that our tendency as a society is to focus on knowledge over action and obedience? Why or why not? Does your faith tend to be more functional or theoretical? How does a person who has mostly a theoretical knowledge of God learn to integrate faith into all aspects of their life experience?

The risk of obedience.   How would life be different for you if you took Jesus more seriously as a literal teacher for life? What seem to be the most challenging or counterintuitive things that Jesus said or did?

Vows and promises.   Making vows and taking common action is a foreign concept to many of us, and to some ears it may sound exclusive or suspicious. The fact that making a commitment is so unfamiliar to our culture doesn't imply that doing so is either exclusivist or cultlike. What makes us so cautious about making verbal commitments to God or to one another? What does this say about the norms and values of the culture we live in?

EXPERIMENTS

An intentional and systematic approach.   Reread the gospel texts, noticing the instructions Jesus gave. Put these teachings into five to seven categories and develop a plan for how you will attempt to integrate them into your life during the next year.

Live with greater intentionality.   Live by a budget. Manage your calendar. Examine how you are spending your time and your money, and journal about what it would mean for you to become more centered and focused in how you are using your life energy.

Experiment by taking small vows. We only find out what is transformational through practice and experimentation. With a friend or in a small group, invite one another to commit to a certain practice or activity as an experiment in applied obedience. Your experiment can be as short as a day or as long as a year. If you don't "cheat" on your commitment, you will be better able to determine if the practice was beneficial.

Find people to share your journey with. If your community is not quite ready for the level of intentionality you seek, consider initiating an experimental group. Some people have found people locally who resonate with their longings by posting on Web sites or attending conferences or events. If you start moving toward what you have imagined, you will find people in your path to journey with. (It might be just five people in a living room.) You may also want to consider visiting or connecting with groups that embody many of the themes in this book. They may be able to encourage you and put you in contact with people closer to where you live. Here is a short list of places to start:

Allelon Foundation sponsors initiatives to help churches and organizations develop missional leadership (www.allelon.org).

The Church of the Sojourners is a residential "church family of disciples" (www.churchofthesojourners.org).

Emergent Village is a Web-based network of faith seekers committed to the Way of Jesus and generative friendship (www.emergentvillage.com).

Innerchange is a global order among the poor (www.innerchange.org).

Mustard Seed Associates (MSA) provide resources and a network for people committed to seeking the kingdom of God and making a difference (www.msainfo.org).

ReIMAGINE is a Center for Life Integration in San Francisco that hosts workshops, projects, and internships (www.Reimagine.org).

Relational tithe is an online community that encourages the global redistribution of wealth (www.relationaltithe.com).

Rutba House is a new monastic community helping to network people exploring radical Christian community (www. newmonasticism.org).

SEVEN is a missional community in San Francisco (www. Sevensf.org).

The Simple Way is an activist residential community of faith (www.thesimpleway.org).

Solomon's Porch is an example of a larger faith community seeking to follow God in the way of Jesus through intentional formation (www.solomonsporch.com).